P9-CCF-265

PRODUCTIVITY AND THE SOCIAL SYSTEM—THE USSR AND THE WEST

PRODUCTIVITY AND THE SOCIAL SYSTEM—THE USSR AND THE WEST

Abram Bergson

HARVARD UNIVERSITY PRESS
Cambridge, Massachusetts
London, England 1978

Printed in the United States of America

Library of Congress Cataloging in Publication Data

Bergson, Abram, 1914-
Productivity and the social system.

Includes index.
1. Industrial productivity—Russia. 2. Russia—Economic policy—1966- I. Title.
HC340.I52B47 338'.0947 77-15493
ISBN 0-674-71165-3

Preface

The chapters of this volume were written and published on various occasions. As with any such collection, an awkward problem is the inevitable repetitiveness in different contexts. In assembling the volume, I have tried to minimize duplication, but it was not feasible to avoid it altogether. Except to excise repetition, I have sought to limit rewriting. In an initial footnote to each chapter, I explain briefly the nature of the revisions, if any, involved.

A number of the chapters were developed as lectures. The original publications contained technical notes setting forth certain supplementary data that I had considered in interpreting summary measures. I refer to data of a usual, rudimentary sort that bear on the statistical significance of observed "regression" relations among those measures. In republishing the lectures, I again include the technical notes.

I also republish, sometimes in expanded versions, footnotes that were added to clarify complexities that could not easily be handled in lecture texts. Thus the technically inclined reader can turn to the footnotes for further elucidation of such matters as the extent of the divergence between Western data used and corresponding Soviet official statistics on the rate of growth of Soviet output; the nature of the "production functions" employed in the calculation of summary measures of "factor productivity" considered in the text, and the degree to which the measures are altered should some other "production function" be employed instead; the rationale of relevant Soviet policies on urbanization; and so on.

In the original publication of the lectures and essays, I made available appendixes elaborating on sources and methods used in compiling the more basic statistical data for Chapters 6, 7, 9, 10, and 11. These appendixes, of interest primarily to specialists, are not reproduced here, though I have included for reference a number of supplementary tables. Detailed explanations of sources and methods are thus available for Chapter 6, Table 6.1; Chapter 7, Tables 7.1, 7.2, 7.4-7.7; Chapter 9, Tables 9.1-9.4; Chapter 10, Tables 10.1-10.5; and Chapter 11, Tables 11.1-11.4, 11.6. Should appendixes on sources and methods not be accessible as published, copies will be supplied on request. For Chapter 5, an unpublished appendix on sources and methods for Tables 5.1-5.3 and 5.5 is also available.

I am deeply grateful to Professor Simon Kuznets for invaluable advice regarding the selection of essays for inclusion in this volume and the manner of their editing. The manuscript also benefited from careful editing provided in press by Judith Plitt. Where in order, acknowledgment for permission to reprint an essay has been made to the original publisher in an initial footnote. The kind cooperation elicited in every case is much appreciated.

Cambridge, Massachusetts
November 1977

A.B.

Contents

TABLES

FIGURES

ABBREVIATIONS

CDSP	*Current Digest of the Soviet Press*
CIA	Central Intelligence Agency
Gosplan	Gosudarstvennaia Planovaia Komissiia
JEC	Joint Economic Committee, United States Congress
National Income 1966	U.S. Department of Commerce, *The National Income and Product Accounts of the United States, 1929-1965* (Washington, D.C., 1966)
OECD	Organization for Economic Cooperation and Development, Paris
RAND	The RAND Corporation, Santa Monica, California
Real SNIP	Abram Bergson, *The Real National Income of Soviet Russia Since 1928* (Cambridge, Mass., 1961)
TSU	Tsentral'noe Statisticheskoe Upravlenie, USSR

PRODUCTIVITY AND THE SOCIAL SYSTEM—THE USSR AND THE WEST

1. Introduction

The twentieth century will be known to history for many things, but not least for the emergence and rapid spread of a radical alternative to the previously expansive capitalist economic order. The rise of socialism has provoked various reactions among contemporaries; for the economist it also provides an intriguing opportunity and challenge: to explore, in the light of an increasingly extensive experience, an issue long debated in theoretical discussion—the comparative economic merit of socialism.

The opportunity is limited, for in economic affairs experience is rarely easy to interpret. This seems especially true in reference to alternative social systems of a complex, modern sort and, in economic matters, where both the kind of society in question and the great rival with which it is compared exist in many variants in countries with differing cultures and histories. Yet the attempt to gain further insight into comparative economic merit through empirical inquiry need not be abandoned.

The chapters of this volume cover diverse topics. They will be of interest, I hope, from more than one standpoint, but taken together they may properly be regarded as an inquiry into the comparative economic merit of the two competing systems. I often focus expressly on that theme. Even when I do not, the discussion still contributes to analyses more immediately bearing on it.

Economic merit is a notion that may be seen from a number of normative standpoints. In any conventional view it has many facets. Where appropriate, I explain and defend particular standards that are applied. Suffice it to say here that I focus mainly on "economic efficiency." Reference is made to that standard not only in the "static" sense in which it is most often understood but also in the "dynamic" sense, which likewise is familiar. If the chapters shed light on relative economic merit of the two rival systems, as so viewed, they do so chiefly through quantitative appraisals and analyses of comparative performance in the context of levels and growth of productivity. Attention to comparative growth more generally, especially in the sphere of consumption, and to the nature and operating patterns of socialist economic institutions may also be illuminating.

Without being conversant with the technicalities, one can see that such inquiries may contribute to an assessment of comparative efficiency. The appraisal of efficiency, however, is almost necessarily incomplete, and the inquiry does not extend at all to performance in other areas such as income distribution. Viewed as a study in comparative economic merit, then, this volume is hardly comprehensive. Nevertheless, a limited inquiry into a complex theme can be of value.

Empirical studies of the economic merit of rival systems may be and have been conducted in diverse ways. Investigation of that theme here, as implied, is often characterized by summary quantification. I try at many points to measure performance for the economy generally and for the major sectors. That is a formidable task for any economy. It is especially problematic when the concern is to measure performance comparatively and when analyzing socialist economies—economies in which, even with the waning of the Cold War, the ruling governments are notably secretive and their published statistical data are all too often tantalizingly difficult to assess and interpret. Under these circumstances, as the chapters do not leave in doubt, precise results cannot be expected. Even crude calculations, however, can limit speculation on an important subject.

I understand socialism throughout this book as a social system in which ownership of the means of production is predominantly public and capitalism as a social system in which ownership is more or less mixed, but in which the private sector is substantial. Granting the status of ownership, the specific institutions, policies, and practices shaping a country's economic affairs may still vary, and that is indeed so in practice. On the socialist side, I focus for the most part on a single country, the USSR. At one point, however, I am able to consider also most of the countries of Eastern Europe. Among capitalist countries, although I refer generally to the United States, I often consider also a number of other Western countries.

Among socialist countries the USSR surely is especially interesting. Moreover, Soviet economic working arrangements have been widely emulated in the socialist world. Extension of our inquiry to Eastern Europe suggests that Soviet economic performance may be more nearly representative of socialist performance in general than is often supposed. In any event, the more inclusive inquiry enables us to gauge how performance varies among countries that, in applying the "Soviet model," have almost inevitably put their own stamp on it.

The fact remains that this volume focuses on the Soviet model and hence on the famous system of "centralist planning," which stresses bureaucratic processes (as distinct from markets), that originated in the USSR, and the development strategy that emphasizes growth and limited economic dependence on the capitalist West, also first pursued systematically in Russia. I leave for separate inquiry the experience in Yugoslavia, where the alternative form of planning organization that has come to be called "market socialism" has long prevailed. Yugoslavia has also deviated somewhat from the Soviet model in its development strategy. Since 1968, although in a rather different form from that in Yugoslavia, market socialism has also prevailed in Hungary. My discussion does not reach into the particular experience of that country with market socialism either.

Among socialist nations those in Asia are still shrouded in mystery. In planning organization and development strategy the chief of those countries, China, probably has not departed quite as far from the Soviet model as is often imagined; still, it is obviously a case by itself.

The Soviet model has been evolving in the course of time. The change in the USSR is especially noticeable when we compare recent circumstances with conditions during Stalin's reign. Some of the differences are discussed in this volume. The radical break with the past with respect to planning organization that many once anticipated still has not materialized. However, centralist planning has undergone some reform, perhaps most notably in the area of managerial incentives and the increasing use of mathematical economics and computers. Development strategy, too, has been in flux. As the daily news suggests and as the chapters that follow emphasize, the preoccupation with economic growth and self-sufficiency is no longer as all-consuming as it once was. Let me note, therefore, that I consider primarily the more recent circumstances in the USSR. Brief attention to the Stalin years, however, may provide some perspective on that extraordinary period.

The Western economies considered are all decidedly mixed and rather remote from the pure laissez-faire, private-enterprise system of textbooks. The mixture varies among countries, so quite a range of working arrangements is considered. Yet I have not really been able to pursue the interesting question of the extent to which economic merit differs correspondingly.

Differences in economic working arrangements may significantly affect economic merit under socialism or capitalism. Hence we must have in mind, if only in a general way, the kinds of arrangements in the particular countries that exemplify each system. Economic merit may also be influenced by historical and cultural factors. That counters a seemingly not unusual presupposition: given the economic working arrangements, economic merit is essentially determined. True, the conception of economic merit itself may vary, but once that notion has been delineated, any particular working arrangements, regardless of the circumstances, must achieve one and only one normative score.

That such a view is untenable, this volume, I think, will demonstrate clearly enough. Indeed, a recurring concern is the need, in comparing performance between systems, to take due account of one aspect in particular: the stage of economic development as measured against one or another conventional yardstick. For clarity, however, let me record here that I assume as is usually done that economic merit turns ultimately on the relations of the actual configuration of resource use to some theoretical ideal that is deemed optimal. As the primers teach, even in a fully determinate theoretical model, the actual configuration of resource use must depend not only on the general nature of the model but also on underlying parameters relating to "technologies," "tastes," and the like. So far as the economy is at all dynamic, further parameters to delineate the initial position and the path and speed of "convergence" also become relevant. Unless the working arrangements are seen as embracing both the model and the different magnitudes or states of such parameters, then, diverse scores are quite conceivably dependent on those magnitudes or states.[1]

All this means only that the economic merit of particular working arrangements may depend on the circumstances, but what has been said may also suggest why historical and cultural factors may be among the more important of those circumstances. That there must, in fact, be such a connection with historical and cultural data should become evident in the following essays.

So far as economic merit depends on development stage, there is greater reason to be cautious about extrapolating our findings to Asian socialist countries, including China. In the USSR and, with one or two exceptions, in Eastern European countries, socialism came into being when the econo-

1. So far as consumers are "sovereign," however, efficiency, at least of the static sort, is usually construed as "Pareto optimality." That is the construction throughout this volume. Yet, in terms of efficiency as so understood, does not perfect competition always score 100 percent without regard to the parameters determining actual resource use at any moment? As is well known, it does so only when there are no "externalities." Given such externalities, not only is there no Pareto optimality, but the degree of departure from it must depend both on the nature and incidence of the externalities and on parameters such as are in question. That is so in equilibrium; when the economy is dynamic, even in the absence of externalities, there will be departures from Pareto optimality of varying kinds and degrees, depending on the parameters in question.

mies in question were hardly advanced by Western standards. The introduction of socialism in Asia, however, came at a far earlier stage. China, no less than other Asian socialist countries, conforms to this rule, and its experience with socialism must be seen in that perspective.

As Schumpeter has rightly observed, socialism is a protean concept. The interpretation of socialism adhered to in this book is conventional. Especially lately, however, it has often been challenged. While such dissent could not be accommodated here, it does remind us that the socialist experience, extensive as it is, is still limited in at least one important way: we have, to date, examples only of authoritarian socialism. Whether socialism can be other than authoritarian is, needless to say, a much-debated question. So far as it can be, there presumably may be yet another dimension in which the economic performance of socialist economic working arrangements may vary, namely, that delineated by the comparative roles of authoritarian and democratic political institutions. For the present, however, socialist economic merit along that dimension must be gauged on the basis of theoretical speculation rather than empirical inquiry.

In sum, our inquiry often raises questions rather than answers them. Nevertheless, it may stimulate further research in an important and relatively unexplored area.

A few words are in order on the individual essays and on their relation to one another. Chapter 2 deals with reforms in the Soviet planning system initiated in September 1965. Coming nearly a year after Khrushchev's downfall, the reforms, it is argued, were not nearly so earthshaking as many commentators supposed at the time. Since their introduction Soviet planning has continued to evolve, but the September 1965 reforms retain interest as one of the first and more significant revisions in planning introduced since Stalin. In Chapter 3, I explore trends in Soviet development strategy since Stalin. While somewhat topical, the essay offers a prognosis that now appears to be in the process of being validated. Chapter 4 deals briefly with forces affecting entrepreneurial activity in the important sphere of innovation in the USSR.

This first part of the volume in one way or another provides perspective for the discussions in the two later parts. As the titles of Parts Two and Three indicate, the component chapters consider, respectively, levels of output and productivity and the growth of output and productivity. Chapter 5 compares national income in the Soviet Union and the United States. The calculations relate principally to 1955, but cardinal aspects are extrapolated to 1970. The inquiry should be useful in various connections, but it also serves as an essential basis for the calculation of comparative productivity levels in the USSR and the West in Chapters 6 and 7.

In Chapter 6, I again focus on the USSR and the United States. I try to formulate a methodology appropriate to inquiry into comparative productivity levels, where the concern is with economic merit, as it is here. Such a methodology seems hitherto not to have been very adequately developed. In applying the methodology to the year 1960, moreover, I am able for the two countries in question to explore diverse complexities that are not easily dealt with in any more inclusive study.

Comparative productivity levels are also the subject of Chapter 7, and there the inquiry is extended to cover, on the Western side, not only the United States but a number of other Western countries as well. On that basis it is possible, among other things, to explore the important question posed above concerning the variation of economic performance with the stage of economic development.

In Part Three Chapter 8 examines the comparative growth of output and productivity in the USSR under the five-year plans into the late fifties, and in the United States over both contemporary and earlier post-Civil War years. While it does not probe deeply into economic merit, the survey provides additional background for the remaining chapters, all of which relate to more recent years.

Thus, in Chapter 9, I inquire for post-World War II years into the comparative tempos and sources of productivity growth in the USSR on the one hand, and in the United States and a number of other Western countries on the other. Inclusion of a number of Western countries again permits inquiry into the role of the development stage, though now with respect to productivity growth. Such growth could be measured not only for the economy generally but also separately for "material" (as distinct from "service") sectors and for industry. For fairly obvious reasons, such a disaggregation is of much interest. As a companion piece to Chapter 9, Chapter 10 explores related postwar trends in the volume and structure of consumption. Part Three concludes with a further inquiry into comparative post-World War II productivity growth. I consider in Chapter 11 the performance of a relatively large number of countries on each side, particularly the COMECON and the OECD nations. The numerous countries considered permit examination of the role of the development stage on each side, but available data do not allow here the kind of disaggregation just described.

In comparing productivity levels under socialism and capitalism I focus on the year 1960. How matters stand more recently can be judged from the parallel results set forth on comparative productivity growth in post-World War II years. Inquires into that theme reach as far as 1970.

As the attentive reader will see, I often refer to a brief study of comparative productivity that originated in some lectures I gave in 1967 (*Planning and Productivity under Soviet Socialism,* New York, 1968). Drawing on that study here, I have been able, I think, to improve on and go beyond it in significant ways. As a result, the persent book may be considered to supersede that earlier work, though none of its essentials have been invalidated.[2]

2. Among the principal advances, I feel, are the relatively explicit formulation of a methodology of productivity measurement; sector disaggregation of results; the increase in coverage of the calculations by country; extension of inquiries into post-World War II productivity growth to more recent periods; and the attempt to deal more systematically than before with the question of interpretation posed by the multiplicity of causes affecting a country's economic performance. I refer especially to the role of the development stage.

PART ONE

PLANNING AND POLICY

2.

Soviet Planning Reform

Recently announced intentions of the Soviet government to reform its planning system have been greeted in the West as decisions of momentous international significance. The changes being made are not so dramatic as this reception would indicate, but the government is reorganizing, often in novels ways, its proverbially centralized arrangements for industrial planning. It has good reason to do so.

Although some of the reforms are innovative, one of them, concerning the administrative structure of industry, is hardly so. Prior to May 1957, branch ministries were preeminent in industry, but

Originally a lecture, this essay on the September 1965 Soviet planning reform was first published in Alexander Balinky, Abram Bergson, John N. Hazard, and Peter Wiles, *Planning and the Market in the USSR: The 1960's* (New Brunswick, N.J., 1967). The initial footnote explained, "To my profit, Gregory Grossman kindly commented on a preliminary draft. I also benefited from discussion with other colleagues." I reproduce the essay, by agreement with the Rutgers University Press, with only minor editing, but observe here that the reform in prices of industrial goods that the essay anticipated in fact did materialize in 1967. The government since September 1965 has continued to tinker with managerial incentives, though broadly within a framework established by the planning reform of that date. The enterprise, which seemed to gain authority under that reform, appears more recently (especially under a reorganization initiated in April 1973) to have been losing it. As these more recent developments suggest, the problems described in the essay seem still to affect Soviet planning.

On the developments in question, see Gertrude Schroeder, "The 1966-67 Soviet Industrial Price Reform," *Soviet Studies*, April 1969; Joseph Berliner, *The Innovation Decision in Soviet Industry* (Cambridge, Mass., 1976), pt. 3; Alice C. Gorlin, "The Soviet Economic Associations," *Soviet Studies*, January 1974; Paul R. Gregory and Robert C. Stuart, *Soviet Economic Structure and Performance* (New York, 1974).

Khrushchev at that time supplanted this traditional apparatus with one in which regional authorities became primary. Khrushchev acted with much fanfare, but his successors apparently have concluded that the branch-ministerial form of organization is superior, and no doubt with some basis, though Khrushchev may not always have been so harebrained as charged. In any event the government has now decreed reestablishment of the branch ministries. As the latest example of the familiar Soviet proclivity for bureaucratic reshuffling, this reversal is not without interest, but Western attention has properly been focused on other changes being made in industrial planning that are relatively novel.

THE REFORMS

Of the reforms in question, the principal ones were initiated at a meeting of the Central Committee of the Communist Party held September 27-29, 1965. As elaborated in a report submitted to the Central Committee by Premier Alexsei N. Kosygin,[1] and in the numerous, although not always revealing, decrees, instructions, and commentaries that characteristically followed immediately in the wake of the Central Committee action, the September 1965 program is more complex than many reports might suggest.

To refer only to bare essentials, the agency at the lowest bureaucratic level in Soviet industry, and hence the one immediately in charge of operations, is the *predpriiatie,* or enterprise. This has been so whether branch-ministerial or regional agencies have been preeminent, and will still be so now that the branch-ministerial system is again the order of the day. Under centralized planning, enterprise management has not been subject to control from above to quite the minute degree often supposed, but its authority has been severely limited. Under the new program such authority is to be expanded. This will occur through a reduction in the number of the enterprise's plan targets that must be approved by superior agencies and in other ways. For example, in utilizing available wage funds, enterprise management previously was much constrained by targets for wage payments, for employment, and for average earnings of different categories of workers. Now management will be subject to only one such target, for total wages paid to all workers. Within the limits of the total fund assigned it, management may employ labor as it wishes. Scales of basic wage rates for different categories of workers, however, will continue to be determined primarily by superior agencies.[2]

1. *Pravda,* September 28, 1965.

2. Dismissals of workers presumably will still require, as they have since 1958, the consent of the trade union factory committee. Also, under the new charter for the enterprise promulgated by the Council of Ministers on October 4, 1965, the director of the enterprise appar-

Decisions on capital investments hitherto have been especially centralized. Through charges to profits and depreciation each enterprise is now to establish a "fund for the growth of production," which it may use with some discretion to finance modernization, automation, and various other capital investment projects. For industry generally, funds for the growth of production are expected in time to finance about 20 percent of state capital investment. Hence the additional authority gained at this point could be of some consequence.[3]

Enterprise management is also to be allowed greater discretion in other, related ways. It may now decide whether and to what extent piece (rather than time) work is to be employed in determining wages, it has more authority than before in respect to custom production, and so on.

Plan targets in the USSR constitute standards of performance, or "success criteria," for enterprise management, but necessarily not all targets can have equal weight. Interestingly, then, not only are targets approved by superior agencies being reduced in number, but to some extent they are being changed in character and apparently in relative importance. Among other things, previously stressed targets for output, including unfinished goods and stocks, are to give way to a target for "realized production," or sales.[4] Contrary to many reports profits have long been calculated in the USSR; now the target for profits is also to become an important test of performance.

Along with success criteria, changes are being made in arrangements for managerial bonuses. These affect managerial behavior under Soviet socialism no less than elsewhere. Bonuses, hitherto based chiefly on performance relative to the plan target for output, are henceforth to depend primarily on performance relative to plan targets for sales and profits. Bonuses are to

---

ently will still have to observe some average wage schedule for salaried workers, though the precise meaning of this constraint is not clear. See *Ekonomicheskaia gazeta,* No. 42 (October 1965).

On enterprise management's authority generally under the new reform program, in addition to the new charter and Kosygin's report cited above, see the Central Committee resolution in *Pravda,* October 1, 1965; discussions of the program in *Pravda,* October 29 and November 12, 1965; and *Ekonomicheskaia gazeta,* No. 47 (November 1965), p. 10; No. 7 (February 1966), pp. 31 ff.; No. 13 (March 1966), p. 29.

3. *Ekonomicheskaia gazeta,* No. 47 (November 1965), p. 10.

4. In addition to sales to others, according to *Ekonomicheskaia gazeta,* No. 6 (February 1966), p. 32, "realized production" includes transfers to the enterprise's own capital construction work and "nonindustrial economic activities." An example of the latter presumably would be a factory restaurant. The source cited is not entirely clear regarding the treatment of changes in inventories of finished goods, but the reform program derives its meaning in part from the fact that "realized production" represents output net of such inventory changes. My identification of "realized production" with sales, therefore, seems appropriate.

vary according to the degree of fulfillment of one of these two targets but will be conditional on fulfillment of the other. The bonuses will also be conditional on satisfactory performance in other areas, such as the assortment of goods produced.

Such managerial bonuses, together with some premiums for workers generally, are to be paid out of a new "fund for material encouragement," which is to be maintained to a considerable extent through charges from profits. The charges are to vary according to an intricate system that is not easily summarized and that perhaps will not always be readily grasped even by managerial personnel. Suffice it to say that appropriations will depend not only on sales and profits but also on other indicators of performance, including "profitability," a Soviet euphemism for the rate of return on capital. Regarding sales and profits, what will count is performance relative not only to the plan but to preplan levels. The government is also establishing new arrangements for rewarding the introduction of new products and hopes to heighten interest in satisfactory performance generally through changes in procedures for financing housing, nurseries, and the like, which are administered by the enterprise.[5]

Last but not least, the changes in success criteria are to be accompanied by revisions in financial and price-fixing practices.[6] According to a strange but long-standing policy, new capital in the past has been made available to enterprises largely in the form of interest-free grants from the government budget. In the future enterprises will have to pay a charge out of their profits on their capital (typically 6 percent). The enterprises will also have to finance their capital needs increasingly through repayable loans. A firm that enjoys an especially favorable position with respect to natural resources may also be subjected to a fixed "rental" payment.

For the rest, the manner in which price-fixing practices will be changed is still under study. Industrial wholesales prices, which usually are fixed to allow a standard markup over average branch cost, but which for the most part have not been changed since July 1, 1955, are apparently at long last to be updated. In the process prices presumably will also be altered to allow for the novel charges on capital and rental payments.

In advancing the new program, Kosygin was careful to explain that it will be implemented only in the course of time. Although the government has committed itself to the reform, it expects to review it as it goes into effect. In fact, the new arrangements affecting enterprise autonomy, success

5. On the new incentive arrangements, see *Ekonomicheskaia gazeta,* No. 6 (February 1966), p. 33; No. 7 (February 1966), pp. 31-32; No. 8 (February 1966), pp. 21-22; No. 11 (March 1966), p. 23; and P. Krylov et al., "O poriadke i usloviakh perekhoda k novoi sisteme," *Planovoe khoziaistvo,* April 1966, pp. 55 ff.

6. *Pravda,* September 18, 1965; November 12, 1965; *Ekonomicheskaia gazeta,* No. 6 (February 1966), pp. 31 ff.; and Krylov et al., in *Planovoe khoziaistvo,* April 1966, pp. 55 ff.

criteria, and finance began to be introduced only in January 1966, and at that time only for forty-three enterprises. In April 1966, however, the new arrangements were extended to an additional two hundred enterprises, and Kosygin explained in his report to the twenty-third Party Congress that by the beginning of 1967 enterprises operating under the new reforms would employ one-third of all industrial workers.[7] The reform in industrial prices was to be carried out in 1967 and 1968.

I have been referring to the reform program initiated by Kosygin at the Party Central Committee meeting of September 1965. Before this meeting the government had already experimentally initiated changes in planning for consumer goods industries much like the changes now being instituted in industry generally. The experimental changes were first introduced in two clothing firms, the Bol'shevichka and Maiak, in the summer of 1964 and in 1965 were extended to several hundred enterprises producing clothing, shoes, leather, and textiles. Under this earlier experiment procedures different from those introduced under the September 1965, program were sometimes employed. For example, the enterprises affected were given much discretion to determine the assortment of goods produced in response to orders received from wholesale and retail trade outlets. Often such enterprises also gained more authority in other spheres than is being given industrial enterprises generally under Kosygin's later reform. Procedures employed under the experiment, however, varied in the course of time and between enterprises and are in any event often difficult to judge from the incomplete information available. The experiment remains of interest because the government intends to continue its operation and probably will broaden its scope while it reorganizes industry generally in the manner projected by Kosygin in September 1965.[8]

RATIONALE

In sum, the Soviet government is scarcely dismantling wholesale its system of centralized industrial planning, as sometimes has been suggested in the West, but it is adapting this system measurably in the direction of decentralization and increased use of market-type controls.[9] The adaptation, moreover, cannot be very palatable to a political group that has been bred

7. *Pravda,* April 6, 1966. See also *Ekonomicheskaia gazeta,* No. 18 (May 1966), p. 8.

8. For an informative survey of the 1964-1965 experiment, although it may overstress the resulting autonomy of enterprises, see CIA, *An Evaluation of Experimental Economic Reforms in the Consumer Industries of the USSR,* ER 65-35 (Washington, D.C., December 1965).

9. That the measures on which I have focused decentralize authority to some degree is evident, but a question might be raised as to whether the reorganization referred to at the outset did not have a contrary effect. Since branch ministries were often located in Moscow, did not the supplanting of these agencies by regional authorities under Khrushchev's reorganization of May 1957 represent a form of decentralization? And by the same token, does not

ideologically to view market institutions as a source of anarchy and is sensitive to the threat to its authoritarian rule and the bureaucratic status of superior personnel that is inherent in any consequential economic shifts in the direction now taken. Why is the government at long last initiating such changes?

The USSR, it has been reported, is "going through a crisis as profound, if not as eye-catching, as capitalism's crisis in the 1930's."[10] This is hardly accurate, but the government is manifestly concerned about the onerous responsibilities that superior agencies in the bureaucratic structure must bear under centralized planning. Subject to approval at the highest level, such agencies must determine the volume and direction of capital investment. They also have a major responsibility for the coordination of myriads of plan targets and for the control of current factor inputs, especially of materials, fuel, power, and machinery required to implement the plan.

With such responsibilities the superior agencies understandably find it difficult to cope, and one must read partly in this light complaints that lately have become commonplace even in the USSR; for example:

> The basic flaw in planning and management was that every detail was supposed to be decided from the center and, since it was impossible to know the circumstances at each enterprise, the center proceeded from average conditions that did not exist in reality in any one enterprise, and added an approximate average rate of growth, which was low for some and intolerable for other enterprises.[11]

Or:

> There are also irregularities in deliveries and incomplete deliveries; the grades, types and sizes of materials ordered are frequently re-

---

the reestablishment of the branch-ministerial system now mean recentralization? Khrushchev's reorganization has sometimes been construed in the manner suggested, perhaps with some basis, but the reorganization was quite complex and any shift in authority from Moscow must have been relatively limited. The current sequel to Khrushchev's reorganization is still too new to be fully understood, but the recentralization resulting from abandonment of Khrushchev's regional authorities would also have to be limited. In any event, shifts in the locus of authority resulting from either the May 1957 reorganization or its current abandonment occur only among superior agencies. Other reforms on which I have focused, whereby authority is transferred in a limited degree down to the enterprise, seem more significant economically. On the reorganization of May 1957, see Oleg Hoeffding, "Soviet Industrial Reorganization of 1957," *American Economic Review,* May 1959, and Abram Bergson, *The Economics of Soviet Planning* (New Haven, Conn., 1964), chap. 3. On the current change, see *Pravda,* October 3, 1965.

10. *The Economist,* March 19, 1966, p. 1100.

11. A. Birman, in CDSP, April 13, 1966, pt. 2, p. 3.

> placed by other less economic ones. For example, the Ukraine Chief Supply and Marketing Administration sent the Novo-Kakhova Electrical Machinery Plant a large amount of 750 x 1,500 mm. sheet steel for dynamos instead of 860 x 1,720 mm. sheet; as a result the coefficient of use of the metal dropped by 23 percent.
>
> Shortcomings in supply also affect the economics of enterprises . . . At the Rostov Farm Machinery Plant, for example, there were approximately 11,000 substitutions of rolled metal shapes and dimensions in five years—that is, an average of seven substitutions a day; this resulted in an overexpenditure of more than 22,000 tons of metal. Frequently there are also hugh losses from the low quality of products supplied, in particular cast parts.[12]

Or:

> Because of the absence of equipment, there are now about 1.5 million square meters of deserted productive floor space. In the textile department of the Kursk Synthetic Fiber Kombinat more than 3,000 square meters of floor space have been empty since 1960. In the "Tadzhiktekstilmash" Factory around 5,000 square meters of productive floor space . . . have been idle for more than two years because of the lack of specialized equipment.[13]

The government understandably is seeking to lighten the responsibilities of superior agencies. Since managers of enterprises have often complained of the "petty tutelage" to which they are subject, it is also hoped that the authority transferred to them will be exercised more effectively than it was by their superiors.

The government has no less reason to reform managerial success criteria, for within their limited sphere, enterprise managers also act wastefully, and curiously they are even impelled to do so by the success criteria that have prevailed.[14] Even with a "visible hand" replacing an "invisible" one, as it has turned out, what is good for the individual enterprise is by no means always good for the country.

Thus a familiar feature in the USSR is the infamous "safety factor": enterprise managers of necessity are allowed to negotiate with superior agencies regarding their plan targets and in doing so seek to limit their assignments. In this way they hope more easily to earn bonuses for plan fulfill-

12. E. Lokshin, cited in Bergson, *Economics of Soviet Planning,* p. 156.

13. *Pravda,* January 11, 1965.

14. Joseph Berliner, *Factory and Manager in the USSR* (Cambridge, Mass., 1957); Bergson, *Economics of Soviet Planning,* pp. 72ff., 287ff.; and Leon Smolinski, "The Soviet Economy," *Survey,* April 1966, p. 94.

ment. The Managers also hesitate to overfulfill targets, for fear that subsequent goals will only be made higher.

In trying especially to meet the target for gross output, managers also often find it possible, and even expedient, to stress goods that bulk large physically. Alternatively, where gross output is calculated in value terms, emphasis may be placed on products that have relatively high ruble prices; such prices also have their limitations, so the resulting assortment again may be strange. This explains the unending reports of difficulties of the Soviet consumer in shopping for particular items: for example, in buying large-size boys' shoes, as distinct from small-size men's shoes; or shirt, as distinct from bandage, cloth; or small-size, as distinct from large-size, electric bulbs; and so on.

Almost inevitably shortcuts are taken regarding quality: as in Russian Soviet Federated Socialist Republic, where among products examined by inspectors of the Ministry of Trade in the first half of 1962, 32.7 percent of the clothing articles, 25 percent of the knitwear, and 32.6 percent of the leather shoes were rejected or reclassified in a lower quality category; or in the Ukraine, where 20 to 25 percent of the clothing and knitwear examined by the Ministry of Trade during 1963 were condemned as defective; or in a factory manufacturing tractor parts which found it advantageous to overfulfill its output goal by 60 percent while lowering the quality of its products and so reducing their useful life by 40 to 50 percent. In order to meet the current target for output, managers also hesitate to introduce new products and find it profitable to abuse their machinery. The list of managerial aberrations could easily be lengthened.

In the determination of wholesale prices for industrial goods, the rule has long been simply to cover average branch cost.[15] Whereas a modest planned profit is also allowed, no charge has been included in cost for interest on fixed capital or rent for scarce resources. The rule nevertheless has often been honored in the breach, and sometimes the prices must be closer to underlying "scarcity values" than they otherwise would be, but often, too, they must tend rather to be more distorted. Most important, as noted, prices generally have been left unchanged since the last major price reform of July, 1955. For this reason alone, prices must frequently differ greatly from costs as well as from scarcity values generally.

Determined in these ways, ruble prices bear the earmarks of obsolete doctrines, particularly the Marxian labor theory of value, as well as of cumbersome central planning. Prices tend to be distorted economically in both cases, and curiously such incogruities are a major reason why the task of superior agencies is so difficult. For such agencies to calculate in terms

15. Bergson, *Economics of Soviet Planning,* chap. 8.

of such prices is not easy, but it is no easier for them to calculate differently. The dubious prices have also been a source of malfunctioning by enterprise management and they promise only to become more of a problem as far as sales and profits become the cardinal success criteria. Therefore, regarding prices too there is both room and need for improvement, though the government has yet to commit itself on the precise changes that will be made. Furthermore, it is seeking to make success criteria more valid by revising procedures for financing capital investment.

WHY REFORM NOW?

These deficiencies in centralized planning are hardly new; they became manifest in the early five-year-plans under Stalin. Why is the government only now taking consequential action to alleviate them? Even though reform might have been in order long ago, it has become especially so lately because of the ever-increasing complexity of the task with which the cumbersome system of industrial planning must grapple. In Western comment on the current Soviet economic scene, this trend is often referred to. The task is becoming more complex because of the continually growing number of industrial enterprises (recently 200,000 of "census" size[16]), whose interrelationships must be planned; because of the ever-increasing variety of commodities that such plants supply (according to a "complete" classification, an estimated 20 million items are now in production[17]); and because of the ever more exacting requirements of modern technology.

The complexity is also greater because the governement's own aim is no longer simply to produce steel and then more steel, as it was under Stalin. In his famous attack on Gosplan men in "steel blinkers," Khrushchev, of course, meant to urge not merely a greater use of plastics but a more flexible outlook on alternative industrial branches generally. Despite their criticism of Khrushchev, his successors probably will hesitate to abandon altogether this particular policy.[18] Moreover, the government, which in the face of crop shortages has been importing about 20 million tons of grain since mid-1963, is more attentive to consumers than it was under Stalin. For the dictator, food shortages did not preclude exports. And the task of directing economic activity has become more intricate because, though still not affluent, consumers themselves have become more choosy —witness the quite new phenomenon in the USSR of overstocks of consumer goods of less desirable sizes and styles.[19]

16. Smolinski, "The Soviet Economy" p. 90.

17. Ibid., p. 93.

18. N. S. Khrushchev, in CDSP, December 19, 1962, p. 9; Leonid Brezhnev, in *Pravda,* March 30, 1966.

19. A. Kosygin, in *Pravda,* December 10, 1964.

If prevailing priorities reflect a greater awareness of alternatives, it must be owing partly to another development that has been favorable to economic reform in other ways as well. The pretensions of poor Comrade Yaroshenko notwithstanding, Stalin held that "the directing bodies" must reserve for themselves consideration of the "rational organization of the productive forces, economic planning, etc." Hence these vital topics could not be the subject matter of a "political economy of socialism" open to inquiry by economists generally.[20] Yet the government has now found it expedient to allow economists to explore these very same questions. In doing so, the economists are even permitted to use forms of analysis, especially of a mathematical sort, formerly regarded as bourgeois and so taboo.

The invigorated economics that has quickly emerged has itself been a factor in the equation indicating economic reform. Much of the Soviet criticism of planning procedures that has been referred to is to be found in the writings of Soviet economists. The reforms being implemented, it has been reported, were largely shaped by the ideas of the Kharkov economist Evsei Liberman. In fact, many other Soviet economists have contributed, but the current reforms bear the stamp of the "new economies."[21]

Scarcely less momentous than these developments has been another: the rate of economic growth has declined markedly, according to both official Soviet and Western calculations. I cite measures of the annual average percentage increase in real national income:[22]

	Soviet official data	Western data
1950-1958	10.9	7.0
1958-1959	7.5	4.2
1959-1960	7.7	4.9
1960-1961	6.8	6.8
1961-1962	5.7	4.3
1962-1963	4.1	2.6
1963-1964	9.0	7.2
1964-1965	6.0	3.0

20. J. V. Stalin, *Economic Problems of Socialism* (New York, 1952), p. 55.

21. On the more recent currents in Soviet economic thought, see Marshall Goldman, "Economic Controversy in the Soviet Union," *Foreign Affairs,* April 1963.

22. For official Soviet data, see TSU, *Narodnoe khoziaistvo v 1964 g.* (Moscow, 1965), p. 575; *Pravda,* February 3, 1966. Western rates through 1962-1963 from JEC, *Current Economic Indicators for the U.S.S.R.* (Washington, D.C., 1965), pp. 12-13; and for 1963-1965, from U.S. Department of State, "U.S.S.R. Falters in Economic Growth Race with the United States," September 1965. For 1958-1963, State Department estimates are slightly below those issued by the JEC. Western data refer to the gross national product as usually understood, whereas Soviet figures refer to the net material product as that is construed in Soviet usage.

Even the reduced rates are still respectable, but the decline must be disconcerting for proponents of a social system whose asserted economic superiority is held to be observable, above all, in its ability to generate rapid growth. And, still worse, the rival capitalist system in the West lately has shown unexpected capabilities in this regard, first in Western Europe and most recently even in the United States. To "overtake and surpass" the advanced capitalist countries economically can no longer seem the easy task that the ebullient Khrushchev assumed not so long age.

By all accounts, economic growth has declined in the USSR for diverse reasons. Among them some of the most important, such as those that are causing the continued stagnation in agriculture,[23] are remote from deficiencies in industrial planning. By repairing these deficiencies the government hopes to assure an increasingly effective use of productive factors in industry and on this basis to offset more successfully the retarding forces that affect the economy generally.

As Kosygin made clear in his September 1965 report, the government seeks increased effectiveness in the use of all productive factors, especially capital. Even when growth was rapid, it could be achieved only by a disproportionately rapid increase in capital stock. Now that growth has slowed, the increase in capital stock has become inordinate. To continue to rely so heavily on capital inputs as a source of growth necessarily would mean that the share of total output going to current capital investment, which already may be one-third, must rise still higher. Only in this way could the government hope to find the wherewithal to assure a continuing increase in capital stock more rapid than the increase in output.[24] By implication, supplies of goods available to provide long-promised gains for consumers would likely be meager. Through improved planning procedures the government seeks to arrest the rise in capital coefficient and so to limit increases in the investment rate and encroachments on consumption that will be needed for future growth.

APPRAISAL

In reporting to the Party Central Committee in September 1965, Kosygin expressed confidence that "with tireless work" the measures being undertaken would yield "beneficial results."[25] Although he referred primarily to the reforms that he had proposed to the Central Committee, the government obviously is of the same view regarding the rearrangement that al-

23. Abram Bergson, "The Great Economic Race: U.S.S.R. versus U.S.A.," *Challenge,* March 1963; and A. Nove, "Soviet Economic Progress," *Lloyds Bank Review,* October 1965.
24. Bergson, "Great Economic Race," p. 5.
25. *Pravda,* September 28, 1965.

ready had been made experimental for consumer goods enterprises. How beneficial will the result be?

Under the reforms the responsibilities of superior agencies will be somewhat diminished, but they will still be onerous. Still, the experiment in consumer goods industries has brought a marked improvement in quality and assortment in many enterprises. Often this has been achieved in the face of adverse profit margins, which could be discouraging under other than experimental conditions. Difficulties have also been encountered in procuring through the still cumbersome supply system materials needed for an improved assortment. Under the September 1965 reforms, appropriations to the enterprise's bonus fund are to depend partly on the projected improvement in performance over the previous year, and the government hopes on this basis to weaken the "safety factor." Perhaps it will; but it remains to be seen to what extent, under the intricate incentive procedures being established, management will be interested in forgoing use of that device. Successes in this regard have been reported among the forty-three enterprises placed under the reforms in January 1964, although one wonders how typical such initial experiences will prove to be.

Under both the experiment in consumer goods industries and the September 1965 reforms, the government expects managerial performance to improve in other spheres. Here too, however, difficulties have arisen that may prove more than episodic: a wholesale oil supply base seeking to meet its target for sales compelled its customers, by the threat of fines, to fulfill their contracts, even though as a result of operating economies the customers' requirements had declined; management's newly won discretion in the matter of investment has been balked by difficulties in obtaining needed services of construction agencies; and enterprise autonomy generally is reportedly still constrained by red tape and improper encroachments of superior agencies.[26]

When adversities have been encountered, the still dubious prices are sometimes a factor, and the projected reform in prices should be to the good. The principles to be observed in fixing the new prices are not yet settled, however, and even after such prices prevail, the bureaucratic reluctance to change them will remain deleterious.

In sum, time alone can tell what will be achieved. Even a proponent of

26. Whether the oil supply base and its customers operated under the new planning procedures is not clear, but apparently enterprises functioning under such procedures have had similar experiences. On the experience with the reforms to date, see CIA, *An Evaluation;* CDSP, February 23, 1966, pp. 25-26, and April 6, 1966, p. 29; *Pravda,* January 19, 1966, March 9, 1966, and April 20, 1966; *Pravda Ukrainy,* March 18, 1966; *Soviet Studies, Information Supplement,* July 1965, p. 11, and January 1960, pp. 23, 30; and issues of *Ekonomicheskaia gazeta* for March, April, and May 1966.

Western market institutions may feel that resort to these sort of arrangements in such a limited fashion in a strange environment is apt to yield only limited gains. The government may soon find the system of industrial planning again on its agenda, though in changed circumstances. Possibly it will refrain from further reforms, but this would not be promising—nor would it be auspicious to abandon the reforms now in progress, even though that, too, is possible.

The government is presently promoting the use of mathematical economics and advanced computers, and some enthusiastic proponents of these tools have held that they will permit centralized planning to work after all, so that decentralization and market-type controls can be obviated. The government thus far has properly been guided by a more responsible view that mathematical analysis and computers can be helpful but are hardly a solution to the problem of planning organization. In a complex modern economy, with myriads of unknowns to be determined, "perfect computation" is conceptually intriguing as the electronic analogue of the perfect competition of economic theory. Nevertheless it is scarcely a practicality.[27] The government is not about to restore capitalism, and Soviet economists have rightly criticized commentators, both in China and in the West, who have suggested as much, but it may not be easy to confine the market to limits now being observed. Another suggested characterization of the current reforms therefore, may not really be amiss: "creeping capitalism." It will be fascinating to see how in the years ahead the government grapples with its complex problem of planning organization.

27. On recent developments in the use of mathematical economics and advanced computers in the USSR and the possible economic impact of such developments, see J. P. Hardt, M. Hoffenberg, N. Kaplan, and H. S. Levine, eds., *Mathematics and Computers in Soviet Economic Planning* (New Haven, Conn., 1967); and Egon Neuberger, "Libermanism, Computopia and Visible Hand," *American Economic Review,* May 1966. The expression "visible hand," which I use above, first came to my notice in Neuberger's article, but Neuberger points out that the expression was used previously by Joseph Berliner.

3.

Toward a New Growth Model

An attempt to peer into the long-term future of the Soviet economy is always timely, but it is especially so after the launching of a new five-year plan proclaiming rather novel priorities. Such an attempt should properly rest on substantial statistical projections of a kind that still remain to be made for the USSR. Even on the basis of limited inquiry, however, it is clear that the Soviet economy has been in a high degree of flux for some time. The resulting change in structure may be more profound and enduring than many commentators on the new plan suppose. The famous Soviet model of economic growth that Stalin initiated with the five-year plans appears at long last to be passing from the Soviet scene.

Originally a concluding discussion presented at a NATO symposium held in Brussels on April 14-16, 1971, this essay appeared in *Problems of Communism,* March-April 1973. It is reproduced with minor editorial changes. The essay represented a response to the ninth five-year plan (1965-1970), but the reported trends in post-Stalin Soviet development strategy, which are held likely to persist in the future, appear clearly manifest in the new tenth five-year plan (1975-1980), which has recently been promulgated. See Abram Bergson, "The Russian Economic Planning Shift," *Wall Street Journal,* May 17, 1976.

In Table 3.2 I cite data on the GNP by final use in 1970. One of the final uses in question is "government and defense." The underlying estimate of defense expenditures, rather speculative to begin with, now seems more speculative in light of the CIA's sharp upward revision last year in its calculation of such outlays. The allocation of the GNP by final use in 1970 serves here primarily as a point of departure for projection of future trends in consumption levels under alternative hypotheses for capital stock growth. Moreover, I assume throughout that the share of "government and defense" is constant at the 1970 level. Consequently, the results are little affected by the precise magnitude of that share.

Like any relatively modern economy, that of the USSR consists of myriad components, which are summarized in the country's real national income. Hence the trends that are relevant to the present inquiry may be explored by focusing on movement in that cardinal indicator and particularly its best-known variant, the gross national product (GNP).

PAST TRENDS

Inquiry into the future must begin with an analysis of the past. Therefore, let us at the outset look at trends in Soviet national income since the completion of the initial postwar five-year plan in the year 1950. After 1950 national income at first increased rapidly, though probably not quite as rapidly as is often supposed. From 1950 through 1958, according to Stanley H. Cohn's calculations, it grew at an average rate of 6.4 percent a year (Table 3.1). That is somewhat lower than the rate indicated by other Western data, but there are reasons to think it is still much nearer the mark than the official Soviet claim of 10.9 percent.[1]

Even according to Western calculations, the tempo of Soviet growth much exceeded that of the United States (2.9 percent). But it is worth noting that the Soviet growth rate was nearly equaled or surpassed by the growth rates of Italy (5.6 percent) and West Germany (7.6 percent). Moreover it fell well shy of Japan's growth rate. In these early years, although Japan had not quite achieved the economic miracle that is now a hallmark there, its rate of growth was already an impressive 8.0-9.0 percent.

Since 1958, as is well known, Soviet growth has slowed. As Table 3.1 shows, the retardation is manifest in both Cohn's and Soviet official data (curiously enough, it is more marked in the official figures than in Cohn's). The reasons for the slowdown have often been discussed, but there may still not be general understanding that no corresponding retardation occurred in the growth of inputs of the two principal productive factors generating output—capital and labor. According to both Soviet official and Western data, the available stock of capital increased during 1958-1967 at about the same rate as during 1950-1958, and the tempo was extraordinarily rapid. Similarly, Murray Feshbach's calculations with regard to employment show that it also rose at much the same rate during 1958-1967 as during 1950-1958.

The slowdown in output growth, then, was due essentially to a decline in

1. By Western standards, the Soviet official data are partial because they relate only to "material output." For a recent appraisal of the official data, including the nature of the Soviet concept of national income, see Abraham S. Becker, "National Income Accounting in the USSR," and Stanley H. Cohn, "National Income Growth Statistics: Summary and Assessment," in V. G. Treml and John P. Hardt, eds., *Soviet Economic Statistics* (Durham, N.C., 1972).

TABLE 3.1 Selected economic indicators for the USSR, 1950-1975 (average annual rates of growth, in percent)

Indicator	1950-1958	1958-1967	1967-1970	1970-1975 (planned)
National income (Soviet official data)[1]	10.9	7.2	7.3	6.7[2]
GNP (Cohn calculations)	6.4	5.3	3.4[3]	—[4]
Capital investment (Soviet official data)[5]	12.9	7.6	7.5	6.7
Gross investment, fixed capital (Moorsteen-Powell calculations)	11.4	6.9[6]	—	—
Gross investment (Moorsteen-Powell calculations)	12.2	6.1[6]	—	—
Fixed capital stock, including livestock (Soviet official data)	8.3[7]	8.3[7]	7.5	—
Net fixed capital stock (Moorsteen-Powell calculations)	10.0	9.4	—	—

(*cont.*)

the rate of productivity increase. While that is already evident from the trends in output and factor inputs, it becomes even more obvious if we average the rates of growth of capital and labor in a way that has become a standard practice in economics. Using this method, we can calculate the rate of growh of output per composite unit of labor and capital together, "factor productivity" as it has come to be called. During 1958-1967, that rate was significantly below the corresponding one for 1950-1958. A computation of factor productivity for a nonmarket economy such as that of the USSR, it is true, is almost inevitably rather arbitrary, but the results obtained are still illuminating.[2]

2. The arbitrariness derives in part from the difficulty of obtaining for the USSR meaningful factor income shares, such as are generated in a market economy, to use as weights in averaging the rates of growth of labor and capital. This paper employs weights of 0.6 and 0.4, respectively, for the two factors—weights suggested by relevant Western experience.

At least for the technically initiated, I should explain that I felt it appropriate, in the case

TABLE 3.1 (cont.)

Indicator	1950-1958	1958-1967	1967-1970	1970-1975 (planned)
Net capital stock (Moorsteen-Powell calculations)	9.0	9.0	—	—
Employment (Feshbach calculations)	1.8	1.7	1.7	—
Total input of capital and labor	4.6	4.6	—	—
Factor productivity (GNP per unit of labor and capital)	1.7	0.7	—	—

Sources: TSU, *Narodnoe khoziaistvo SSSR v 1960 g.* (Moscow, 1961), p. 85, and subsequent volumes in the same series for 1962, p. 535; for 1967, p. 613; for 1968, p. 49; and for 1970, pp. 60, 478, 533; TSU, *Kapital'noe stroitel'stvo v SSSR* (Moscow, 1961), p. 40; *Gosudarstvennyi piatiletnii plan razvitiia narodnogo khoziaistva SSSR na 1971-1975 gody* (Moscow, 1972), pp. 62-75, 345, 352. Stanley H. Cohn, "General Growth Performance in the Soviet Economy," in JEC, *Economic Performance and the Military Burden in the Soviet Union* (Washington, D.C., 1970), p. 17; Richard Moorsteen and Raymond P. Powell. *The Soviet Capital Stock, 1928-1962* (Homewood, Ill., 1966), pp. 323, 341, 360; Richard Moorsteen and Raymond P. Powell. *The Soviet Capital Stock, 1928-1962: Two Supplements* (New Haven, Conn.: Yale University, Economic Growth Center, 1968), pp. 11, 18, 24; Murray Feshbach, "Estimates and Projections of the Labor Force and Civilian Employment in the USSR: 1950-1980" (Washington, D.C.: U.S. Bureau of the Census, processed, February 1970).

[1]National income *produced* unless otherwise indicated.

[2]National income *utilized for consumption and accumulation.* For 1965-1970, such income grew at an average annual rate of 7.1 percent. The corresponding figure for national income produced was 7.7 percent.

[3]This figure is for 1967-1969.

[4]Not applicable or not available.

[5]Investment in fixed capital only, exclusive of investment in private housing as well during 1950-1958.

[6]These figures cover 1958-1966.

[7]For 1950-1959 and 1959-1967.

---

of capital, to adopt an income share that is gross of depreciation even though what is in question here is the growth of net capital stock over time. Also, inputs have been averaged "logarithmically"; hence I have assumed, in effect, a so-called Cobb-Douglas production function, in which the "elasticity of substitution" of inputs of capital and labor is taken to be unity. However, the elasticity of substitution in Soviet circumstance may be less than unity. If so the growth of calculated total inputs would tend to slow down, even though the rate of increase in inputs of individual factors remained unchanged, and the tempo of factor productivity growth would not decline as much as it does in the present calculations. The problem of

There are, perhaps, too many reasons for the decline in the growth of factor productivity. For one, in 1956 Nikita Khrushchev initiated a reduction in working hours that ultimately led to the establishment of an approximately forty hour week in industry in place of the forty-eight hour week that had prevailed in the early 1950s. That reform had already had some impact before 1958, but its principal effect came in subsequent years. Since employment, as calculated, does not allow for varying hours, the reduction in time worked should have tended to reduce productivity growth in the post-1958 period compared to the pre-1958 one.

Another cause lay in the proverbial vicissitudes in agriculture, the most important of which were Khrushchev's heroic interventions, notably the great New Lands Program. This innovation produced favorable results at first, but progress became relatively slow and uncertain after the great crop of 1958.[3]

Still another element in the slowdown possibly has been the well-known deficiencies of the Soviet system of central planning: the failure of enterprise managers to behave as desired because of ineffective incentives, and the often fallible direction and coordination of superior agencies. These difficulties are by no means new. They date virtually from the earliest days of Soviet planning. As often argued, however, they may have become increasingly costly as Soviet central planning had to cope with the ever-growing complexities associated with continuing industrialization: the increasing number of plants that have to be coordinated, the increasing number and variety of products whose output has to be determined, and so on.

Last but not least, the so-called "catch-up" phenomena that came in the wake of World War II may have affected factor productivity. Countries ravaged by the war experienced a speedup of economic growth because of such factors as the restoration of partially destroyed productive capacity at

---

declining factor productivity, then, is transformed, at least in part, into one of a declining rate of return on capital, and much of what is said, I believe, is still relevant.

Inasmuch as we shall later employ the Cobb-Douglas function to project future Soviet economic growth, a word or two about the impact that an elasticity of substitution less than unity would have on these projections seems to be in order. Because under such a circumstance the calculated tempo of factor productivity growth is raised for past years, one might assume that a higher rate would result for the future, too, but there are indications that the rate of growth of total inputs of labor and capital will decrease. Trial projections of total GNP growth based on the assumption of an elasticity of substitution less than unity suggest that such calculations may be less favorable to the USSR than those made here on the assumption of an elasticity of unity.

3. Note that chiefly as a consequence of the New Lands Program, the cultivated land area increased sharply during the years 1950-1958. If my calculation of productivity were extended to include agricultural land as an input (as might be proper), productivity growth during 1950-1958 would be somewhat reduced compared with 1958-1967.

relatively limited investment cost, the acceleration of technological progress through application of innovations made in other countries less affected by the war, and so on. By the same token, the progressive exhaustion of such advantages could prove a source of retardation in later years. By 1950 the USSR surpassed its prewar level of national income, but recovery from war damage remained to be completed in some areas. Thus "catch-up" phenomena may still have exerted an appreciable influence on growth until the 1960s, when they no longer were as potent as they had been.

SOME ALTERNATIVE PROJECTIONS

So much for past trends. What of the future? One possible answer may be found in the new five-year plan: during 1970-1975 national income is to grow at nearly the same rate as it did in the 1960s (Table 3.1).[4] Interesting as a Gosplan projection is, however, we must seek somehow to arrive at an independent evaluation. We may best begin with Feshbach's forecast that employment will grow in the 1970s at a rate of 1.2 percent a year, or somewhat less rapidly than during the 1950s and 1960s.

What of the other principal input, capital? Can Soviet capital stock be expected to grow at the notably high rates that prevailed during the 1950s and 1960s? A clue is provided by available data on the rate of growth achieved in the volume of capital investment in those years. According to both official Soviet and Western data, the rate of growth of investment, while fully comparable to the rate of growth of capital stock during 1950-1958, fell well below the tempo of the latter in later years (Table 3.1). During any year, investment represents new additions to total capital stock. The rate of investment growth is not at all the same thing as the rate of growth of the capital stock itself. Indeed, the two might temporarily tend to diverge widely. But in the course of time they must tend to converge. Hence, if investment continues to increase at a reduced rate like that of the 1960s, the rate of growth of total capital stock will inevitably tend to drop. In fact, if the official data are accurate, the latter began to decline in the late 1960s. Moreover, the new plan apparently projects a tempo of investment growth actually somewhat below that of the 1960s.

To arrive at our own assessment let us look at several alternative projections (see Table 3.2). While these projections are quite hypothetical and

4. As noted in the table, official rates of growth cited for past periods relate to national income produced, but the growth rate planned for 1970-1975 relates to national income utilized for consumption and accumulation. The growth rate for the latter is only 0.4 percentage point below the actual growth rate of national income utilized for consumption and accumulation during 1965-1970. Therefore, the projected retardation of growth is less than a comparison with rates of growth for national income produced in past years suggests.

could properly be viewed as exercises, they may help to clarify the implications and facilitate appraisal of alternative hypotheses regarding the future growth of the Soviet stock of capital. They may also serve to structure speculation about the future increase of national income.

The projections begin with estimates—sometimes rather crude—of the GNP and its disposition in terms of major uses in 1970 and of capital stock

TABLE 3.2. The Soviet economy in 1970 and alternative projections for 1975 and 1980[1]

Item	1970	λ = 3.0 percent[2] 1975	λ = 3.0 percent[2] 1980	λ = 2.0 percent 1975	λ = 2.0 percent 1980	λ = 1.0 percent 1975	λ = 1.0 percent 1980
		With capital stock growing at 9.0 percent a year					
Consumption	56.5	71.1	96.5	65.8	80.0	60.2	65.2
Government and defense	13.3	19.0	27.1	18.1	24.6	17.2	22.3
Gross investment	30.2	52.1	80.2	52.1	80.2	52.1	80.2
Net investment	20.2	36.9	56.8	36.9	56.8	36.9	56.8
Depreciation	10.0	15.2	23.4	15.2	23.4	15.2	23.4
GNP	100.0	142.8	203.8	136.0	184.8	129.5	167.7
GNP, average yearly increase in percent from previous date	—	7.4	7.4	6.3	6.3	5.3	5.3
Net stock of capital, Dec. 31	290.4	446.9	687.7	446.9	687.7	446.9	687.7
		With capital stock growing at 6.0 percent a year					
Consumption	56.5	81.8	111.0	76.3	96.2	70.8	82.8
Government and defense	13.3	18.0	24.2	17.1	22.0	16.3	19.9
Gross investment	30.2	35.2	47.1	35.2	47.1	35.2	47.1
Net investment	20.2	22.2	29.4	22.0	29.4	22.0	29.4
Depreciation	10.0	13.2	17.7	13.2	17.7	13.2	17.7
GNP	100.00	135.0	182.3	128.6	165.3	122.3	149.8
GNP, average yearly increase in percent from previous date	—	6.2	6.2	5.2	5.2	4.1	4.1
Net stock of capital, Dec. 31	290.4	388.6	520.1	388.6	520.1	388.6	520.1

[1]All figures except those for average yearly increase in GNP from the previous date are in percent of total GNP of 1970 (i.e., total 1970 GNP = 100.0 percent).

[2]λ is the projected rate of increase in factor productivity.

in that same year,[5] and they assume that employment will grow subsequently at the already mentioned rate of 1.2 percent a year. As for capital stock, two hypotheses are explored. The first postulates that it will continue to grow at a rate of 9.0 percent a year in the 1970s, the second that the rate of growth will be only 6.0 percent. In effect, the former assumes that the decline in the rate of growth of investment in the 1960s will prove to be transient, while the latter assumes that the decline will persist and indeed become more pronounced.

For each hypothesis, three possible alternative rates of increase in factor productivity are explored. Specifically, it is assumed that factor productivity will increase at alternative rates of 3.0, 2.0, and 1.0 percent a year (these rates compare with actual growth rates in factor productivity of 1.7 percent in 1950-1958 and 0.7 percent in 1958-1967). In conjunction with the average rate of growth of inputs of labor and capital combined (a figure calculated in the manner previously described), each of these hypothetical rates of factor productivity growth results in a praticular rate of increase in GNP (Table 3.2).

To carry the projections somewhat further we can calculate hypothetical levels of output for 1975 and 1980 from the indicated rates of growth of GNP. The stock of capital in these years can be determined once the rate of increase from that of 1970 is specified; so can the annual net investment in 1975 and 1980 if capital stock is to rise by the required amount each year.[6] Net investments must be financed, and in real terms such finance must, of course, come from the very output that the mounting capital stock makes possible. Hence the volume of current output that must be allocated to net investment in 1975 and 1980 can be established. With depreciation calculated at the 1970 average rate, gross investment can likewise be determined. To complete the tabulation of the GNP by use in 1975 and 1980, it remains merely to allow for dispositions to government administration and defense. I assume provisionally that these will absorb the same share of output as they did in 1970. The residual thus represents the volume of output available for consumption.

5. The absolute figures underlying the percentages in Table 3.2 are in 1964 adjusted rubles and are taken or estimated from data in a variety of Western sources, including principally the works of Cohn and of Moorsteen and Powell, cited in Table 3.1, and various RAND studies of Soviet national income. I also draw upon my own calculations of Soviet national income in Chapter 5, and Stanley H. Cohn, "The Economic Burden of Soviet Defense Outlays," in JEC, *Economic Performance and the Military Burden in the Soviet Union,* (Washington, D.C., 1970). But note that the correspondence between the tabulations of GNP by use in 1970 for this paper and those for 1967 in Cohn's essay is misleading to some extent. Cohn's data are in current adjusted rubles, while those for this article. as indicated, are in 1964 adjusted rubles.

6. See n. 8, this chapter.

This residual is of particular interest, along with the growth rate of output. (Note that in Table 3.2 all data on output uses and on capital stock, including those for 1975 and 1980, are expressed as percentages of total 1970 GNP; this facilitates comparisons.) Under each of the two assumed rates of capital stock growth, the rate of increase of both GNP and consumption varies with the rate of increase in productivity. For any praticular productivity rate increase, the rate of growth of output, logically, is always greater when capital stock rises at 9.0 percent a year than when it rises at 6.0 percent a year. On the other hand, the increase in consumption when capital stock grows at 6.0 percent is always greater than it is when capital stock grows at 9.0 percent. Although consumption rises markedly in the latter case when productivity grows by 3.0 percent, the gains in consumption are quite modest at lower rates of productivity growth. For instance, when productivity increases by only 1.0 percent, there is hardly any gain to speak of in per-capita terms, for the indicated growth in consumption would barely exceed the rise in population, which is expected to amount to 3.9-6.1 percent over the period 1970-1975 and 3.4-6.6 percent over the period 1975-1980.[7]

In effect the extra increments of output produced when capital stock grows at 9.0 rather than 6.0 percent a year are, in every instance, more than totally offset by concomitant increases in requirements—chiefly those for investment to render possible the higher rate of growth of capital stock in the first place. These additional requirements are always incongruously large, but they become larger and larger the slower is the rise in productivity and output.

The inordinate demand on output to meet current investment requirements is just a corollary of a primary feature of Soviet economic growth that is already evident but merits emphasis: capital stock has risen not only rapidly but also distinctly more rapidly than output. This was already true in the 1950s when output increased at a relatively rapid pace, but it was even more the case in the 1960s after the growth of output had slowed. In any economy, such an incongruously rapid growth of capital stock can be assured only through the allocation of an ever-increasing share of output to current investment. To be sure, this observation is simply an arithmetic truism, but it does help to explain the rising share of output that, as our data clearly imply (Table 3.1), investment was already absorbing in the 1950s and 1960s.

We must also see in this light the further projected increase in investment—that is, from 30.2 percent of 1970 GNP to between 39.4 and 47.8 percent of GNP in 1980—that is indicated when we extrapolate to the

7. Murray Feshbach, "Population," in JEC.

future on the basis of a 9.0 percent tempo of growth in capital stock. At that rate, capital stock rises more rapidly than output even with the most favorable hypothetical rate of productivity increase, and the disparity between the growth of capital stock and the growth of output only widens if we interpret the rise in productivity less optimistically.

What about the alternative projection that assumes that capital stock will increase at only 6.0 percent a year? In that case, the tempo of growth of capital stock is fully matched by that of the GNP when the rise in productivity is 3.0 percent; when the rise in productivity is just 2.0 or 1.0 percent, the rate of growth of GNP will be less than that of capital stock. In neither of these instances is the difference nearly as marked as when capital stock rises by 9.0 percent. Thus, though gross investment as a share of GNP may rise, its projeced level for 1980—25.8 to 31.4 percent, depending on the increase in productivity—turns out to be much lower than required when capital stock grows by 9.0 percent a year.[8]

IMPLICATIONS

The foregoing exercise may afford insight into why the Soviet government has lately been acquiescing to a retardation of the extraordinarily rapid expansion of the country's capital stock despite the fact that such expansion has been the primary means by which the government has endeavored over the years to achieve a rapid growth of output. More important, the projections suggest that retardation will probably be allowed to continue.

To expand captial stock by 9.0 percent a year has always been an oner-

8. For 1970-1975 the differences between the two sets of projections with respect to the growth rates of investment and, by implication, of consumption could be deemed to be somewhat understated because of the manner in which net investment in 1975 and 1980 has been arrived at. Thus net investment in each of those years has been taken as simply equal to either 9.0 or 6.0 percent of the capital stock on January 1 of the given year, the particular figure depending on the rate of growth of the capital stock in question. In effect, then, under each hypothesis regarding the growth of capital stock, net investment would increase from 1975 to 1980 at the same tempo as that of capital stock.

The correspondence of the rates of growth of net investment and capital stock is to be expected over the long run, but inasmuch as we start with 1970—a year when, at the current rate of net investment, the capital stock rose by 7.5 percent—net investment, at least for a time, must increase at an even higher rate than 9.0 percent if capital stock is to grow at an average annual rate of 9.0 percent from 1970 to 1975. Similarly, net investment could rise for a time at less than 6 percent and still assure a 6 percent rate of growth of capital stock from 1970-1975.

While there is no logical bar to the achievement of the rates of investment listed in Table 3.2, it may be more reasonable to assume that investment will grow at a constant rate during 1970-1975—that is, at a tempo that would produce the hypothesized rate of increase in

ous undertaking for the USSR, but it would become a greater burden should the government seek to maintain the tempo in the future. The chief costs, of course, have been and would continue to be borne by Soviet consumers. Although Stalin sanctioned such deprivation, soon after his death the Soviet government avowedly committed itself to a different policy, which has been reaffirmed in the five-year plan promulgated for 1971-1975. According to the text of the plan its "chief test" will be whether or not it assures "the rise of the material and cultural level of life of the population."[9]

The Soviet people, to be sure, have come to understand that improvements in consumption standards do not inexorably follow government commitments to provide them. Nevertheless, these standards by all accounts have tended to rise since Stalin, sometimes markedly. It would be surprising if, in the years ahead, the government decided, except under great duress, to suspend these rewards for any length of time for a population that is relatively educated as well as conscious of Western living standards and whose elite groups have become increasingly materialistic. Such a governmental decision would be especially surprising under circumstances in which a full reversion to the techniques of rule of the days of the "cult of personality" no longer appears to be a feasible alternative.

The implementation of the government's commitments to consumers obviously will not be made easier by the 1972 crop failures, which are still much in the news as these lines are written, but the government's reaction to these failures indicates that at least a partial shift in priorities has occurred. Reportedly, nearly $2 billion of scarce foreign exchange has been allocated for the importation of some 28 million tons of grain. In

---

capital stock, on the average, over the five-year period. Under this assumption, investment in 1975 would have to constitute 40.6 percent of the GNP, instead of the 36.9 percent shown in the table, to guarantee a rise of 9.0 percent a year in capital stock; it would need to be only 19.2 percent of GNP, rather than the 22.0 percent shown in the table, to ensure a growth of 6.0 percent a year in the capital stock.

According to the same reasoning, the calculations for 1975-1980 contain an element of bias, too, though of a contrary nature. Thus, if we alter investment's projected share of total GNP in 1975 as just indicated and then apply to 1975-1980 the same methodology for computing investment as we just did for the 1970-1975 period, we come up with the following results: investment in 1980 would need to be only 53.7 percent of the GNP, instead of the 56.8 percent shown, to assure an increase of 9.0 percent a year of capital stock; it would have to be 31.9 percent of GNP, rather than the 29.4 percent shown in the table, to guarantee a rise of 6 percent a year in capital stock.

9. *Gosudarstvennyi piatiletnii plan razvitiia narodnovo khoziaistva SSSR na 1971-1975 gody,* p. 73.

Stalin's time concern for alleviating the impact of harvest losses was hardly so intense.[10]

If the tempo of capital stock growth is permitted to decrease, of course, the growth of output will likely do the same. Our projections only underline what is evident at this point. Yet the government has already acquiesced in a retardation of output growth. Given its heightened interest in consumer goods, it may find it expedient to continue this policy in the future.

What about productivity? Do our projections not show that if productivity grows rapidly enough—say, by 3.0 percent—capital stock and output could continue to grow at high rates even as the needed improvement in consumption standards is realized? Theoretically, that is a possibility, and the Soviet government, which is always concerned about raising productivity, has understandably become increasingly so as the investment costs of sustaining the further growth of the capital stock have continued to climb. As the just-concluded Soviet-American economic accord indicates, the USSR, once so uneasy about economic relations with the West, is now actively seeking to promote them. It hopes that productivity growth will be helped by the increased exchanges and especially by the more accelerated importation into the USSR of advanced Western technology that the agreement makes possible. The Soviet government has been trying to speed up productivity growth in other ways, as well. Of late it has placed increasing stress on domestic technological innovation, and at the same time it has sought, through much-discussed planning reforms launched in the fall of 1965, to remedy the perennial deficiencies in economic administration and thereby to increase the efficiency of the system.

Thus far the planning reforms do not appear to have been highly effective.[11] Moreover the acceleration of technological progress in any whole-

10. This is not the first occasion since Stalin's death that the government has imported grain on a large scale to offset harvest losses. The current imports much exceed even the purchases made in response to the exceedingly bad harvest of 1963 (16.8 million tons during 1963-1965), and they apparently will suffice to make good all the 1972 losses.

In the aftermath of the recent harvest failures, the government is also reportedly revising its investment program in order to assure more funds for agriculture. This initiative should be taken into account when we come to a consideration of the prospects for productivity growth in the economy generally, although its implications in that regard are perhaps not so evident as is sometimes assumed. Thus, while some analysts have argued that substantial revision of investment allocations under the current five-year plan in itself may tend to impair efficiency, it is also possible that additional allocations to agriculture might be relatively productive in view of the chronic shortage of capital there.

11. See Chapter 2; and Gertrude E. Schroeder, "Organization and Management as Factors in Soviet Economic Growth in the 1970's," in Y. Laulan, ed., *Prospects for Soviet Economic Growth for the Seventies* (Brussels: NATO, 1971).

sale way in a complex, modern economy such as that of the USSR is not an easy task. Productivity may increase more rapidly in the future than it has recently, but that is not saying a great deal. Certainly the government would have difficulty achieving a much higher tempo of productivity improvement than the buoyant rates of the 1950s. Should the government seek to sustain a super-high rate of capital stock growth at the expense of consumption, big gains in productivity would be all the harder to attain, inasmuch as frustration of consumer aspirations for rising standards of living could affect labor incentives adversely.

Though the changes introduced in the wake of the planning reforms announced in the fall of 1965 were hardly revolutionary, the reforms themselves did represent something of a break with the past. Hence we should not be too surprised if, in search of additional sources of productivity gains, the government initiated still further reforms in planning. Perhaps at long last it will even make the kind of wholesale shift to "market socialism" that many thought was taking place in 1965. Only time will tell just what further changes will be introduced and how they will affect productivity.

My projections have assumed throughout that the Soviet government will devote to public administration and defense a constant share of output corresponding to that of 1970. Defense is far more important than administration, and the USSR could obviously find additional resources for both investment and consumption if it were prepared to limit allocations to that competing use. While the Soviet government has always seemed reluctant to restrict defense expenditures on purely economic grounds, it may in the future—political circumstances permitting—find such grounds more impelling than it has found them in the past. Possibly it has already come to this point if the apparently increased flexibility that it manifested lately in arms control negotiations, for example, is any indication.

To conclude, I have referred often to the extraordinarily high tempo of capital stock growth that has prevailed in the USSR—a tempo that has surpassed that of output growth even when output was increasing relatively rapidly. I have also discussed a corollary of that incongruity: the rising share of output absorbed by the investments required to sustain such rapid growth of capital stock. Although the pattern of economic growth that emerged in the USSR under Stalin's five-year plans—and has come to be called the Soviet model—has many facets, a central characteristic has been the imbalance manifested in such disproportionately rapid growth of capital stock in combination with a rising share of output going into investment. (The latter phenomenon may be more familiar in the alternative guise of an inordinately high tempo of growth in "heavy" as opposed to "light" industries.) The Soviet model has clearly been undergoing a process of erosion lately. Notably unbalanced growth has apparently been giving way to relatively balanced growth in the very sphere—capital formation—where the imbalance had previously been most striking. The prospect is that this erosion will continue. In the USSR at least, the Soviet model may not survive its dictatorial architect much longer.

4.

Entrepreneurship and Profits in the USSR

In this chapter I propose to consider profits briefly in the context of socialism of the thoroughgoing sort, in which there is predominant, if not universal, public ownership of the means of production. Such socialism theoretically may be organized in various ways, but in practice one form of organization is common. It is the scheme that has come to be known as "centralist planning": essentially, production units to a great extent are coordinated and directed by superior agencies in bureaucratic structures and through the use of extra-market devices, such as physical quotas. Why centralist planning is preeminent is an interesting question that I cannot pursue here, but so far as it is prevalent, our attention inevitably turns to that scheme. Of particular interest too is the experience of the USSR, the country where centralist planning originated, where it has accordingly had the most time to mature, and where its operation has been studied in some depth.

While the USSR has largely dispensed with private enterprise and markets as we know them, certain institutions characterizing the Western mixed economy are present there. I refer particularly to money, prices, and financial accounting. Indeed it is evidently only because of the persistence of those features that there is in the USSR such a thing as profits for us to discuss at all. The survival of those institutions together with profits sometimes occasions surprise, al-

A contribution to the Diebold Symposium on profits that was held in Cambridge, Massachusetts, on February 27-28, 1976, this essay is reproduced here essentially as it will appear in a forthcoming volume of symposium proceedings.

though they are hardly novelties. Some Soviet theoreticians, it is true, once urged their abolition, and at one time they were nearly abolished, but that was long ago. Money, prices, financial accounting, and profits are established features in the USSR that are rarely, if ever, challenged today.

Like profits in the Western mixed economy, profits in the USSR are necessarily integral to financial control over the activities of economic entities. Under Soviet centralist planning such controls are no less needed than they are in the West. The question that arises is: What is the role of profits in Soviet economic life more generally? We also want to know how, if at all, the Russians perform economic functions that are rewarded by profits in Western mixed economies.

These are very broad questions. Consequently I shall focus on one fundamental aspect of the system. As Schumpeter taught us long ago, among the different activities rewarded by profits in the West, not the least is entrepreneurship. Entrepreneurship, moreover, is seen essentially as the initial introduction and diffusion of productive technologies and products of the sort that we usually call innovations. It seems fitting to consider here, if only in the most summary way, the Soviet experience in this sphere.

Regarding that experience, a common supposition today, I think, is that Soviet centralist planning has been shown not to be especially impressive in the area in question. I may as well say at once that I have no quarrel at all to pick with that view. On the contrary, all that I know seems to confirm it. It may be instructive, nevertheless, to probe the question a bit further. To begin with, if the record of Soviet centralist planning in encouraging innovation has been unimpressive, what is the reason? The answer, I think, is a very simple and familiar one: bureaucracy. Of course, bureaucracy is not exactly unknown in the West, and up to a point it obviously must have its rationale economically. Under Soviet centralist planning, however, there are reasons to think that bureaucracy often goes beyond that point in economic affairs generally. It seems especially so in the context of innovation.

The resulting difficulties are frequently a subject of complaint in the USSR itself. To mention some of the more outstanding ones,[1] there is the need to keep accounts and to calculate in terms of the proverbially dubious administered ruble prices, a practice that only compounds risks inherent in innovation; the notable multiplicity of agencies often concerned with any project and the correspondingly complex task of coordination thus encountered; the related difficulties of integrating a novel vector of productive inputs and outputs into an economy in which such supplies are often

1. On the nature and effectiveness of Soviet methods to encourage innovation, see R. Amann, M. J. Berry, and R. W. Davies, *Science and Industry in the USSR* (Birmingham, England: University of Birmingham, Centre for Russian and East European Studies, n.d.); Joseph Berliner, *The Innovation Decision in Soviet Industry* (Cambridge, Mass., 1976); and A. F. Garmashev, ed., *Izobretatel'stvo i ratsionalizatsiia SSSR* (Moscow, 1962).

rationed and unavailable in markets; and last but not least, the apparently less-than-energizing incentives often offered for overcoming such hurdles. The last item calls for further comment.

In the USSR, in the sixth decade since the October revolution, egalitarianism in income distribution is still an avowed goal, but no one supposes that it is a fact. On the contrary, incomes continue, as they long have been, to be differentiated systematically to reflect skill levels and the nature of the task. That is true for workers generally and also for scientific workers and managerial personnel in economic organizations. In short, circumstances affecting incentives on the face of it, seem to favor rather than to inhibit innovation. On closer scrutiny, they turn out, I think, to be inhibiting.

True, individuals responsible for useful inventions might be granted special rewards. Though of a modest one-time sort, the rewards are no doubt beneficial. Much more important from the present standpoint managerial personnel in the economy, depending on their performance, customarily receive bonuses in addition to basic salaries. Determined by intricate schemes that almost defy summarization, bonuses depend first and foremost on meeting more or less general plan targets for sales, profits, and the like. Should an innovation favor that result, it would be to the good and the bonuses for overall performance could be somewhat larger than they would be otherwise. Special bonuses could be earned also for the innovation itself. But these rewards too have tended to be of a relatively modest one-time-only kind. Should disruption attendant on the innovation impair fulfillment of more general targets, there may be no gain to speak of. Disconcertingly, an innovation, if successful, can also result in the imposition of unduly taxing plan targets in the future.

Not too surprisingly, therefore, managerial personnel seem again and again to prefer the quiet life to innovation, or so we infer from ever-recurring Soviet complaints, such as this one by Z. Sirotkin, chief design engineer, Bielorussian Motor Vehicle Plant, and USSR State Laureate:

> Unfortunately the "mechanism" of the Economic Reform has proved insufficiently effective when applied to the question of putting new equipment into production. After all, the manufacture of a new machine means, first of all, new concerns and difficulties. The work rhythm is disrupted, and many new problems appear. Under the existing situation, this causes the performance indicators to decline and the enterprise incentive funds grow smaller. It is for this reason that some plant executives brush aside innovations proposed by science.
> . . . This is especially true if the plant has achieved a stable work rhythm and high quality output and has all the benefits the Economic Reform provides; as for material incentives to induce changes, there are none.

> In a time of general well being the plant manager would have to be a very far-seeing person indeed to feel any concern or anxiety, and to undertake the preparatory work for producing a new model of the machine. For in the next few years that promises many difficulties.[2]

I have been discussing primarily the system of rewards for managerial personnel in the "enterprise (*predpriiatie*), the agency immediately in charge of a production unit.[3] At all levels of the economic bureaucracy successful innovation can be favorable to a managerial career, but what counts above all apparently is performance with respect to more general plan indicators. If in the Soviet system incentives to innovate have limitations, to be sure, that must also be true of the corresponding rewards that are familiar in the West. Nevertheless, can the latter as often be so ineffective?

Despite all its shortcomings as a mechanism to generate innovation, Soviet centralist planning must be credited with some virtues. Most important, while the inventor is rewarded, he receives no restrictive entitlement whatever to his invention, so limitations on use such as are possible under Western patents are quite avoided. Commercial secrecy too cannot be at all consequential. Yet, in the realm of innovation it seems difficult to avoid concluding that Soviet centralist planning must often be at a disadvantage compared with the mixed economies that we know in the West. If so, an outstanding feature of the Soviet growth process that is otherwise difficult to understand can be explained in part.

Over a protracted post-World War II period the rate of growth of output per worker in the USSR has no more than matched Western countries at comparable economic levels, despite the fact that capital stock per worker has grown at an extraordinarily rapid rate. Under the circumstances, the USSR might have been expected markedly to outpace, rather than merely to match, the growth of output per worker in the West. Among Western countries, in only one, Japan, has capital stock per worker grown at a rate similar to that in the USSR. But Japanese output per worker has grown by 8.8 percent yearly, more than twice the corresponding 4.2 percent rate in the USSR. It is not necessary to be informed about problems of productivity measurement to be aware that results such as these may be construed variously, but there is, I think, at least a presumption

2. Quoted in Berliner, p. 490.

3. Under the reorganization initiated in April 1973, enterprises in industry are in the process of being merged into branch and regional associations (*ob'edineniia*), and in important ways the latter are apparently supplanting the former as the primary operating agency in industrial administration.

that innovation in the USSR is not contributing to the growth of output at nearly the rate that Western experience indicates.[4]

The bonuses paid to innovative managerial personnel in Soviet enterprise are probably the nearest counterpart in the USSR of the entrepreneurial profits on which Schumpeter focused. Moreover the bonuses are financed in good part, though not entirely, by appropriations from the accounting category "profits." To what extent the economic gain from innovation is actually captured in the profits of the responsible enterprise is an interesting question; given the oddities of ruble prices, it is not easily answered. In any event, profits from whatever source for the most part are transferred to the government budget rather than retained within the enterprise. The limited amounts retained are used principally to finance inventories and small-scale fixed investments, diverse "social-cultural" measures, and bonuses.

In the great debate on the economic merit of socialism that was waged in the interwar years, a principal issue was comparative performance with

4. If Soviet performance has been substandard as described, Soviet centralist planning cannot be considered to be solely at fault. Innovation in the USSR undoubtedly has suffered also from the quasi isolation from the West into which the Soviet economy was plunged by the autarkic policies of the early five-year plans, an isolation from which the USSR, despite all the attendant fanfare, has still only partially emerged. Even so the USSR has always tried assiduously to replicate Western technological developments, but the adaptation of those developments to Soviet circumstances and their introduction into the USSR must often have been impeded by the constraints on economic relations with the West generally. To be sure, the quasi isolation has been fostered to a degree, in well-known ways by Soviet centralist planning, yet it has also reflected the government's more basic development policies and the deleterious effect on innovation must be read in that light. Western strategic controls, of course, have also been a limiting factor in Soviet economic connections with the West.

It is sometimes suggested too that innovation in the USSR has suffered because of the Soviet preoccupation with military R and D. At least, civilian innovation, it is held, must have suffered simply because of the resultant diversion of scarce scientific talents and resources to military work. That could well be so, and so far as it is, Soviet performance with respect to productivity growth would have suffered the more because available data probably reflect only very imperfectly innovation in final products, whether civilian or military. But note that Soviet outlays for R and D have been very large and, even after due allowance for allocations to military-related activities, probably still compare favorably with corresponding outlays in Western countries at similar economic levels. The military R and D must also have had some favorable civilian spillovers.

On the subject of comparative productivity growth in the USSR and the West, see Chapters 9 and 10, this volume. For discussion of Soviet expenditures for R and D, see C. Freeman and A. Young, *The Research and Development Effort* (Paris, 1965); OECD, *The Overall Level and Structure of R & D Efforts in OECD Member Countries* (Paris, 1967); Nancy Nimitz, *The Structure of Soviet Outlays on R & D in 1960 and 1968,* R-1207-DDRE (Santa Monica, Calif.: RAND Corporation, June 1974); and Abram Bergson, Statement to Subcommittee on Science, Research and Development, the Committee on Science and Astronautics, U.S., House of Representatives, Ninety-Second Congress, Second Session, *Science, Technology and the Economy,* no. 23, April 11, 12, 13, 18, 20, 1972 (Washington, D.C., 1972), pp. 127 ff.

respect to innovation under that system. Thus, in Oskar Lange's economic case for socialism[5] a cardinal contention is that the system would provide a solution to the problem posed by the asserted tendency of "monopoly, restrictionism, and interventionism" to limit introduction of new technologies under capitalism. On the other hand, critics such as Hayek,[6] while not seeking to rebut the proponents too explicitly on the question, have obviously held a different view: apparently innovations were expected to be hindered under socialism by the difficulties encountered by overburdened superior agencies in planning new investments and by the general aversion of managers to risks, which is probably unavoidable.

If Soviet experience is at all representative of socialism in practice, perhaps the critics have been nearer the mark than the proponents. The USSR has been able to avoid some restrictive arrangements, particularly patents, which, Lange argued, impede innovation under capitalism. On the other hand, bureaucratic difficulties such as the critics adumbrated have obviously taken a considerable toll under socialism.

The critics have often focused on an asserted managerial reluctance to take chances. If only for clarity, it should be observed that for risky projects such as the ones in question, theory seems to prescribe only that socialist managerial personnel, while seeking their own benefit, must be induced also to heed expected economic returns, whatever those returns may be. With appropriate rewards for success, I believe, there is no bar, in principle, to approaching that desideratum. There is no obstacle to that even if managers are risk averse, as they apparently are in the USSR. For overcautious managerial personnel whose careers as well as earnings depend on success, however, the rewards may have to be large even though losses of capital almost inevitably have to be borne by the community generally.[7]

The Soviet government, one can infer, has not found it expedient to bestow managerial rewards of the required magnitude. Very possibly the reasons are ideological, though such scruples manifestly have not generally been overpowering. But any inducements for managerial personnel to stress plan fulfillment over innovation cannot be entirely accidental. Given

5. "On the Economic Theory of Socialism," in B. Lippincott, ed., *On the Economic Theory of Socialism* (Minneapolis, Minn., 1938), pp. 110 ff.

6. Friedrich A. Hayek, *Individualism and Economic Order* (Chicago, Ill., 1948), chaps. 8, 9.

7. For an approach to the "Pareto optimum," the expected returns strictly speaking must be calculated net of managerial rewards. Also managerial estimates of such returns are understood to be acceptable, if only provisionally, to the community generally. Managerial rewards apart, gains and losses from individual projects supposedly are widely distributed and do not fall inordinately on any particular individuals. These, I believe, are essentially the conditions under which socialist managers are properly guided, as it is usually assumed they should be, by expected returns. Compare Kenneth J. Arrow, *Essays in the Theory of Risk Bearing* (Chicago, Ill., 1971), pp. 131 ff, 138 ff, 149, 239 ff.

the difficulties that innovation poses for planning, the government must hesitate on that account, too, to offer large rewards for innovation.

The methods of achieving innovation under Soviet centralist planning are surely open to improvement, but the deficiencies seem to be deep-seated. One suspects that the government will continue for some time to have reasons to stress plan fulfillment rather than innovation. Whether on that account or for ideological reasons, so long as managerial rewards for innovation remain relatively restricted, it is reasonable to doubt that Soviet performance in that sphere can approach the level that proponents of socialism seem to expect.

PART TWO

LEVELS OF OUTPUT AND PRODUCTIVITY

5.

The Comparative National Incomes of the Soviet Union and the United States

Economic theory teaches that comparisons of real national income in different countries, like those within a single country for different times, may have to proceed according to which of two analytic purposes is in mind: appraisal of comparative "production potential" or appraisal of comparative "welfare." In trying to relate Soviet and American real national income, I take as a desideratum the assessment of comparative production potential. To what extent such an abstract desideratum can be achieved is another matter, but the inquiry is usefully organized with it in mind.

Because basic data are relatively available for 1955, I calculate national income for both countries initially for that year. Comparative magnitudes that are derived for that year may be extrapolated to more recent years by use of published indexes of the change over time in physical volume.

While national income purportedly represents the sum of "final" goods and services produced by a community, it almost inevitably omits diverse activities that contribute to final output, and includes others that, at least in part, may properly be considered intermediate rather than final. This is a familiar theme and need not be elaborated here, but it should be observed that in 1955 the USSR was still

This essay was originally published in D. J. Daly, ed., *International Comparisons of Prices and Output* (New York, 1972), and is reproduced with the permission of the National Bureau of Economic Research. In that version I extrapolated to 1965 comparative data on Soviet and American output compiled for 1955. Here I extrapolate to 1970. For brevity I have deleted a section comparing my results with those obtained in previous inquiries. I have also made some minor revisions.

much behind the United States in terms of degree of industrialization, although, of course, not nearly as far behind as in 1928 on the eve of the five-year plans. Thus, in 1955 nearly two-fifths of the Soviet labor force was still employed in agriculture. For the United States, the corresponding figure was 8.0 percent.

The degree to which national income omits final activities or includes intermediate ones depends on the degree of industrialization. On balance, output of a less industrialized country tends to be understated relative to that of a more industrialized one. That should be the case here, except that the two countries considered have different social systems. Curiously this distinction probably has tended to limit rather than compound the understatement of output in the USSR relative to the United States. Thus one of the most important omissions from national income is home processing. Because of the notably extensive employment of women in the USSR, the volume of home processing there must be less than normal for a country with a comparable degree of industrialization.[1] Because of the wholesale socialization in the Soviet Union, many independent activities of a kind that tend to escape reporting, hence inclusion in national income, have also been drastically curtailed there, if not wholly eliminated.

THE CALCULATIONS

Comparative data have been compiled on Soviet and American national incomes by final use and in a highly summary way on Soviet and American national incomes by industry of origin. The former data are the more basic here. Following the path blazed long ago by Gilbert and Kravis,[2] I have tried to compile measures in terms of the prices in both countries; that is, I take as a point of departure data for each country on its national income by final use in terms of its own prices and in each case derive corresponding figures in terms of the prices of the other country.

Tables 5.1 and 5.2 show the data on national income by use with which I began and the corresponding figures derived in terms of prices in the other country. In measuring national income I focus particularly on gross national product. The final use categories are to be construed as the designations usually imply, but it should be observed that for the United States the figures on defense cover practically all of the relevant outlays whereas the corresponding data for the USSR refer essentially to the so-named category in the government budget. The precise scope of this category is still contro-

1. In the USSR in 1960 women accounted for more than half of all civilian employees and for some 47 percent of all civilian employees outside agriculture. In the United States in the same year women accounted for 29 percent of all civilian employees.

2. Milton Gilbert and Irving B. Kravis, *An International Comparison of National Products and the Purchasing Power of Currencies* (Paris, 1954).

TABLE 5.1. Gross national product by final use, USSR and United States, 1955

Final use	Prevailing rubles			Adjusted rubles			Dollars		
	USSR (bil.)	U.S. (bil.)	USSR/ U.S. (%)	USSR (bil.)	U.S. (bil.)	USSR/ U.S. (%)	USSR (bil.)	U.S. (bil.)	USSR/ U.S. (%)
Household consumption	659.2	3267.4	20.2	473.5	2376.8	19.9	64.4	239.28	26.9
Communal services, including health care and education	102.5	198.1	51.7	93.2	160.9	57.9	34.7	29.86	116.2
Consumption, all	761.7	3465.5	22.0	566.7	2537.7	22.3	99.1	269.14	36.8
Government administration	29.5	42.8	68.9	27.4	36.4	75.3	8.8	8.29	106.2
Defense	105.4	212.1	49.7	99.5	205.9	48.3	29.9	38.06	78.6
Gross investment	246.6	628.7	39.2	238.1	605.6	39.3	43.0	84.07	51.1
Nonconsumption, all	381.5	883.6	43.2	365.0	847.9	43.0	81.7	130.42	62.6
GNP	1143.2	4349.1	26.3	931.7	3385.6	27.5	180.8	399.56	45.2
GNP, excluding selected final services[1]	1016.3	4273.8	23.8	809.7	3312.7	24.4	124.0	364.0	34.1

[1] Labor outlays for communal services, government administration, and military pay and subsistence under defense.

TABLE 5.2. Gross national product per capita by final use, USSR and United States, 1955[1]

	Prevailing rubles			Adjusted rubles			Dollars		
Final use	USSR	U.S.	USSR/ U.S. (%)	USSR	U.S.	USSR/ U.S. (%)	USSR	U.S.	USSR/ U.S. (%)
Household consumption	3359.8	19,766.5	17.0	2413.3	14,378.7	16.8	328.2	1447.5	22.7
Communal services, including health care and education	522.4	1,198.4	43.6	475.0	973.4	48.8	176.9	180.6	98.0
Consumption, all	3882.2	20,964.9	18.5	2888.3	15,352.1	18.8	505.1	1628.1	31.0
Government administration	150.4	258.9	58.1	139.7	220.2	63.4	44.9	50.2	89.4
Defense	537.2	1,283.1	41.9	507.1	1,245.6	40.7	152.4	230.2	66.2
Gross investment	1256.9	3,803.3	33.0	1213.6	3,663.6	33.1	219.2	508.6	43.1
Nonconsumption, all	1944.5	5,345.3	36.4	1860.4	5,129.4	36.3	416.5	789.0	52.8
GNP	5826.7	26,310.3	22.1	4748.7	20,481.5	23.2	921.5	2417.2	38.1

[1]USSR population, 196.2 million; United States, 165.3 million. Differences between indicated totals and sums of items are due to rounding.

versial. Nevertheless there are clearly significant omissions, one of which is the support of quasi-military internal security forces. Tables 5.1 and 5.2 include this, along with internal security generally, in government administration. Much defense-related research probably falls under communal services rather than defense, while atomic weapon development and stockpiling, at least in part, may be omitted from defense and find its way instead into gross investment. Under communal services, health care and education for the United States include private as well as public outlays. The private outlays are accordingly excluded from household consumption. For the USSR reference is only to public outlays, which are nearly comprehensive in that country. Communal services in the USSR include under the budget heading "science" the defense-related research just mentioned and probably often research outlays that in the United States are treated as expense and hence are not included in the GNP to begin with. In 1955, however, total budgetary outlays recorded as "science" were still relatively limited: exclusive of capital expenditures classified here as investment, they amounted to perhaps 7.0 billion rubles, or 6.8 percent of all outlays for communal servics in Table 5.1.

These are perhaps the more interesting incongruities affecting our final use categories. The reader with special interests may want to refer to separate appendixes mentioned in the Preface of this volume, that elaborate on the calculations, and to the principal sources from which I have drawn data on national income in national prices.[3]

When output is calculated in ruble values I have compiled data in terms of prevailing and adjusted prices. The latter are essentially prevailing ruble prices after deduction of the famous turnover tax and the additon of subsidies. I have explored at length in previous studies the problem posed for the valuation of Soviet national income by the proverbial limitations of prevailing ruble prices.[4] Suffice it to say that in approaching the problem I take as a point of departure the factor cost valuation standard that theory teaches is appropriate where production potential is the object of interest. The calculation in adjusted prices is to be viewed in that light. In fact, even adjusted rubles are rather remote from the factor cost standard of theory, but they still seem preferable to prevailing rubles if production potential is of concern and are by no means lacking in merit as a practical expendient.

3. Abram Bergson, *The Real National Income of Soviet Russia Since 1928* (Cambridge, Mass., 1961), hereafter *Real SNIP;* Oleg Hoeffding and Nancy Nimitz, *Soviet National Income and Product, 1949-55,* RM-2101 (Santa Monica, Calif.: RAND Corporation, April 6, 1959); Nancy Nimitz, *Soviet National Income and Product, 1956-1958,* RM-3112-PR (Santa Monica, Calif.: RAND Corporation, June 1962); and U.S. Department of Commerce, *The National Income and Product Accounts of the United States, 1929-1965* (Washington, D.C., 1966), hereafter *National Income, 1966.*

4. See *Real SNIP,* chap. 3; and Chapter 6, this volume.

Where output is calculated in dollar values, I have considered only prevailing prices. A further computation in terms of dollar factor cost would have been to the good, but the results probably would not be very different from those where valuation is in prevailing prices.[5] Even dollar factor cost, of course, is not the same thing as the factor cost of national income valuation theory. It no doubt does not diverge as much from the latter ideal, however, as do adjusted rubles.

For Soviet national income, I draw on earlier studies primarily for data in prevailing rubles, although corresponding data in adjusted rubles have been compiled previously. I do little more here than revise these figures to make them conform to the data used for national income in terms of prevailing rubles. Moreover, once American national income is calculated by use in terms of prevailing rubles, corresponding data in terms of adjusted rubles may be derived by applying to the outlays in different use categories appropriate coefficients obtained for the calculations of Soviet national income in prevailing and adjusted rubles.

As an element in national income in prevailing prices, farm income in kind is valued throughout at average realized farm prices. For each country farm income in kind is valued initially in terms of average realized farm prices in the country in question and then in terms of average realized farm prices in the other country. In the calculations in adjusted rubles, average realized farm prices are adjusted for taxes and subsidies along with prices generally.

Outlays in prevailing prices of one country are translated into outlays in prevailing prices of the other primarily by deflation, that is, by application of ruble-dollar price ratios for different groups of goods that were compiled from corresponding ratios for different commodities. In the case of outlays on commodities I rely chiefly on ruble-dollar price ratios that I have either taken from or calculated from data in unclassified reports of the U.S. Central Intelligence Agency[6] and in a study by Abraham S. Becker for the RAND Corporation.[7]

5. See Abram Bergson and Hans Heymann, Jr., *Soviet National Income and Product, 1940-1948* (New York, 1954), p. 103, n. 18; and Morris Bornstein, "A Comparison of Soviet and United States National Product," in JEC, *Comparisons of the United States and Soviet Economies,* 86th Cong., 1st sess., 1959, pt. 2:380.

6. *A Comparison of Consumption in the USSR and US,* ER 64-1 and ER 64-1-s, (Washington, D.C., January 1964); *1955 Ruble-Dollar Price Ratios for Intermediate Products and Services in the USSR and US* (Washington, D.C., June 1960); and *1955 Ruble-Dollar Ratios for Construction in the USSR and the US,* ER 64-26 (Washington, D.C., August 1964). I have satisfied myself that these reports are scholarly studies and have utilized them as such. It will be evident at important points that the results would not have been greatly affected if I had referred to alternative sources.

7. *Prices of Producers' Durables in the United States and the USSR in 1955,* RM-2432 (Santa Monica, Calif.: RAND Corporation, August 15, 1959).

In these studies, ruble-dollar parities have been compiled from ruble price quotations obtained mainly from Soviet price handbooks and observers' reports and corresponding American price data compiled by the U.S. Bureau of Labor Statistics. American price data were obtained also from the Sears, Roebuck catalog and by special inquiry. For construction, reference was made to Soviet cost estimates used in revaluation of capital assets and to American reported contract prices.

In translating farm income in kind, commodity components of one country are valued directly in realized farm prices of the other. Average realized farm prices for the USSR are Nancy Nimitz's, as given in cited RAND studies, and for the United States are those reported in government publications.

In the foregoing ways I also obtain parities for translation of commodity components of outlays for final services, such as health care, education, and government administration. Corresponding expenditures for labor services are converted by reference to data from diverse sources on employment and average earnings in the two countries. Outlays for services of military personnel, including military subsistence, are translated in the same way as expenditures for labor in outlays for health care, education, government administration, and the like.

As is proper, I try throughout to use price ratios with Soviet weights to deflate ruble outlays and ratios with American weights to deflate dollar outlays.

APPRAISAL

Calculations like the ones made here are almost inevitably inexact. Apraisal of their reliability may be facilitated by a summary examination of more important sources of error and consideration of the likelihood of a bias in one direction or the other. Of particular interest is the translation of outlays from one currency to another. I focus, therefore, on the ruble-dollar price ratios for different groups of goods used in the translation. Where one currency is translated into the other by procedures other than deflation, reference is to the implied rather than to the explicit parities. It should be borne in mind that where the error in parities takes the form of an overvaluation of the ruble, Soviet outlays in dollars are overstated and American outlays in rubles are understated. Undervaluation of the ruble has a reverse effect.

Price quotations. In each country the price of any commodity considered in the compilation of parities ideally should correspond to the average unit value at which the commodity is delivered to its final use. In fact, many of the price quotations considered in compiling the parities used here do not correspond to such values. Ruble retail prices, for instance, often refer to Moscow, whereas dollar retail prices for many non-food items came from a Sears, Roebuck catalog. Use of Moscow retail prices probably does not lead to any very consequential error.[8] The validity of calculations based on Sears, Roebuck prices remains to be tested systematically.[9] Except for alcoholic beverage prices, the dollar retail prices considered omit state and local sales taxes. The resulting undervaluation of the ruble for all household consumption may be on the order of 1 or 2 percent.[10]

For producers' durables, the values to be deflated in both countries include freight charges, as is customary in national income calculations and proper, at least where the concern is to appraise production potential. Ruble-dollar price ratios, however, are compiled from FOB shipper prices. Moreover transportation and distribution charges probably account for a larger share of delivered prices in the United States than in the USSR.

8. Such prices are used without correction primarily in the case of food. According to data assembled by Janet Chapman, however, Moscow prices for twelve major foods averaged 101 percent of corresponding all-USSR average prices in 1936. Also Moscow and all-USSR average prices have moved closer together since that date. See Janet Chapman, *Real Wages in Soviet Russia Since 1928* (Cambridge, Mass., 1963).

9. In response to an inquiry regarding the representativeness of Sear's prices, the late Arthur M. Ross, when he was commissioner of the U.S. Bureau of Labor Statistics, commented in a letter dated January 30, 1967:

> Unfortunately, it is not possible to make a positive statement in this regard, nor have we made any definitive study of the subject. Sears' prices for various items are set according to various marketing strategies, availability of resources, and a variety of other competitive factors. As a result, prices for some items may be higher than average; others may be lower. Sears' catalog prices are used on a limited basis in the Consumer Price Index, particularly for the small cities (under 50,000 population) where mail-order buying is still important. On the basis of our own observations, we would conclude that Sears' prices are generally somewhat lower than are prices for nationally advertised brands having comparable descriptions, but are about the same as private brands offered by other stores.
>
> If the foregoing has not really answered your question, I would hasten to add that we in the Bureau of Labor Statistics, as well as researchers in the academic world and in private industry, have extensively used prices from the Sears' catalog as a general indicator to retail price levels for many commodities, particularly in making international comparisons.

10. For household retail nonfood purchases, I use a Soviet-weighted parity of 17.4 rubles to the dollar and a U.S.-weighted parity of 18.4 rubles to the dollar. Adjusted to omit state and local sales taxes from dollar prices, these parities might have fallen to, say, 16.8 and 17.7 rubles to the dollar, respectively. The omitted state and local sales taxes, I believe, are those of a general sort, as distinct from excises on tobacco and gasoline. On the possible magnitudes involved, see *National Income, 1966,* pp. 54-55. The indicated reduction in ruble-dollar parities for household retail nonfood purchases would cause the corresponding adjusted ruble-dollar parities for household consumption to fall by 0.6 and 1.7 percent. The parities for household nonfood purchases also figure somewhat in my calculations at other points.

Hence the ruble is undervalued here too, perhaps appreciably. Thus, for gross investment as a whole, the adjusted ruble may be undervalued as much as 5 percent where Soviet weights are applied and 3 percent where American weights are applied. A similar undervaluation occurs for the defense ruble, for which the parity of producers' durables is taken as a surrogate for that of munitions.[11] An additional error of uncertain nature appears wherever American price quotations were obtained from selected manufacturers.

Parities for construction are compiled from Soviet cost elements rather than final prices. Since such estimates are based on established input norms, which are often exceeded, the ruble must be appreciably overvalued in this case.[12] Although average construction prices could not be compiled for either country, an attempt was made to pair projects that were "similarly" located in the two countries.

Comparability of commodities. In compiling ruble and dollar price quotations for different commodities, studies on which I draw have sought to correlate relevant economic features of commodities in the two countries. This desideratum was often difficult to realize. Resulting errors in calculation must vary in different cases, but we must consider that the production of defective or otherwise substandard goods, while a feature in any modern economy, is by all accounts notably pervasive in the USSR. For example, among products examined in the first half of 1962 by inspectors of the Ministry of Trade of the Russian Soviet Federated Soviet Republic, 32.7 percent of clothing articles, 25 percent of knitwear, and 32.6 percent of leather shoes were rejected or reclassified to a lower-quality category. Among clothing and knitwear inspected by the Ministry of Trade of the Ukraine during 1963, 20 to 25 percent was condemned as defective.[13] All of these products are consumer goods, but substandard producers' goods are often reported as well.

How does production of low-quality items affect comparability? If substandard goods are rejected or reclassified to a lower-quality category, their production need not affect comparability at all, but it would be surprising to learn that such goods were not often sold simply as standard goods. Although this could be so in any case it is more likely in the USSR where both consumer and producers' goods have been chronically disposed

11. On the possible importance, for the parity for producers' durables, of the omission of transportation and distribution charges, see Becker, *Prices,* pp. 16-17.

12. CIA, 1955 *Ruble-Dollar Ratios for Construction,* pp. 9-10; A.I. Kats, *Proizvoditel'nost' truda v SSSR i glavnykh kapitalisticheskikh stranakh* (Moscow, 1964), p. 56.

13. Abram Bergson, *The Economics of Soviet Planning* (New Haven, Conn., 1964), p. 295.

of in a seller's market.[14] By implication, goods in the USSR that are nominally comparable to those in the United States frequently must be inferior in fact. At this point, therefore, ruble-dollar price ratios should tend to overvalue the ruble. The overvaluation could be significant.

What I have said primarily about commodities should also apply to construction. Thus an attempt has been made to pair quotations for comparable projects. Nevertheless, at least in the case of housing, the end products of Soviet construction work have been notoriously deficient in quality. This factor could be only partly allowed for in pairing quotations. Hence, in this area, too, the ruble should be overvalued.

Comparability of Services. While the parities used for construction, including housing, probably overvalue the ruble, differences in quality are taken into account in the derivation of a parity for current services of housing. The allowance is arbitrary, but the direction of any resultant error is conjectural.

On the other hand, for a variety of other final services, the calculations expressly or by implication take comparative wages as an appropriate parity for deflation of labor outlays. Hence labor inputs are taken to be of the same quality in the two countries. This is, of course, a conventional assumption in national income accounting, but it may be materially incorrect. The calculations in question are a case in point, for the ruble very possibly is often overvalued with respect to the labor component of final services. Overvaluation seems likely if we consider, for example, that the average level of education of labor employed in final services must usually be less in the USSR than in the United States. Also relatively more women are employed in such services in the USSR than in the United States, and one perhaps need not be an antifeminist to feel that quality is sometimes inferior on that account.[15]

At any rate, as would be expected, the parities used in the translation of outlays for final labor services are far more favorable to the ruble than are those used to translate expenditures for commodities. Hence, relative to

14. There are many signs, though, that, at least for consumer goods, this is no longer as true as it was in past years.

15. In 1960, according to computations of a Denison type (see Chapter 6), one Soviet worker was comparable on the average to 0.97 high school graduate. The corresponding figure for the American worker was 1.17. Soviet labor must tend to be of relatively higher quality in final services than in other sectors, but it should often be inferior to that in the United States. See, for example, CIA, *A Comparison of Consumption,* p. 38.

For the services considered, an additional source of bias favorable to the USSR is the use of inputs as a surrogate for output and the omission of allowance for capital inputs. But this is a deficiency in the initial computation of national income in national prices rather than in the deflation.

total output, Soviet outlays for final labor services became quite large in dollars and American outlays for such services are notably small in rubles (Table 5.3). An overvaluation of the ruble at this point, therefore, could be important. Partly for this reason, in Table 5.1 I have compiled comparative data on GNP exclusive, as well as inclusive, of final labor services. Among the use categories considered, final labor services are especially important in communal services. The comparative results obtained for such outlays must be examined accordingly.

TABLE 5.3. Labor outlays in selected final services, USSR and United States, 1955[1]

	Ratio of labor outlays to GNP (%)	
Output valuation	USSR	U.S.
Prevailing rubles	11.1	1.7
Adjusted rubles	13.2	2.2
Dollars	31.4	8.9

[1]The services included are health care, education, government administration, and defense (military personnel only).

A word about one other source of incomparability, namely, that resulting from the treatment of retail trade services. In each country prices of goods purchased at retail include trade markups. When commodities are paired in the two countries, however, the characteristics of the commodities alone are considered. Hence no allowance is made for differences in the quality of trade services through which the commodities are supplied. As even the casual observer soon becomes aware, quality of trade services does differ in the two countries. Partly because of the relatively limited facilities available, partly because of the difference in trade technology, and partly because of the chronic shortages of goods in relation to demand, trade services in the USSR must be, by any standard, markedly inferior to those in the United States per unit of goods sold.[16] Consequently, in these calculations, too, the ruble must be overvalued.

Representativeness. Ruble-dollar price ratios for different groups of commodities (as distinct from labor services) were compiled from more or

16. Marshall I. Goldman, *Soviet Marketing* (New York, 1963).

less extensive samples of price relatives. While an attempt was made to assure that the samples were representative, it was a difficult task, for the price relatives for different kinds of commodities sometimes varied widely. Resulting sampling errors could be correspondingly large. The dispersion is especially great in the case of producers' durables. The sample considered for these goods comprises over five hundred items representing more than half of American purchases of producers' durables, but the parities derived could still be erroneus. For construction only twenty-five pairs of projects could be considered; curiously though, the resultant price ratios do not vary very much.

As for the direction of error, it is conjectural, but the samples tend almost inevitably to be more representative of varieties of goods produced in the USSR than of those produced in the United States. Thus higher-quality commodities produced in the United States often had to be omitted because they had no counterpart in the USSR. Such omissions do not affect the representativeness of parities compiled with Soviet weights; they do affect the representativeness of those compiled with American weights. Very possibly, in these calculations too there is a tendency toward overvaluation of the ruble. Commodities not produced in the USSR properly should be covered in the American-weighted parity and ideally at ruble prices corresponding to costs of producing very limited supplies in the USSR. For goods that are of high quality in the United States, the ruble prices in question presumably would be especially high. Hence ruble-dollar parities would tend to shift against the ruble with the inclusion of such goods.[17]

As indicated, ruble price quotations used in compiling ruble-dollar ratios were very often obtained from Soviet price handbooks. In appraising the representativeness of the sample of commodities studied, therefore, we must consider that handbook price quotations in the USSR necessarily relate to more or less standarized goods. While such goods usually constitute the bulk of sales, nonstandard products have been important, especially in machinery industries. Moreover there are reasons to think that extra-handbook prices for such goods tend to be inflated by almost any yardstick; indeed many of the nonstandard products seemingly are only nominally nonstandard, limited variants being introduced simply in order to evade the price controls established by the handbooks. Similar phenomena are, of course, not unknown in the United States, and some price quotations available for this country in 1955, a prosperous year, could also be overstated. Nevertheless these figures probably constitute yet another source

17. The deficiency in parities at this point, it should be observed, is independent of that due to incomparabilities resulting from matching American products with substandard Soviet products.

of overvaluation of the ruble, possibly a significant one, though less so for 1955 than for other years. The year 1955 witnessed a major price reform in the USSR, and extra-handbook prices probably were less important then than at other times.

Substitutions. Ruble-dollar price ratios compiled for one category of outlays frequently had to be used to deflate another. The effect on the results is uncertain, but it should be observed that the most important example is the ratio for producers' durables, which was also used to deflate munitions procurement.

Appraisal concluded. In sum, the parities used are subject to error at many points. The direction of error is not always clear, and insofar as it is, it is sometimes adverse and sometimes favorable to the ruble. Errors of the latter sort seem decidedly more important (Table 5.4). By implication, whether the calculations are in rubles or in dollars, Soviet output probably is overstated relative to that of the United States.

In appraising the calculations, I have focused on the parities applied. The comparative data on national income in national prices from which I started have limitations, as does the translation into adjusted rubles, whether for the USSR or for the United States. In any event the adjusted

TABLE 5.4. Biases in ruble-dollar price ratios applied or implied in deflation

Source of bias	Probable direction, whether undervaluation (−) or overvaluation (+) of ruble
Defective price quotations:	
Omission of state and local sales taxes from U.S. retail prices; use of f.o.b. shippers' prices for producers' durables	−
Use of Soviet cost estimates for construction	+
Mismatching of inferior-quality goods	+
Noncomparability of labor services	+
Noncomparability of retail trade services	+
Underrepresentation of high-quality goods	+[1]
Overvaluation of nonstandard Soviet machinery products	+

[1]For ratios with United States weights only.

rubles leave something to be desired analytically and so do U.S. dollar prices, though not to the same degree.[18]

These deficiencies are fairly familiar. Can they, however, offset or compound the relative overstatement of Soviet output? This question could be the subject of an essay in itself, and I will raise only one outstanding aspect: the widely suggested possibility that Soviet real national income suffers relative to that of the United States because of the undervaluation of farm labor services and so of farm output, insomuch as it reflects the undervaluation.

How to value farm labor services is a matter on which students of national income do not always agree. It is usually assumed, however, that such services are accounted for ideally at a "real" wage corresponding to that of industrial labor of the same skill and at a money wage corresponding to differential rural living costs. The principle, I think, is correct; at least where, as here, the purpose is to appraise production potential. It should be observed, therefore, that, in money terms, the typical Soviet farm worker in 1955 earned some 5244 rubles per man-year, or 55 percent of the average industrial wage: his American counterpart earned some $1762 per man-year, or 40 percent of the average industrial wage. Differentials in real earnings between farm and industry in the two countries presumably are less than those in money earnings indicated by these data. And, especially in the USSR, skill levels in the rural areas must be markedly below those in the city.

Even so, farm labor services may be undervalued. While undervaluation may occur in both countries, it necessarily would be disadvantageous to the USSR in view of that country's relatively large farm sector.[19] Additional data suggest that the distortion cannot be serious:

	GNP: USSR/U.S. (%)	
	With adjusted ruble valuations	With U.S. dollar valuations
As initially computed (Table 5.1)	27.6	45.2
With farm value added in each country increased to 1.5 times initial level	29.5	46.0

18. So far as my comparative data in national prices are in error, that is presumably attributable more to the data in rubles than to those in dollars. On the reliability of ruble data such as the ones I have used, see *Real SNIP.* I also discuss in that study the nature and limitations of other data, such as those compiled here in adjusted rubles.

19. The desideratum, to repeat, is that farm labor services be valued at the same "real" wage as that of comparable industrial labor and at a money wage corresponding to differen-

An increase in the average prices, net of materials cost, at which farm output is valued to as much as 150 percent of the initial level apparently would increase Soviet national income relative to that of the United States, but to a limited extent.[20]

NATIONAL INCOME BY INDUSTRIAL ORIGIN

Comparative data on gross national product by industrial origin are set forth in Table 5.5. The contribution of a sector to that output consists, therefore, of its "value added," as usually understood, although reference here is, of course, to additional value gross of depreciation.[21]

Data on gross national product in different valuations are the ones derived in the calculations of output by final use, as are the figures on the value added of selected final services—for, except for housing, value added consists only of wages. Data on wages paid in the services in question have been compiled in the calculations on output by final use.[22] With regard to housing for present purposes it seemed best simply to refer to final outlays, rather than to try to disentangle value added from materials inputs in these outlays.

In Table 5.5 nonfarm value added (exclusive of selected final services) was calculated as a residual. Hence in computing national income by industrial origin it remained only to determine the value added of agricul-

---

tial rural living costs. As not always considered, a corollary is that, in deflating one country's output in terms of another country's prices, one should treat rural and urban consumption as separate commodities, the former being valued at rural and the latter at urban prices. Or that is so if, as seems proper, production potential is construed as representing capacity not only to produce goods but also to deliver them to different localities. In practice, however, what probably matters most in this connection is that farm income in kind be treated separately from consumption generally, as has been done here, so there should not be any serious additional distortion at this point. For more about data on farm and nonfarm earnings see Chapter 6.

20. The recalculation, in effect, increases farm factor charges generally by 50 percent. In terms of adjusted rubles, farm factor charges consist almost exclusively of wages, so the recalculation results in a more or less corresponding increase in labor charges alone. In terms of dollar prices, farm factor charges include sizable nonlabor charges; so the implied increase in labor charges alone is appreciably greater than 50 percent. The recalculation uses the estimates of GNP by industrial origin presented later in this chapter.

21. As Kuznets made clear to me, at least for the United States, the sectoral data sometimes more nearly represent "gross domestic product originating" than "value added." That is so insofar as the principal sectoral contributions are net not only of materials but also of productive services obtained outside the sector.

22. In Table 5.5, I consider "defense" to be the earnings, including subsistence, of military personnel only. Wages paid civilians under "defense" in the United States are assumed to be more correctly classified as nonfarm income.

TABLE 5.5 Gross national product by industrial origin, USSR and United States, 1955

Industrial sector	Prevailing rubles			Adjusted rubles			Dollar prices		
	USSR (bil.)	U.S. (bil.)	USSR/ U.S. (%)	USSR (bil.)	U.S. (bil.)	USSR/ U.S. (%)	USSR (bil.)	U.S. (bil.)	USSR/ U.S. (%)
Farm	185.3	280.1	66.2	212.6	321.8	66.1	13.8	18.59	74.2
Nonfarm excluding selected final services	822.6	3949.2	20.8	588.8	2946.8	20.0	103.8	311.69	33.3
Selected final services									
Other than housing[1]	126.9	75.3	168.5	122.0	72.9	167.4	56.8	35.54	159.8
Housing[2]	8.4	44.5	18.9	8.3	44.1	18.8	6.4	33.74	19.0
All	*135.3*	*119.8*	*112.9*	*130.3*	*117.0*	*111.4*	*63.2*	*69.28*	*91.2*
Total GNP	1143.2	4349.1	26.3	931.7	3385.6	27.5	180.8	399.56	45.2

[1]Health, education, government administration, and defense.
[2]Gross outlays before deduction of materials inputs.

ture. Essentially, such value added is obtained as the excess of net farm output (that is, farm output net of production expense in kind) over other material inputs to agriculture. Net farm output and material inputs to agriculture, other than production expenses in kind, are determined for each country initially in terms of its own currency and then translated into the other's currency by applying suitably weighted ruble-dollar parities. Here and in the additional translation from prevailing to adjusted rubles, I rely on sources and methods such as were used in the compilation of comparative data on output by final use.

These calculations are often crude, and any error at this point necessarily affects also the calculation of nonfarm output as a residual. The resultant error in nonfarm output would not be at all proportionate, however, for the nonfarm sector is by far the larger one in both countries (Table 5.5). Since the figures on selected final services are likewise subject to error, the data compiled on national income by industrial origin are, in general, relatively tentative.

CONCLUSION

My calculations, although inexact, may shed further light on the comparative volume and structure of output in the USSR and the United States. In 1955, at the end of the fifth five-year plan, the USSR lagged far behind the United States in total output. Thus Soviet GNP is found to be but 28 percent of that of the United States if valued in rubles[23] and 45 percent of that of the United States if valued in dollars (Table 5.1).

Relations of different uses and sources of output in the two countries are very broadly similar to that for the GNP itself, but there are quite a few incongruities. Of particular interest is the fact that the special nature of the growth process in the USSR—as represented by the "Soviet model"—and related defense policies, causes that country to compare much more favorably with the United States in nonconsumption than in consumption. Soviet nonconsumption is 43 percent of American nonconsumption in rubles and 63 percent in dollars. Soviet consumption, however, is just 22 percent of American consumption in rubles and 37 percent in dollars (Table 5.1).

As late as 1955, application of the Soviet model had only very partially compensated for the "late start" by the USSR. The result, which is not always understood, was that the USSR compared much more favorably with the United States in farm output than in nonfarm output. In agriculture, the Soviet Union produced 66 percent as much as the United States in

23. Here and later, ruble data cited are of the adjusted variety.

rubles and 74 percent as much as the United States in dollars. In the nonfarm sector, however, the USSR was only 20 percent as productive as the United States in rubles and 33 percent as productive in dollars (Table 5.5).

Because of the larger population in the USSR, comparisons in per capita terms are necessarily less favorable to that country than those of an absolute sort. Suffice it to say that the Soviet GNP per capita is 23 percent of that in the United States in rubles and 38 percent in dollars. The corresponding figures for per capita consumption are 19 and 31 percent. The per capita nonconsumption of the USSR is 36 percent of the United States in rubles and 53 percent in dollars (Table 5.2).

As the cited findings illustrate, we encounter at almost every point and to a striking degree the familiar phenomenon of index number relativity. Measures in terms of alternative valuations diverge markedly. This gap is perhaps not very surprising in view of the still relatively limited advance of industrialization in the USSR compared with the United States. Moreover the calculation in rubles is less favorable to the USSR than is that in dollars. That trait, of course, conforms with the pattern for Western countries that Gilbert and Kravis observed long ago. It is also the pattern that is theoretically expected.[24] Its appearance here, therefore, is reassuring as to the reliability of the calculations.

Index number relativity reflects differences in price and output structure, and conformity of the relativity to the normal pattern here provides some support for use of ruble prices for national income measurement. It is worth noting, however, that, as revealed in data compiled for this study, the Soviet price structure differs not only from that of the United States but also from that of Italy, a country that seems to be at a similar economic stage to that of the USSR.[25] The differences are sometimes striking (Table 5.6). Perhaps most notable are the low prices of producers' durables relative to foodstuffs in the USSR, compared with not only Italy but even the United States. Expectations of many proponents to the contrary notwithstanding, socialism, as it exists in the USSR, has meant cheap machines rather than cheap food.

Peculiarities in the Soviet price structure have to be interpreted in the context of the distinctive nature of the Soviet model generally. From that standpoint, the peculiarities must often connote a correspondence of ruble prices to Soviet "scarcity values" rather than the reverse, and necessarily it is conformity of a country's prices to its own scarcity values that counts in national income measurement. But, although implications of the present study for the ruble price structure have properly been noted, I cannot re-

24. See *Real SNIP*, chap. 3.
25. See Chapter 7, this volume.

TABLE 5.6. Explicit or implied 1955 ruble-dollar price ratios and 1950 lira-dollar price ratios (ratio for GNP = 100)

Item	Prevailing rubles per dollar		Adjusted rubles per dollar		Lira per dollar[1]	
	With Soviet quantity weights	With U.S. quantity weights	With Soviet quantity weights	With U.S. quantity weights	With Italian quantity weights	With U.S. quantity weights
GNP	100	100	100	100	100	100
Consumption						
All	*122*	*118*	*110*	*111*	*102*	*102*
Food[2]	197	160	—	—	122	88
Housing	21	12	25	16	36	21
Health care and education	48	61	52	64	—	—
Health care	44	71	—	—	96	55
Education	49	46	—	—	56	40
Government administration						
All	*54*	*48*	*60*	*52*	*41*	*64*
Wages	43	21	52	27	35	20
Other	168	141	160	139	202	154
Defense						
All	*56*	*51*	*63*	*64*	*72*	*91*
Military personnel	38	22	42	26	37	21
Other	81	61	96	76	136	125
Gross investment						
All	*90*	*69*	*106*	*85*	*139*	*103*
Producers' durables	65	59	—	—	247	159
Construction	111	65	—	—	90	56

[1]Source of ratios is Milton Gilbert and Associates, *Comparative National Products and Price Levels* (Paris, n.d.).

[2]For ruble-dollar ratios includes alcoholic beverages.

open the large issue concerning the limitations of ruble prices for national income valuation.

I took as the ultimate desideratum the compilation of data on national income that might illuminate comparative production potential. However the ruble-dollar price ratios are read, the national income measures compiled are certainly remote from the sort ideally prescribed by theory for that purpose. On an analytic plane, however, divergent index numbers such as have been observed imply a related divergence in capacity to produce different output mixes. Thus, relative to that of the United States, Soviet output is, to repeat, smaller in rubles than in dollars. Theoretically, the implication is that Soviet productive capacity compares more favorably with that of the United States in terms of its own output mix than in terms of the American one. In spite of the limitations of our measures, that seems a plausible result.[26]

I have focused on 1955, a year for which available data are favorable to calculations such as mine. It may be hoped that further research will allow similar calculations for more recent dates. Meantime, we are able to extrapolate some of the major findings by using available related measures of changes in physical volume over time in the two countries.

If the results (Table 5.7) are at all near the mark, we may conclude that over the fifteen years 1955-1970 the USSR has gained on the United States in every sphere, but very unevenly. Hence structural differences that prevailed initially are sometimes ameliorated; for instance, the Soviet relative standing in nonfarm output has risen more than its relative standing in farm output. But they are sometimes compounded. For example, the Soviet relative standing in consumption, if anything, suffers in comparison with that in nonconsumption. As often reported, Soviet consumption has risen sharply since the midfifties. So has American consumption. As it turns out, the USSR still surpasses the United States much more in the growth of nonconsumption than in that of consumption. In total volume of nonconsumption the USSR actually surpassed the United States in 1970.[27]

26. It must be assumed that "production possibilities," or more correctly the "feasibility locus," is concave or at least not very convex to the origin. See Richard H. Moorsteen, "On Measuring Productive Potential and Relative Efficiency," *Quarterly Journal of Economics,* August 1961; and *Real SNIP,* chap. 3.

27. In extrapolating comparative data on output in the two countries from 1955 to 1970, I refer for the USSR to data on the change in physical volume from 1955 to 1970 in ruble prices and for the United States to such data in dollar prices. It is well known that such a procedure is subject to error, but if recent computations for Western countries in Irving B. Kravis et al., *A System of International Comparisons of Gross Product and Purchasing Power* (Baltimore, Md., 1975), pp. 8-11, are at all indicative, the error should be small (for GNP, perhaps not more than several percentage points on the down side) in the case of comparative output data for the United States and other countries in dollar prices. The error, however, apparently could be larger for corresponding data in prices of other countries. For that reason, comparative data in Table 5.7 are in dollar prices only. In extrapolating, I use data in Appendix Tables 19, 24, and 25.

TABLE 5.7. Soviet-American output ratios, dollar valuations, 1970

Item	USSR/U.S. (%)
Gross national product	62.9
Consumption	45.2
Nonconsumption	110.0
Value added, farm	97.2
Value added, nonfarm excluding services	59.9
Gross national product per capita	53.0
Consumption per capita	38.1
Nonconsumption per capita	92.7

6.
Comparative Soviet and American Productivity and Efficiency

This chapter examines the extent and sources of differences in productivity between the Soviet Union and the United States. One possible source is a variation in efficiency between the two social systems that the two countries exemplify, so the inquiry also bears on the comparative efficiency of those two systems. This approach to the study of the comparative efficiency of socialism and capitalism seems to be relatively new, and a principal concern is, by applying the approach in a particular case, to explore diverse methodological problems that arise.[1] Perhaps my substantive findings will arouse interest too, although I can hardly hope to dispose of the great issue in question.

The comparison is made for a single year, 1960. For present purposes, 1960 does not seem to have been an especially unusual one in the USSR, despite the fact that farm output was several percent be-

This chapter is a revised version of an essay originally published in Alexander Eckstein, ed., *Comparison of Economic Systems* (Berkeley, Calif., 1971), and drawn on here by permission of the Regents of the University of California. I have redrafted much of the original text, especially section 2, "Theoretical considerations." In a much restated and expanded form, that section has been republished as Abram Bergson, "Index Numbers and the Computation of Factor Productivity," *Review of Income and Wealth,* September 1975. I draw from that article material that is of particular interest here. Research for the study, in its original version, was done with the aid of a grant from the National Science Foundation.

1. Broadly similar inquiries were made in Abram Bergson, *The Economics of Soviet Planning* (New Haven, Conn., 1964), pp. 340 ff.; Joseph Berliner, "The Static Efficiency of the Soviet Economy," *American Economic Review,* May 1964; and Abram Bergson, *Planning and Productivity Under Soviet Socialism* (New York, 1968).

low the peak level of 1958. In the United States in 1960 total output expanded to levels appreciably above the previous cyclical peak of 1957. Unemployment, however, was 5.6 percent. These facts should be kept in mind.

THEORETICAL CONSIDERATIONS

The data to be considered relate to comparative levels of productivity at one time but are formally similar to data that are used in measuring the change in productivity over time and that are by now familiar in Western quantitative economics. Thus, as with the latter measurements, output is related to an aggregate of major factor inputs, and both outputs and inputs are more or less comprehensive in scope. Nevertheless, in any but a formal sense, my data are still rather novel, and that is also true of the use to which they are put. I have explored such an application theoretically elsewhere.[2] While the analysis is notably abstract and seems only to underline limitations of whatever can be achieved in practice, the bare essentials will serve as a point of departure.

The efficiency of an economic system is a many-faceted thing. If comparative levels of factor productivity are at all indicative of relative performance from that standpoint, they evidently must bear chiefly on one facet in particular, namely, realization of "production possibilities." Let us consider two hypothetical communities, Marxiana and Smithiana. In Marxiana production conforms to this formula:

$$F^m(x_m; g_m) = 0. \tag{6.1}$$

Here x_m represents the amounts of n final goods produced, that is, $x_{m1}, \ldots, x_{mi}, \ldots, x_{mn}$; g_m represents the amounts of t primary inputs employed in their production, that is, $g_{m1}, \ldots, g_{mi}, \ldots, g_{mt}$. Similarly, for production in Smithiana we have the formula:

$$F^s(x_s; g_s) = 0 \tag{6.2}$$

where x_s represents the amounts of the n final goods that Smithiana produces, that is, $x_{s1}, \ldots, x_{si}, \ldots, x_{sn}$; g_s represents the amounts of the t primary inputs that are employed in their production, that is, $g_{s1}, \ldots, g_{si}, \ldots, g_{st}$.

In each case, reference is not necessarily to production possibilities that are delineated by available technological knowledge. Rather each formula supposedly depicts a "feasibility locus" that reflects not only such knowledge but also prevailing inefficiency. In other words, for any given volume of employment of the different factors and given outputs of all but one

2. Reference is again to Bergson in *Review of Income and Wealth,* September 1965.

product, (6.1) indicates the amount of the remaining one that may be produced in Marxiana with due regard to both available technological knowledge and inefficiency. Formula (6.2) has a similar meaning for Smithiana.

As for production possibilities, let us assume for the present that technological knowlege is the same in the two communities. Thus a single formula

$$F(x; g) = 0 \tag{6.3}$$

may be taken to represent such possibilities in both communities. Depending on the community in question, appropriate subscripts must be added to the arguments in the function. On that understanding, (6.3) indicates for the community, for any given volume of employment of the different factors, and any given output of all but one product, the maximum output of the remaining one that can be produced with available technological knowledge. With respect to (6.3), then, there is no inefficiency.

Consider now some standard mix of inputs and outputs, x^*; g^*. For Marxiana, for any scalar $\beta_m > 0$, there should be some scalar $a_m > 0$ such that

$$F^m (a_m x^*; \beta_m g^*) = 0. \tag{6.4}$$

Consider also the ratio

$$K_m = a_m / \beta_m \tag{6.5}$$

which indicates the volume of outputs per unit of inputs that it is feasible for Marxiana to produce relative to that implied by the standard mix.

Proceeding similarly for Smithiana, we have for any scalar $\beta_s > 0$, some scalar $a_s > 0$ such that

$$F^s (a_s x^*; \beta_s g^*) = 0. \tag{6.6}$$

Also,

$$K_s = a_s / \beta_s \tag{6.7}$$

is construed in the same way for Smithiana as K_m is for Marxiana.

Consider the ratio

$$K_{ms} = K_m / K_s. \tag{6.8}$$

Unless there are scale economies (for the moment let us pass these by), K_m and K_s are independent of the magnitudes of β_m and β_s, respectively. The coefficient K_{ms}, therefore, is independent of both those magnitudes. As is readily seen, the coefficient also precisely represents the feature of immediate interest, relative efficiency in Marxiana and Smithiana, or, more precisely, the comparative degree of realization of production possiblities in the two communities.[3]

Reference is to inputs and outputs in each country that conform structurally to the standard mix. Conceivably, technological change may be of a "neutral" sort where variation in production capacity does not depend on the structure of either outputs or inputs. If technological change should be neutral in that sense, K_{ms} would also be invariant of the structure of inputs and outputs. But so far as circumstances are otherwise, K_{ms} is relative to that structure. As reflected in production capacity, in other words, a difference in efficiency between Marxiana and Smithiana depends on the mix. For any two communities, a ratio such as K_{ms} has been designated as the coefficient of factor productivity (CFP).

How might we observe the CFP. In question is measurement by use of comparative data on quantities of inputs and outputs in the two countries and the corresponding prices. As shown in an earlier essay of mine cited above, under certain conditions we obtain precise measures by applying, in turn, two formulas. Both formulas are familiar and each, in effect, yields a ratio of factor productivity (RFP) in the two countries. Thus, in one,

$$\text{RFP}_s = [(p_s x'_m)/(p_s x'_s)]/(\prod_i g_{mi}^{\varrho_{si}} / \prod_i g_{si}^{\varrho_{si}}) \tag{6.9}$$

and in the other,

$$\text{RFP}_m = [(p_m x'_m)/(p_m x'_s)]/(\prod_i g_{mi}^{\varrho_{mi}} / \prod_i g_{si}^{\varrho_{mi}}) \tag{6.10}$$

where p_s and p_m are vectors of prices of products in the two communities and ϱ_{si} and ϱ_{mi} are earnings shares of the *ith* factor input in Smithiana and Marxiana, respectively; it is understood that shares of all inputs add to unity in each community.

In both formulas, then, the ratio of aggregate output in the two countries is compared with a corresponding ratio of aggregate inputs. Outputs of different products, however, are aggregated arithmetically, while inputs are aggregated logarithmically. Also, in (6.9) aggregation involves Smithiana's prices as weights; that is, outputs are aggregated in terms of the prices of that country and inputs, with Smithiana's shares as weights. In (6.10) a corresponding use is made of Marxiana's prices as weights.

3. Let $\bar{a}_m, \beta_m$ be determined for (6.3) in the same way that a_m, β_m were determined for (6.1) and similarly for $\bar{a}_s, \beta_s$ as compared with a_s, β_s. Then,

$$K_{ms} = \left(\frac{a_m}{\bar{a}_m} / \frac{a_s}{\bar{a}_s}\right)\left(\frac{\bar{a}_m}{\beta_m} / \frac{\bar{a}_s}{\beta_s}\right)$$

If there are no economies of scale, the term on the far right reduces to unity. The remaining term on the right evidently represents relative efficiency. Note that if there are no economies of scale, this term itself is independent of scale, that is, of the magnitudes of β_m and β_s.

Formulas (6.9) and (6.10) give precise measurements for the CFM relating to particular standard mixes: in the case of (6.9), the standard mix corresponds to that actually experienced in Marxiana; in the case of (6.10), it corresponds to the mix actually experienced in Smithiana. As for the conditions under which such observations result, essentially the feasibility locus for each country must be of the famous Cobb-Douglas sort. The Cobb-Douglas function, however, is usually supposed to relate to the production of a single commodity. Here reference is to a linear aggregation of all products instead, so the production function for Marxiana is of the form:

$$a_m x'_m = A_m \prod_i g_{mi}^{\bar{\varrho}_{mi}} \tag{6.11}$$

where a_m is a vector of constants, $a_{m1}, \ldots, a_{mi}, \ldots, a_{mn}$, and A_m and $\bar{\varrho}_{mi}$ are also constants. The latter add to unity. Similarly, for Smithiana,

$$a_s x'_s = A_s \prod_i g_{si}^{\bar{\varrho}_{si}} \tag{6.12}$$

The notation corresponds to that for Marxiana, and here too the exponents of input terms add to unity.

In each country, furthermore, prices must conform to these principles: for final products, they must correspond to marginal rates of transformation; for primary inputs, to marginal rates of substitution. Reference is to rates of transformation and substitution given by the feasibility locus. Hence for product prices we have:

$$\begin{aligned} p_{mi} / p_{mj} &= a_{mi} / a_{mj}; \\ p_{si} / p_{sj} &= a_{si} / a_{sj}. \end{aligned} \tag{6.13}$$

For earnings of inputs,

$$\begin{aligned} v_{mi} / v_{mj} &= (\bar{\varrho}_{mi} / \bar{\varrho}_{mj})(g_{mj} / g_{mi}); \\ v_{si} / v_{sj} &= (\bar{\varrho}_{si} / \bar{\varrho}_{sj})(g_{sj} / g_{si}). \end{aligned} \tag{6.14}$$

Here v_{mi}, v_{mj}, v_{si} and v_{sj} are earning rates for the *i*th and *j*th inputs. We also have

$$\begin{aligned} \bar{\varrho}_{mi} / \bar{\varrho}_{mj} &= \varrho_{mi} / \varrho_{mj} \equiv v_{mi} g_{mi} / v_{mj} g_{mj} \\ \bar{\varrho}_{si} / \bar{\varrho}_{sj} &= \varrho_{si} \varrho_{sj} \equiv v_{si} g_{si} / v_{sj} g_{sj} \end{aligned} \tag{6.15}$$

In other words, in each country product prices are proportional to output coefficients in the feasibility locus, and earnings shares, as often supposed for a Cobb-Douglas function, correspond to factor exponents in that locus.

How do the foregoing pricing principles compare with the "factor cost" standard familiar in national income valuation theory? That standard, as usually construed, ideally involves valuation at marginal cost where input prices themselves conform to "competitive norms." With such valuation, prices obviously also conform to the principles set forth here. According to familiar reasoning, however, in order to be realized ideally, the theoretic factor cost standard presupposes that there is no inefficiency to begin with; in other words, the feasibility locus and production possibilities come to the same thing. Where the concern is to appraise comparative efficiency, evidently we must allow for the possibility that in at least one of the two countries considered there is a consequential shortfall from production possibilities. The pricing principles that have been set forth here are equally valid whether there is inefficiency or not, although, especially at this point, theory seems to be one thing and practical work quite another.[4]

With such pricing, (6.9) and (6.10) are the formulas indicated for the computation of RFP where the feasibility locus is of the expanded Cobb-Douglas sort in (6.11) and (6.12). As explained in my cited essay, however, should that locus conform to some other formula, the computation of the RFP properly should proceed correspondingly. Thus, in the Cobb-Douglas function the elasticity of substitution (σ) between any two inputs is unity. Should σ instead be $\neq 1$, then in the computation of RFP outputs should be aggregated as before; inputs, on the other hand, should be aggregated in accord, not with Cobb-Douglas, but with the well-known CES alternative to that function.[5]

Other possible departures from (6.11) and (6.12) do not seem to lend themselves so readily to analytic representation and corresponding adaptation of (6.9) and (6.10). Still something can be—and indeed has been—said a priori about their impact should (6.9) and (6.10) be employed.[6]

4. With factor cost as formulated, there could still be inefficiency inasmuch as there are "externalities" involving interrelations of production functions of different production units. But, in that case, factor cost can no longer be considered the ideal in national income valuation or for purposes of the productivity computations at hand.

5. Considering, for simplicity, the case in which there are only two inputs, we may use this formula:

$$[(\Phi g^{\varepsilon}_{m1} + g^{\varepsilon}_{m2}) / (\Phi g^{\varepsilon}_{s1} + g^{\varepsilon}_{s2})]^{1/\varepsilon}.$$

Where computations are in Smithiana's prices, $g_{s1} = g_{s2} = 1$, and g_{m1} and g_{m2} are the corresponding relatives for Marxiana. Also,

$$\Phi = \varrho_{s1} / \varrho_{s2}.$$

Where computations are in Marxiana's prices, $g_{m1} = g_{m2} = 1$, and g_{s1} and g_{s2} are the corresponding relatives for Smithiana, while

$$\Phi = \varrho_{m1} / \varrho_{m2}$$

Finally,

$$\varepsilon = (\sigma - 1) / \sigma$$

6. In addition to entailing $\sigma = 1$, the expanded Cobb-Douglas function presupposes that each country's transformation locus is linear and that marginal rates of transformation be-

I have been abstracting from economies of scale and differences in the technological knowledge of two countries. So far as these economies and differences exist, the CFM necessarily reflects those aspects as well as comparative efficiency, a fact that will have to be considered.

THE CALCULATIONS

Factor productivity in the USSR in 1960 is found to have been far below that in the United States. Thus output per unit of factor inputs in the USSR is calculated at but 30.6 or 42.0 percent of that in the United States; the particular figure depends on which computation is considered. I refer to computations for the economy generally. Corresponding measures compiled for the nonfarm sector alone are 39.1 and 58.7 percent.

Table 6.1 shows, together with the foregoing measures, underlying data on comparative outputs and inputs in the two countries and related results. For the present I shall focus on figures outside parentheses and on those that include unadjusted employment measures.[7] The alternative computations for the economy in general and for the nonfarm sector alone are given both

---

tween final products are independent of the factor input structure, while the marginal rate of substitution between inputs is independent of the output structure. According to reasoning set forth by Bergson in *Review of Income and Wealth,* September 1975, if in fact the transformation locus should be, say, concave from below, (6.9) would tend to be biased favorably to Smithiana and (6.10) favorably to Marxiana. There is perhaps also a presumption that because of the interrelations between rates of transformation and input mixes and between rates of substitution and output mixes, (6.9) and (6.10) are subject to biases of a sort contrary to those resulting from concavity of the transformation locus. Curiously, where the standard mix is a hybrid of outputs of one country and inputs of another, an appropriate combination of relatives of aggregate outputs and inputs, one in one country's weights and the other in the other's, is not subject to any bias due to interrelations like the ones in question. I will return to this point later.

In thinking about the possible shape of the feasibility locus, well-known theoretical considerations regarding the shape of the production possibility schedule inevitably come to mind, but for reasons explained by Bergson in *Review of Income and Weath,* September 1975, such a procedure could be misleading.

When the feasibility loci are given by (6.11) and (6.12), could the CFP be >1 for one mix of inputs and outputs and <1 for another? Possibly and indeed it is certain whenever factor earnings shares differ in the two communities. Perhaps the moral is that there are always some mixes of inputs and outputs in which any community will excel another, but to conclude that that is so in any particular case one may have to extrapolate (6.11) and (6.12) far beyond the range of mixes actually observed. It would seem only to compound doubts already attending the application of those formulas within the observed range. In applying (6.9) and (6.10), therefore, it seems best to think of those formulas as presupposing (6.11) and (6.12) for the feasibility locus only within the observed range. That, in any event, is the understanding here.

7. In this section and the following one I explain only summarily the data in Table 6.1. Further details on sources and methods are available. See the Preface.

in dollars and in rubles and are intended to represent applications of formulas (6.9) and (6.10). The formulas are applied on the understanding (I trust, not a surprising one) that the USSR is Marxiana and the United States, Smithiana.

Gross product for all sectors listed in Table 6.1 corresponds to gross national product as it is usually understood in national income accounting. For the nonfarm sector, gross product corresponds to its contribution to gross national product. For each sphere, I focus on two broad inputs, labor and reproducible capital, and data on these are intended to correspond in coverage to output. Provisionally, I exclude from the calculations certain final services: education, health care, defense, other government services of a more or less conventional sort, and housing. More precisely, for both the economy in general and the nonfarm sector, I omit from output the value added by the services in question (for housing, the contribution of material inputs had to be omitted as well). From inputs of labor and reproducible capital I omit the amounts of those factors employed in the provision of such services. These omissions apart, for countries at rather different stages, such as the USSR and United States in 1960, delimitation of my calculations in conformity with conventional national income accounting poses some familiar questions as to comparability in a deeper sense. But what could be said on this matter is fairly evident and need not be labored.[8]

Where ruble valuations are called for, I have sought to compile data in terms of ruble factor cost rather than prevailing ruble prices. For practical purposes, valuation is at prevailing ruble prices less the so-called "turnover tax" plus subsidies. Where dollar valuations are in order, I have simply compiled data in prevailing dollar prices. In both cases, 1955 is taken as the valuation year.

I refer primarily to the valuation of output. In the table, the index numbers of reproducible capital refer to stocks but are assumed also to represent capital services. Each index number is the average of two relatives, one with fixed capital included gross of depreciation and the other with such capital included net of depreciation. In compiling the latter relatives, depending on the required valuation, I have sought to aggregate capital goods in either prevailing ruble prices of 1955 or prevailing dollar prices of

8. To return to the services omitted, for the USSR other government services include an allowance for internal security and Party administration. For both countries, highways are subject to special treatment, which will be discussed later. The national income accounting mentioned is that practiced in the West. According to the national income accounting applied in the USSR, services of the sort under discussion are usually excluded from national income to begin with.

TABLE 6.1. Comparative output, factor inputs, and factor productivity, USSR and United States, 1960

Item	Nature of measurement	USSR/U.S. (%)	
		All sectors	Nonfarm[1]
Gross product	In 1955 ruble factor cost	31.5	26.8
	In 1955 dollars	49.7	47.4
Employment	Workers engaged	164.6	98.1
Employment (adjusted)	Workers engaged (adjusted hypothetically to equivalent male, 8th-grade graduate)[2]	122.3	81.4
Reproducible capital[3]	In 1955 rubles	41.7	37.7
	In 1955 dollars	52.2	48.3
Major inputs (employment plus reproducible capital)	With ruble weights	103.0 (95.6; 116.7)[4]	68.5 (65.0; 73.2)[4]
	With dollar weights	118.2 (107.2)[5]	80.7 (77.9)[5]
Major inputs (employment adjusted, plus reproducible capital)	With ruble weights	84.6 (79.9; 91.6)[4]	60.9 (58.4; 63.7)[4]
	With dollar weights	95.7 (90.8)[5]	70.5 (69.2)[5]
Gross product per worker	With output in 1955 ruble factor cost	19.1	27.3
	With output 1955 dollars	30.2	48.3

Gross product per worker (employment adjusted)	With output in 1955 ruble factor cost	25.8	32.9
	With output in 1955 dollars	40.6	58.2
Gross product per unit of reproducible capital	With 1955 ruble valuations	75.5	71.1
	With 1955 dollar valuations	95.2	98.1
Gross product per unit of major inputs	With 1955 ruble valuations	30.6 (32.9; 27.0)[4]	39.1 (41.2; 36.6)[4]
	With 1955 dollar valuations	42.0 (46.4)[5]	58.7 (60.8)[5]
Gross product per unit of major inputs (employment adjusted)	With 1955 ruble valuations	37.2 (39.4; 34.4)[4]	44.0 (45.9; 42.1)[4]
	With 1955 dollar valuations	51.9 (54.7)[5]	67.5 (68.5)[5]

[1] Here and elsewhere, unless otherwise indicated, selected services are omitted. See text.

[2] See text.

[3] Each index is an average of two indices, one for reproducible capital, including gross fixed assets, and the other for reproducible capital, including net fixed assets.

[4] Of figures in parentheses, the first derive from calculations where the rate of return imputed to Soviet capital is 16 percent rather than 12 percent as originally assumed and the second from calculations where $\sigma = 0.6$ instead of unity, as originally assumed.

[5] Figures in parentheses refer to calculations where $\sigma = 0.6$ instead of unity, as originally assumed.

1955. Finally, capital services are aggregated with employment by use of weights representing, on the one hand, gross capital charges, including interest and depreciation, and, on the other hand, labor earnings. For convenience, rather than aggregate inputs separately for each country, I aggregate intercountry index numbers of the two inputs.

Those are the calculations in bare outline. I will turn now to aspects of particular interest. In the table, output relatives were compiled especially for this study essentially by methods and procedures set forth elsewhere (see Chapter 5). For employment statistics, I rely on U.S. Department of Commerce data on persons engaged, data that are intended to represent full-time equivalent man-years. In compiling comparable figures for the USSR I use the careful studies of Murray Feshbach for the Joint Economic Committee and of Nancy Nimitz. Average annual hours of employment appear to have been similar in the USSR and the United States in 1960, and no translation was made from workers engaged to man-hours.[9] Data on reproducible capital in the United States in dollar prices come essentially from the work of Raymond Goldsmith, and in compiling corresponding data for the USSR, I rely on Norman Kaplan's careful analysis of the results of the Soviet capital inventory of 1959 and on the major study by Richard Moorsteen and Raymond P. Powell. Ruble-dollar parities were obtained by use of data and sources underlying computations of comparative outputs.

In short, in compiling data on outputs and inputs, I drew on a substantial volume of related research. Nevertheless the calculations are unavoidably often inexact. I refer to limitations of data on outputs and inputs apart from those relating to the price weights. As for the latter, in applying (6.9) I valued outputs and capital stocks in prevailing dollar prices and aggregate index numbers of labor and capital inputs with weights given by their prevailing dollar earnings determined in a usual way from national income accounts. Such dollar price weights, needless to say, do not exactly conform to the pricing principles that are theoretically indicated, but in practical work it usually is assumed, at least tacitly, that divergencies between dollar price weights and theoretic norms such as the ones in question are not apt to be so large and systematic as to give rise to consequential error. I proceed on that supposition, though further inquiry into the question at issue would no doubt be to the good. A factor-cost valuation for outputs presumably would be preferable to one in prevailing prices, but the results, I believe, would be little changed by use of the former standard.

Whatever the limitations of prevailing dollar prices from the relevant theoretical standpoint, it is fairly evident from well-known features of the

9. See Bergson, *The Economics of Soviet Planning,* pp. 368-369.

ruble price system that those affecting prevailing ruble prices must be incomparably greater. I have expatiated elsewhere on that system from a similar conceptual perspective.[10] Suffice it to say that, for purposes of valuing output, the ruble factor cost standard that I use in applying (6.10) represents a very real improvement over prevailing ruble prices. Moreover, while ruble factor cost also leaves much to be desired, three outstanding limitations appear to be the omission of a charge for agricultural rent as such (some rent almost inevitably accrues to farmers on better land and is treated here as labor earnings), the absence of any systematic charge also for interest on reproducible capital, and the inclusion of a more or less arbitrary charge for "profits." The importance of these deficiencies may be judged, to some extent, from the following recomputation of output per unit of inputs in rubles. I revalue farm relative to nonfarm output to allow, probably quite generously, for agricultural rent equal to 60 percent of Soviet farm labor income. I also revalue such output to allow for interest on reproducible capital at 12 percent and to exclude profits. These adjustments cause Soviet output per unit of factor inputs to rise from 30.6 to 32.9 percent of that of the United States in all sectors. Productivity in the nonfarm sector alone, of course, does not change.[11]

It seems somewhat reassuring that comparative levels of output are hardly sensitive to the choice even between ruble factor cost and prevailing rubles. Thus, in terms of ruble factor cost, the Soviet GNP in 1955 was 27.5 percent as large as that of the United States. In terms of prevailing rubles, the ratio was 26.3 percent (see Chapter 5).

Where capital goods are a factor input, valuation, to repeat, is in prevailing ruble prices. Such prices may be arguably preferable to ruble factor cost even if they diverge markedly. In fact, they apparently tend not to do so. It follows, however, that they are subject to much the same deficiencies

10. See *Real SNIP,* chaps. 3, 8, 9. In that study, I take as a desideratum a so-called "adjusted factor cost" standard of valuation: essentially, prices correspond to average cost, where services of factors are charged at uniform prices that are proportional, on the average, to factor productivities in different activities. Adjusted factor cost was formulated as a standard of output valuation, but the indicated charges for factor services may serve at once in the aggregation of inputs as well. As will become evident, I also in effect think of adjusted factor cost as a desideratum here. That still seems in order as a practical expedient even though that standard itself is not exactly ideal theoretically. See also Bergson in *Review of Income and Wealth,* September 1975, pp. 271 ff.

11. The recomputation entails increasing ruble value added per unit of farm output by 55.6 percent and reducing that per unit of nonfarm output by 2.6 percent. I take Soviet farm and nonfarm output, in ruble factor cost of 1955, to amount respectively to 260 and 844 billion rubles and use these estimates of relevant charges for the same year: for agriculture rent, 115.6 billion rubles; for interest on farm and nonfarm capital, 30.3 and 120.2 billion rubles, respectively; and for profits and related charges on farm products, 24.4 billion rubles, and on nonfarm products, 135.2 billion rubles.

that affect ruble factor cost generally, although the omission of agricultural rent is no longer among them. Index numbers of reproducible capital in prevailing ruble prices must be read accordingly.

In the USSR, although workers are paid wages for their services, as is well known, no systematic net charge for reproducible capital is included in costs. In addition there has been no market for capital in any conventional sense. Hence, it is difficult even to identify, never mind to calculate, returns to capital that, taken together with labor earnings, may meaningfully represent the factor shares needed to apply (6.10). For purposes of that application, therefore, I allow for a more or less arbitrary rate of return on reproducible capital. The rate used, 12.0 percent, does not seem to be a serious understatement in view of the fact that the computed rate for the United States is but 9.5 percent. Admittedly the USSR's relatively low capital stock per worker (Table 6.1) may signify a relatively high rate. Along with available data on comparative money wage rates and investment goods prices, the indicated rates of return imply a marginal rate of capital substitution for labor in the USSR that is 3.2 to 4.2 times as high as that in the United States; this margin seems fairly generous.[12] It is also illuminating that the share of *net* capital income in the total of labor and *net* capital income combined for the whole economy, excluding selected final services, is 28.7 percent for the USSR and 20.0 percent for the United States. Related but not fully comparable figures compiled elsewhere are 25 percent for the USSR, 14 percent for the United States, 18 percent for France, and 20 percent for Italy.[13]

Yet the assumed rate of return is arbitrary. It should be observed, therefore, that if one imputes to Soviet reproducible capital a still higher rate of 16 percent, Soviet productivity rises to a very limited extent relative to American productivity (see the first of the paired figures in parentheses in Table 6.1, where calculations are in rubles). Only the calculations in rubles, of course, are affected.[14]

12. Derived from the formula:

$$MRS_s/MRS_u = r_{su}W_{us}P_{su}$$

where r_{su} is the ratio of the Soviet to the American rate of return, W_{us} is the ratio of the average money wage in the United States to that in the USSR, and P_{su} is the ruble-dollar parity for investment goods. The second term is found to be 0.45 from data in *National Income, 1966,* p. 108, and TSU, *Narodnoe khoziaistvo SSSR v 1964 g.,* p. 555. Depending on whether weights used are Soviet or American, the ruble-dollar parity for investment goods is found, essentially by procedures described in Chapter 5, this volume, to be 4.7 or 6.1 rubles to $1.

13. The Soviet figure relates to 1955 factor inputs and 1960 earning rates. Others relate to 1960-1962. See Bergson, *Planning and Productivity Under Soviet Socialism,* pp. 87 ff.; and E. F. Denison, *Why Growth Rates Differ* (Washington, D.C., 1967), p. 38.

14. With regard to Soviet pricing as it affects capital, R. H. Moorsteen and R. P. Powell remind us in *The Soviet Capital Stock, 1928-1962* (New Haven, Conn., 1966), pp. 256-257,

Calculations by the formulas applied thus far assume that $\sigma = 1$, but empirical studies suggest that $\sigma < 1$, perhaps appreciably so.[15] Recomputing productivity with σ equal to, say, 0.6, alters the measures again but only by a small amount. As expected, measures in ruble values drop somewhat, while those in dollar values increase somewhat (see figures in parentheses in Table 6.1).[16] As the second of the parenthetically paired figures illustrates, the reductions in the ruble measures evidently produces the opposite effect of a 16 percent rate of return in Soviet capital.[17]

---

that the Soviet failure to account properly for returns to capital means that capital goods tend to be undervalued relative to labor. Unless allowance is made for this undervaluation, rates of return like the ones cited are not as high as they seem. The assumed rates still are generous, however, in the light of other evidence presented.

The Soviet government has found it expedient to allow the publication and prescription of interest-like norms for use in investment-project appraisal, although they omit from prices a charge for capital. These norms, which vary in different branches, do not seem very illuminating as to the rate of return on Soviet capital if it is considered that little is known about the extent of their application and still less is known about the actual returns generated under their use. See Bergson, *The Economics of Soviet Planning,* chap. 11.

I refer to Soviet pricing as it was prior to recent reforms in Soviet planning. Under the reforms, principles of price formation have been changed along with planning arrangements generally. While implications as to the actual return on capital are still obscure, enterprises that previously received much of the capital they required in the form of interest-free budgetary grants now pay into the budget a charge, usually at a rate of 6 percent, on their capital assets. In addition, industrial prices were reviewed in 1967 to allow a planned profit averaging about 15 percent on the enterprise's capital.

15. See K. J. Arrow, H. B. Chenery, B. Minhas, and R. M. Solow, "Capital Labor Substitution and Economic Efficiency," *Review of Economics and Statistics,* August 1961; and P. A. David and Th. van de Klundert, "Biased Efficiency Growth in the U.S.," *American Economic Review,* June 1965.

16. On reasons to expect the indicated sort of effect generally, see Bergson in *Review of Income and Wealth,* September 1975. Given American factor shares and the magnitude of σ, one may compute the corresponding factor shares that would accrue to Soviet factor inputs if they were employed in conformity with the same isoquants as those in the United States. It should be observed, then, that if $\sigma = 0.6$ the implied Soviet share of capital in the earnings of labor and capital together is 48 percent for the economy generally and 44 percent for the nonfarm sector. I include depreciation in the share of capital. The corresponding figures indicated by the assumed rates of return of 12 and 16 percent on Soviet capital are 34 and 40 percent for the whole economy and 38 and 43 percent for the nonfarm sector. These calculations, therefore, seem to provide further support for the assumed rates of return. For purposes of the computations, I take the capital stock index to be a geometric mean of the indices for that item in dollars and rubles.

17. Except for the case just considered where, $\sigma = 0.6$, I have been computing factor productivity in conformity with (6.9) and (6.10). Consequently, where output is valued in dollars, capital stocks are valued in the same currency and the resulting index is aggregated with that for labor in terms of dollar factor shares. Similarly, when output is valued in rubles, capital stock is valued also in that currency and the resulting index is aggregated with that for labor in terms of ruble factor shares. As indicated in footnote 6, however, alternative compu-

To return to selected final services, the reasons for excluding these in the case of housing are chiefly two. First, when valuations are in rubles, the proverbially nominal housing rentals in the USSR must be rejected along with prevailing ruble prices in general, but in view of the immense importance of capital inputs into housing, recourse to ruble factor cost rentals that omit any systematic charge for capital is hardly a satisfactory alternative. Second, meaningful conversion from one currency to another is especially difficult for housing services because of a notable variation in quality in each country.

The exclusion of selected final services other than housing, of course, stems from the need, under the conventional national income accounting procedure observed here, to measure their output by inputs and indeed essentially by inputs of labor alone. Given such a procedure, inclusion of such services, in calculations of comparative productivity is evidently rather pointless. Nevertheless, as Simon Kuznets reminded us long ago, these services are not only "final" but in some degree "intermediate," as well, and so may favorably affect productivity in the economy as a whole. Although I generally ignore these services in my calculations, therefore, I include among the factor inputs covered the sizable amount of capital invested in highways. Intermediate uses of highways are relatively tangible and important and should not be neglected. Highways, furthermore, are incomparably more consequential in the United States than in the USSR, in terms of capital invested and final uses both of which are unrepresented here, so the procedure followed is admittedly favorable to the USSR. Soviet output per unit of factor inputs would fall relative to that of the United States by one or two percentage points if highway capital were omitted from inputs for both countries.[18]

---

tations using "mixed" weights are likewise of theoretical interest. In these computations outputs are aggregated in terms of weights relating to one price system and inputs in terms of weights relating to the other. As seen from Table 6.1, such weighting widens the spread between resulting measures, as it did when $\sigma < 1$ instead of $\sigma = 1$. But note that the extent of the further widening diminishes when $\sigma < 1$. Indeed if there were a single index for the capital stock and if ruble factor shares were determined to conform to U.S. factor shares and the assumed magnitude of $\bar{\sigma}$, no further widening would occur because the first formula in footnote 6 would yield the same relative for inputs, whether calculations were in rubles or dollars.

While applying (6.9) and (6.10) generally, I have departed from those formulas insofar as capital stocks have been computed as linear rather than geometric aggregates. Also employment has been calculated simply in physical units. Later some attempt will be made to allow for differences in the quality of labor, but labor of different qualities will still be aggregated linearly rather than geometrically.

18. In dealing with services in my calculations, I have benefited from discussions with Simon Kuznets.

For similar reasons one may want also to include with inputs covered in my calculations some of the factors employed in providing other services, for example, law and order. It is conceptually and statistically difficult, however, to delineate the relevant employment. I have been considering the contribution of selected final services to productivity apart from their impact on labor quality. The latter aspect I will examine later as it relates to one outstanding service, education.

The data described must be given priority, but I have also calculated the comparative gross national product per unit of factor inputs with the inclusion of selected final services. The results are noted. Attention has been focused on gross product, perhaps with some conceptual justification, but productivity measures relating to net product are noted, too.[19]

PRODUCTIVITY VERSUS EFFICIENCY

Before discussing measures of comparative efficiency as manifested in realization of production possibilities, we must consider some additional limitations of measures of comparative productivity. We have yet to consider, too, sources of divergence between comparative productivity and comparative efficiency that we have discerned on a theoretical plane.

To begin with, although labor is taken as homogeneous, it is not, of course. It is not feasible, however, to factor into measures of productivity the different kinds of labor. Still it is illuminating that a recomputation reducing employment in a Denison-like way to its male eighth-grade equivalent slightly raises Soviet output per unit of factor inputs relative to the American figure (Table 6.1).

I also draw on Denison for the required coefficients evaluating workers of different educational attainment and sex. Denison compiled his coefficients to effect a reduction of employment to its male eighth-grade equivalent in the United States, and they supposedly represent corresponding productivity differentials in this country. Although they hardly do so with

19. With the inclusion of selected final services, gross product per unit of factor inputs for the whole economy in the USSR is 39.1 percent of that in the United States when valuations are in rubles and 56.9 percent of that in the United States when valuations are in dollars. The corresponding figures for net product per unit of factor inputs are 37.0 and 52.6 percent. The omission of selected final services lowers the net product per unit of factor inputs for the whole economy to 28.6 percent when valuations are in rubles and 38.9 percent when valuations are in dollars. In computing net product per unit of factor inputs I use as weights factor shares in which capital charges are net of depreciation. On gross versus net product in factor productivity computations, see E. D. Domar, "On the Measurement of Technological Change," *Economic Journal,* December 1961, pp. 716-717, 722-723; and D. W. Jorgenson and Z. Griliches, "The Explanation of Productivity Change," *Review of Economic Studies,* July 1967, p. 256.

any precision, they are adequate here to compare Soviet and American productivity when valuations are in dollars.

When valuations are in rubles, use should be made of corresponding Soviet coefficients, but the results perhaps would not be much more favorable to the USSR than those obtained. Thus education is scarcer and no doubt more valuable economically in the USSR than in the United States. Hence application of Soviet coefficients should lower employment and increase productivity correspondingly in the USSR relative to the United States.[20] According to Denison, however, a female worker is worth just 0.59 of a male one. One need not be a feminist to feel that this rating is unduly low, if not for the United States then for the USSR, for women do appear, as often claimed, to have had relatively great opportunities to enter the more renumerative professions in the USSR. Women constituted some 43 percent of all workers in the USSR (other than in selected final services) in 1960. American women made up only 29 percent. If female labor is unduly discounted, therefore, the recomputation should favor the USSR.

After allowing for educational attainment and sex, I find that in the USSR a farm worker is equivalent to as much as 0.77 of a nonfarm worker. In the United States, the farm worker is practically on a par qualitatively with a nonfarm worker. These calculations are especially crude, but if they are at all near the mark, they represent decidely higher valuations of farm labor than are implied in the data compiled on output: 0.5 of an industrial worker in the USSR and 0.4 of an industrial worker in the United States.[21] In both countries the farm worker, of course, must have fared better in real terms than the implied money earnings suggest. Yet the following results, obtained when a farm worker in both countries is arbitrarily counted in labor inputs as 0.6 of a nonfarm worker may be of interest:

	Gross product per unit of major inputs, USSR/United States (%)	
	1955 ruble valuations	1955 dollar valuations
Employment adjusted as in Table 6.1	37.2	51.9
Employment further adjusted	38.6	54.1

20. To what extent, we may judge from a further recomputation: when educational attainment is evaluated in accord with coefficients for that aspect Denison has compiled for Italy, Soviet output per unit of factor inputs in rubles rises relative to the United States by two percentage points. Worker educational attainment in Italy is broadly similar to that in the USSR, so the Italian coefficients may serve as something of a surrogate for those for the Soviet Union.

21. I compare here farm labor earnings, as represented in data on national output by industrial origin, with the average money wage of an industrial worker.

The figures include all sectors. The results for the nonfarm sector alone are unaffected.

What of possible differences between the USSR and United States with respect to labor effort? How labor effort compares in the two countries obviously will not be settled here, but according to a familiar socialist claim, public ownership of the means of production should encourage workers to exert themselves with notable diligence. By all accounts the Soviet worker has sometimes done so, but there are reasons to think that among workers, as among the population generally, ideological zeal has been on the wane for some time. We cannot rule out the possibility that effort is, if anything, greater in the United States than in the USSR, as a Soviet economist reportedly has affirmed to a foreign correspondent.

> Really, there is no comparison between the working energy and efficiency of American workmen and Soviet workmen. The Americans are the best workingmen in the world. They possess the best traditions. After all, it was the energetic, able, skilled people who emigrated to America. They took with them the desire and ability to work hard and well.[22]

In contrast, it appears, the Soviet worker is still affected by the "Tom Sawyer tradition," according to which "one man paints, the rest watch."

In whatever way effort differs in the two countries, productivity must differ correspondingly. My comparative data must be read accordingly. Effort may vary because of a difference in incentive arrangements. In that case, it is likely itself to indicate a difference in efficiency, although such efficiency admittedly lies somewhat beyond "realization of production possibilities" as usually understood. The difference in effort may also reflect a difference in the workers' preferences between work and earnings. If it does, it is rather difficult to construe it as indicative of a difference in efficiency of any sort.

The stock of reproducible capital considered in this essay includes all such assets on hand, whether they are in use or idle. In the case of labor, however, it includes only the workers that are actually employed. In appraising comparative performance, therefore, unemployment itself must be considered the source of a shortfall in production possibilities. Despite continuing Soviet claims to the contrary, unemployment, of course, does exist in the USSR. Though chiefly of a transient sort, it can hardly be negligible. In the United States, as indicated, 5.6 percent of the labor force was reportedly unemployed in 1960. The effect on our results of extending our calculations to allow for unemployment must be judged in the light of those facts.

As computed, productivity represents output per unit of labor and re-

22. *The New York Times,* October 2, 1957, p. 18.

producible capital and hence is affected, apart from efficiency, by differences in two other productive factors: industrial resources and farm land. In view of well-known facts about the abundance of industrial resources in the USSR and the United States, a difference in this sphere is probably not very important. Industrial resources, however, often appear to be less conveniently located in the USSR. That may be a reason why, per unit of output, freight traffic in ton-miles in the USSR is 1.5 to 2.4 times as great as in the United States. According to such indices, Soviet transport performance is not especially out of line with indices of Soviet economic performance generally, as reflected in our productivity measures, but a less favorable geographic distribution of industrial resources in the USSR may contribute to the high freight costs there. If it does, it must tend to reduce Soviet productivity without necessarily impairing efficiency.[23]

I doubt, too, that differences in farmland greatly affect productivity measures. The Russians cultivated 1.53 times as much land as we did in 1960. In the light of a careful analysis by Gale Johnson, an average acre of Soviet farmland is qualitatively equivalent to perhaps half an acre of American farmland. Therefore, Soviet farm acreage is equivalent to 77 percent of ours. Inclusion of farmland so measured as a factor input scarcely alters my results where valuations are in dollars. In ruble valuations, Soviet output per unit of factor inputs rises one percentage point relative to that of the United States. The increase is less if labor is adjusted to a male eighth-grade equivalent. In the dollar calculation the weight for farmland is determined in a conventional way.[24] In the ruble calculation I again attribute to farmland income equal to 60 percent of farm labor earnings.

We saw that comparative productivity theoretically must reflect differences not only in efficiency but also in economies of scale. So far as economies of that sort turn on market size, one could suppose that both the USSR and the United States have usually been able to exploit those that are available. True, market size depends not only on the size of the country but also on the magnitude of overall demand, as measured by, say, GNP, transportation costs, and freedom of access to foreign buyers. In none of these features has the USSR been as favorably situated as the United States, but, except where economies continue to be manifested indefinitely with

23. On industrial resources in the two countries, see C. D. Harris, "Industrial Resources," in Abram Bergson, ed., *Soviet Economic Growth* (New York, 1953). On freight traffic, see H. Hunter, *Soviet Transport Experience* (Washington, D.C., 1968), pp. 35 ff.; and H. Hunter "The Soviet Transport Sector," in JEC, *New Directions in the Soviet Economy* (Washington, D.C., 1966), p. 576. In the text, I compare freight traffic with gross national product exclusive of selected final services.

24. As in Bergson, *The Economics of Soviet Planning,* pp. 379 ff.

scale, Soviet market size for the most part ought to be sufficiently large to permit their exploitation. Actually, with respect to industrial plant size, the Russians have frequently surpassed the United States, but, not too surprisingly in view of well-known aberrations of Soviet economic management, the result must sometimes have been diseconomies rather than economies[25] and, where so, seems properly considered as integral to rather than apart from inefficiency. Overall, perhaps productivity in the USSR relative to that in the United States has suffered because of the more limited Russian access to economies of scale; if so, the loss should not have been very consequential.

Inferences from productivity to efficiency, as explained, presuppose ideally that the countries compared have access to the same body of technological knowledge. Among relatively advanced countries technological knowledge developed by one is not easily withheld from another. Any ineptness at gaining access to foreign developments that causes a country's stock of such knowledge to lag in itself constitutes a form of inefficiency. And if productivity should diminish correspondingly, it is of little importance that such inefficiency should perhaps be viewed as "dynamic" rather than "static"—the sort of immediate concern.

Nevertheless technological borrowing takes time, probably more time for the USSR in view of well-known Western policies restricting economic relations with that country. The Russians, for their part, have not been exactly open about their own discoveries, and technological knowledge in the West generally must have suffered somewhat on that account. But the Soviet Union has long relied primarily on borrowing rather than on creation to increase its technological knowledge, and it must still be more of a borrower and less of a creator of such knowledge than the United States. In brief, in terms of comparative productivity the USSR must be at a disadvantage. I wonder, however, whether the disadvantage could come to the productivity equivalent of much more than several years of American technological progress, that is, a number of percentage points in terms of my productivity measures.[26]

25. Leon Smolinski, "The Scale of the Soviet Industrial Establishment," *American Economic Review,* May 1962.

26. But if the USSR borrows rather than creates technological knowledge, is not that fact itself indicative of inefficiency? Perhaps so, but for a country that was backward not so long ago the research and engineering capacities available for innovation as distinct from borrowing may be relatively limited. All things considered, borrowing may be economical from any standpoint.

Productivity may suffer, of course, not only from a lack of technological knowledge, which is the concern here, but also from a failure to apply it. A failure of that kind would imply inefficiency and necessarily of the static sort.

Technological knowledge affects productivity when it limits the outputs producible with

CONCLUSION

Depending on whether computations are in ruble or dollar values, output per worker in the USSR has been found to be either 26 or 41 percent of that in the United States. The corresponding figures for factor productivity are 37 and 52 percent, where labor is adjusted for quality and reference is to the economy generally, exclusive of selected services. For nonfarm sector alone, the corresponding ratios are, for output per worker, 33 and 58 percent and, for factor productivity, 44 and 68 percent.

What may be concluded as to Soviet efficiency? Thanks to Western scholarship, we know a good deal about efficiency in the USSR. This knowledge must be inferred, however, primarily from qualitative information on the nature of prevailing economic working arrangements and the patterns of resource use that they generate. The significance of my comparative data on productivity with regard to Soviet efficiency is beclouded by complexities, and as often is so in empirical work, a principal moral must be simply that more research is in order.

Despite their limitations, the data do seem to shed further light on Soviet efficiency. As is evident from Western research, Soviet economic performance is often faulty, to say the least, but there is, I think, more of a presumption than before that in terms of efficiency the Soviet economy and

---

available inputs. When it is of the "embodied" sort, however, such knowledge also affects the available inputs. To the extent that capital goods produced at different times and hence embody different technologies vary in their productivity, in principle their services should be valued correspondingly in computing productivity measures.

Obsolescence supposedly has been accommodated in the data on capital inputs, but just how is not clear in the case of the data compiled for the USSR, and I wonder whether old assets may not tend to be overvalued. See N. Kaplan, "Capital Stock," in Abram Bergson and Simon Kuznets, eds., *Economic Trends in the Soviet Union* (Cambridge, Mass., 1963), p. 100. That ambiguity probably exists also in the corresponding data for the United States (R. W. Goldsmith, *A Study of Saving in the United States* [Princeton, N.J., 1956], vol. 3, p. 5). Moreover, because of its extraordinarily rapid expansion under the five-year plans, Soviet capital stock was notably young in 1960; it averaged 10.7 years for fixed capital (Moorsteen and Powell, p. 336). Although a corresponding figure is not at hand for the United States, it surely would be higher. If old assets are overvalued, therefore, my calculations should understate capital services and hence overstate productivity for the USSR relative to the United States.

The degree of overvaluation of old assets, it is true, could easily be relatively greater for the USSR, whose embodied technologies often seem to be especially dated. If they are, that may reflect to some extent a Soviet disadvantage compared to the United States in availability of technological knowledge. Probably no less important are the formerly influential Soviet view that obsolescence has no place under socialism and the related policy of producing notably long runs of machines of given design. How to classify the inefficiency resulting from such a policy is an interesting question, which I leave to the reader. But it does not seem too bad that my measures of productivity may reflect it.

the nonfarm sector alone must be markedly inferior to that of the United States. Productivity in the USSR is especially low for the economy in general, possibly in part because of resource misallocation between the farm and nonfarm sectors. The generally low productivity implies also that efficiency is especially low in agriculture. That conclusion is not very surprising in view of commonly known facts about Soviet agricultural organization.

Both for the economy generally and for the nonfarm sector, productivity in the USSR is evidently low whether valuations are in rubles or in dollars, but it is particularly low when valued in rubles. My data are hardly comparable to those considered in theory, but on an analytic plane they seem to imply that the performance of the USSR is better if its own inputs and outputs, rather than those of the United States, are taken structurally as standard. That again is a plausible result.

I have focused throughout on efficiency in the sense of realization of production possibilities. Closely related to that question is the degree of optimality of the output structure. Observe, therefore, that the data set forth bear on the latter as well as on the former aspect. Indeed, inasmuch as the calculations in dollars are in prevailing prices rather than in factor cost, they are readily seen to be more relevant in principle to performance in the two spheres together than to realization of production possibilities alone.[27] Soviet performance does not appear to improve if the inquiry is extended to embrace optimality of output structure along with realization of production possibilities. Optimality, however, is properly the subject for a separate study.[28]

27. I must leave for another occasion extension of the theoretical analysis to the problem posed, but so far as optimality of commodity structure is of concern, one seeks essentially to appraise welfare. According to familiar reasoning, valuation of outputs in that case is more properly in prevailing prices than in factor cost. Viewed as inputs, capital goods seem best valued at prevailing prices rather than factor cost even when attention is focused on realization of production possibilities.

28. When optimality of output structure is in question, not least among the limitations of my data, I think, is the overvaluation of the proverbially large volume of substandard or otherwise undesirable goods, which enterprise managers somehow tend to produce in the USSR. Such overvaluation appears unavoidable in view of the chronic seller's market there, although the condition was not so acute in 1960 as formerly. While only USSR data in rubles are affected in the first instance, the comparative data on output must be partly distorted as well, whether valuations are in rubles or in dollrs. Although comparative data on capital inputs may also be affected, the result should, if anything, be a bias in my productivity measures favorable to the USSR.

At least for consumer goods, optimality of commodity structure is usually seen in terms of consumer preferences. As affected by the aberration of enterprise managers mentioned earlier, Soviet performance in this sphere cannot be much improved by reference instead to any likely "planner preferences."

What of the comparative efficiency of socialism and capitalism generally? While it exemplifies socialism, the USSR represents in well-known ways a particular variant of that social system (see Chapter 1). As an example of capitalism, the United States too is obviously rather special. Moreover we are interested particularly in the comparative efficiency of the institutions, policies and practices shaping resource use in the two countries. One inevitably wonders whether the relative performance of such economic working arrangements as observed here may not in a degree reflect historical and cultural circumstances peculiar to those countries. Who knows, socialism might work better and capitalism worse if circumstances were otherwise.

In short, we need further observations on the working of these two systems. Additional studies would provide evidence on comparative performance in different contexts and presumably would enable us to grapple more effectively with statistical limitations, which must often have a random impact. In this area especially, then, more research is desirable. Let us hope that new analyses will soon become available.

7.

Productivity in the USSR and the West

I report summarily here on the results of an attempt to compare levels of productivity in the USSR and a number of Western countries and to gauge the sources of observed differences. In common parlance, the productivity of an economy is often assumed to be synonymous with its efficiency. In economics, that is hardly so, and to infer one from the other may not be easy.

This inquiry, it is hoped, will nevertheless shed light on comparative efficiency in the USSR and the West. It may thus contribute also to settlement of the long-debated question of the relative efficiency of socialism and capitalism. The two social systems are usually understood primarily in terms of the locus of preponderant ownership of the means of production. Among countries under each system, institutions, policies, and practices for the conduct of economic affairs do vary, however. Economic performance presumably varies likewise. If this analysis should bear on the relative efficiency of the two systems, therefore, it must be understood that reference on the socialist side is primarily to a society where economic affairs conform to the Soviet model, characterized by a system of centralist planning and a development strategy that stresses growth and limited economic dependence on the West. That model has been widely applied in the social-

This essay was originally delivered as a Charles C. Moskowitz lecture at New York University on April 24, 1972, and was published in Jan Tinbergen, Abram Bergson, Fritz Machlup, and Oskar Morgenstern, *Optimal Social Welfare and Comparative Systems* (New York, 1972). With the permission of New York University Press, I republish it here in a somewhat revised form. Research was done partly with the aid of a grant from the National Science Foundation.

world; indeed, until recently it has been almost ubiquitous. Among Western countries I shall refer to the United States, France, Germany (the Federal Republic, of course), the United Kingdom, and Italy. By capitalism, then, I mean economic working arrangements of the proverbally "mixed" sort, although the mix varies.

In technical economic writings efficiency has diverse facets. A cardinal one that is frequently called productive efficiency is the degree to which a country produces the volume of output of which it is theoretically capable. What a country is theoretically capable of depends on the quantity and quality of the productive factors and the knowledge of technologies for combining them that are available to it. Productive efficiency is a somewhat intricate concept, but it is probably sufficient for my purpose to elucidate what, in any event, is rather familiar: a country may indeed fail to realize its theoretical productive capacity because of the nature of its economic working arrangements, that is, because of defective managerial and labor incentives and because of deficiencies of one kind or another in coordination of enterprises and industries, whether the coordination is achieved through markets or planning. So far as our data on comparative productivity illuminate relative efficiency, they do so primarily with respect to productive efficiency. I focus, therefore, on that aspect.

My data are for 1960, which seems to have been a fairly normal year in the USSR. For the Western countries under consideration, 1960 was marked by the expansion of output to new high levels. Yet some countries, especially the United States and Italy, were experiencing significant unemployment. Those facts should be borne in mind.

PRODUCTIVITY IN THE WHOLE ECONOMY

To compare productivity in different countries is a formidable task. The comparative data that I have assembled are necessarily inexact, but productivity in the countries studied should vary broadly, as I have found it does (Table 7.1).[1] The United States clearly surpasses the other Western countries. Next are the three Northwest European countries—France, Germany, and the United Kingdom—which are more or less on a par with each other but far below the United States. And much below these countries is Italy.

1. Sources and methods for the principal data compiled are set forth in a separate appendix, mentioned in the Preface, this volume, but I should note here that I have benefited especially from E. F. Denison, *Why Growth Rates Differ* (Washington, D.C., 1967). In the assembly of appropriate figures for Western countries, that work served again and again as a point of departure.

TABLE 7.1. Gross material product per employed worker and per unit of factor inputs, selected countries, 1960[1]

Country	Gross material product per employed worker	Gross material product per unit of factor (labor and reproducible capital) inputs
United States	100	100
France	51	63
Germany	51	65
United Kingdom	49	64
Italy	34	47
USSR	31	41

[1]Gross material product represents gross domestic product exclusive of output originating in selected final services: health care, education, government administration, defense, and housing. In the comparison of the USSR and the United States, however, it means gross national product.

Employment is, throughout, exclusive of workers employed in the services referred to, except housing. In the calculation of factor productivity, reproducible capital employed in all such services, including housing, was omitted.

Output and, in the calculation of factor productivity, factor inputs are valued at American dollar prices. In the comparison of Western European countries and the United States, valuation of output is at factor cost, and in that of the USSR and U.S., at market price. Employment is adjusted for hours; additional hours beyond those worked by an American nonfarm worker in 1960 were counted less than proportionately.

On sources and methods for this table and Tables 7.2 and 7.4-7.7, see the Preface.

These comparative relations appear in figures on output per worker and output per composite unit of labor and capital, that is, factor productivity. Factor productivity, which is a relatively novel but widely used measure is decidedly the more favorable of the two yardsticks to all the Western European countries in comparisons with the United States.

The USSR ranks with Italy at the bottom of the list, whatever the yardstick. The USSR is essentially on a par with Italy with respect to output per worker but appears to fall perceptibly below that country with respect to factor productivity.

In all these comparisons, a country's output is essentially its national income or output before the deduction of depreciation but exclusive of output originating in diverse services, particularly education, health care, government administration, defense, and housing. Correspondingly, in relating output to employment of labor, on the one hand, and to such employment and available capital stock, on the other, I refer to the amounts of both factors used in the whole economy, exclusive of those service sectors.

My comparative data, then, relate to productivity in the economy generally, apart from the indicated service sectors. International comparisons of productivity often include these services, but in convential national income accounting output in such sectors is actually measured only by factor inputs. For that reason, as practitioners have long been aware, inclusion of such sectors tends only to obscure rather than to illuminate differences in economic performance. They are, therefore, properly omitted here. I refer to services apart from housing, but for one reason or another, that sector seems to be rather special everywhere. Comparative productivity in it, therefore, is best left to a separate inquiry.

In view of the indicated omissions, my comparative data can appropriately be said to relate to gross material product per worker and per composite unit of labor and capital. Those familiar with the Soviet concept of national income will be aware that I have delineated national income here in a manner more or less comparable to that which is customary in the USSR. The Soviet concept of national income frequently has been criticized in the West, with good reason, but for purposes of these productivity calculations it has its point.[2]

In my calculations, output and, where in order, factor inputs are, of course, in comparable prices. Specifically, valuation throughout is in terms of American dollar prices.[3]

2. Housing apart, the services omitted here do not comprise all the components of national income for which output is measured by factor inputs, but they generally represent the bulk of such sectors. From the present standpoint, the case for omission of such services is greater because typically, in national income accounting, output of these services is measured by inputs of only one factor, labor. Inputs of reproducible capital and land usually are not represented at all.

As is proper, I exclude from gross material product only output originating in the service sectors in question. Output originating elsewhere but employed in the provision of services is included. In the case of defense, for example, gross material product excludes the services of military personnel but includes munitions.

Output originating in housing is omitted, along with output originating in the other services in question, but with the available data it was not feasible to exclude from the number of employed workers those engaged in providing housing services. The capital stock represented by housing, however, is left out.

On the scope of national income according to the Soviet concept, see Abraham Becker, "National Income Accounting in the USSR," in V. G. Treml and J. P. Hardt, eds., *Soviet Economic Statistics* (Durham, N.C., 1972).

3. What if in each comparison of a foreign country with the United States, valuation were in terms of the prices of the foreign country? It was not possible to make such calculations

Output per worker is the most usual representation of productivity. But the alternative measure of output per composite unit of labor and capital is the more interesting one here. Output per worker may vary between countries simply because workers in one country are equipped with relatively more capital than they are in another without productive efficiency of economic working arrangements being any greater in one case than in the other. By comparing instead output per composite unit of labor and capital, I in effect allow for such differences in capital stock per worker. My data should be seen in that light.

SOURCES OF PRODUCTIVITY DIFFERENCES

In this analysis, factor productivity too has limitations. To begin with, labor may differ in quality in different countries. So far as it does factor productivity also will vary, although productive efficiency will not necessarily be any greater in one country than in another. Were it not for the difference in labor quality, the economic working arrangements of one country might really function quite as well as even very different economic working arrangements in another. Two outstanding causes of differences in labor quality, however, are levels of education and sex. If we allow for differences in educational achievement and sex in a way made familiar by Edward F. Denison and indeed by use of adjustment coefficients he himself

---

here, but from broadly similar computations made elsewhere, it seems safe to assume that, with substitution of foreign national for American dollar prices, the spread of productivity levels among Western countries would tend to widen. The USSR should be related to those countries, however, essentially as here. That is most clearly indicated for productivity in the economy generally, but most likely the same relations obtain for productivity in industry alone, to which I refer later. See Abram Bergson, *Planning and Productivity Under Soviet Socialism* (New York, 1968); and Chapter 6, this volume.

Reference has been to the effect of valuation in terms of one rather than another price system. As the technically inclined hardly need to be told, factor productivity calculations may vary in other respects. Most important, use may be made of diverse computational formulas. It should be observed, therefore, that I rely here on the so-called Cobb-Douglas formula and its unity "elasticity of substitution" (σ) between factor inputs. As it turns out, the essential results are hardly affected if use is made of a CES formula with a very different σ, say, $= 0.6$. European countries and the USSR, however, then gain on the United States, the increase being relatively marked in the case of Italy. If the United States is again taken as 100 the factor productivity measures in question are: France, 65; Germany, 70; United Kingdom, 68; Italy, 55; USSR, 44.

Later, in calculating factor productivity for industry, I shall also apply the Cobb-Douglas formula. It may be just as well to note now that those results, too, are little affected by substituting the CES formula with $\sigma = 0.6$. For later reference, when the United States is 100, the alternative measures are: France, 73; Germany, 73; United Kingdom, 66; Italy, 65; USSR, 60.

has applied in such calculations, we see that all Western countries other than the United States again gain on that country (Table 7.2). They compare with each other much as before, however, whether the yardstick is labor or factor productivity. The Soviet Union also gains on the United States at this point, but it is still more or less on a par with Italy in labor productivity and somewhat below it in factor productivity.

Denison's adjustment coefficients supposedly represent the comparative earning capacity of workers at different educational levels and of different sexes. I refer to earning capacity in terms of the American experience. Such coefficients are appropriately applied here not only to the United States but also to other countries for, to repeat, my calculations generally are in American dollar prices. As Denison would be the first to admit, however, the coefficients are crude, and my results must be so also. Particularly dubious, I suspect, is the allowance for differences in sex structure because it entails discounting female relative to male workers by 41 percent. That adjustment conforms to the average difference in earning between female and male workers in the United States, but even a male chauvinist must concede that the differential probably reflects limitations in employment opportunities open to women rather than an inherent qualitative inferiority of their labor. To the extent that it does, my calculations tend to be unduly favorable to the USSR. In the Soviet Union, women are employed to a far greater degree than in any other country considered. They now constitute one-half of the Soviet labor force. In the West the cor-

TABLE 7.2. Gross material product per employed worker and per unit of factor inputs (labor adjusted for quality), selected countries, 1960[1]

Country	Gross material product per employed worker	Gross material product per unit of factor (labor and reproducible capital) inputs
United States	100	100
France	60	70
Germany	61	75
United Kingdom	54	68
Italy	44	57
USSR	42	51

[1]Employment adjusted throughout for differences in education and sex and age structure, as well as hours (see text).

responding ratio is one-fourth to one-third. An inordinately high discount for female labor would overstate calculated productivity for the USSR relative to that for other countries.

Factor productivity may also vary because workers do not work as hard in one country as in another. To what extent is that so here? According to Denison:

> It seems to me probable that differences in effort are partially responsible for a higher level of output in the United States than in Europe . . . But the quantitative importance of differences in intensity of work I find impossible to judge, much less to measure by any direct approach.[4]

Reference is only to Western countries, but the degree to which effort might differ between the USSR and the West is, needless to say, also obscure. According to a familiar socialist claim, public ownership of the means of production should encourage the worker to put forth notable effort. The Soviet worker no doubt has sometimes done so, but the extent to which he does so now is a matter for conjecture. If anything, diligence may usually be greater in the United States than in the USSR.

When effort differs among countries, productivity should differ correspondingly. Effort may differ because of differences in incentive arrangements, the arrangements in one country being more beneficent than those in another. If so, the difference in effort might properly be construed as manifesting a difference in productive efficiency as well, so there would be no incongruity after all between such efficiency and productivity. However, effort may vary simply because of differences in worker preferences for labor and leisure, without incentive arrangements being any more or less beneficent in one country than another. In that case, productive efficiency would be the same despite the observed difference in productivity. It would be understood that the economic working arrangements prevailing in different countries simply satisfied different preferences between work and earnings. They might do that just as they might satisfy different preferences among consumer goods. If differences in effort are difficult to gauge, comparative causes of such differences are no easier. My comparative data on productivity must be interpreted accordingly.[5]

In calculating factor productivity, I have referred in the case of labor

4. Denison, *Why Growth Rates Differ,* pp. 113-114.

5. To return to incentive arrangements, as the primers teach, these could conceivably induce too much effort as well as too little. On comparative incentive arrangements and effort generally, see ibid., pp. 112 ff.; and Bergson, *Planning and Productivity Under Soviet Socialism,* pp. 34 ff.

inputs only to workers actually employed. Such a calculation has its point, but in judging comparative productive efficiency we must remember that, at the time studied, the United States and Italy were experiencing significant amounts of unemployment. Relative to the observed gaps in productivity, however, the differences in unemployment rates were very limited (Table 7.3). As for the USSR, it is often claimed that unemployment has been abolished there. In fact, unemployment of the cyclical sort familiar in the West is no doubt little known. But in the USSR, as in the West, there is structural and frictional unemployment, although how much is difficult to judge.[6]

TABLE 7.3. Unemployment rates, adjusted to American definitions, selected Countries, 1960[1]

Country	Unemployed ÷ labor force (%)
United States	5.6
France	1.9
Germany	1.0
United Kingdom	2.4
Italy	4.3

[1]President's Committee to Appraise Employment and Unemployment Statistics, *Measuring Employment and Unemployment* (Washington, D.C., 1962), p. 220.

For capital, inputs have been measured by the entire stock, whether utilized or not. Capital may be utilized with varying intensity, however, and at least beyond a point, more intensive use is by no means costless. Hence high productivity merely as a result of more intensive use need not betoken anything like a correspondingly high productive efficiency. It should be observed, therefore, that productivity in the USSR is low despite the fact that capital is used notably intensively, at least in industry. In the USSR at the time studied, 35 percent of industrial workers were employed on shifts other than the first. In the United States the corresponding figure was 23 percent, in Northwest Europe about 10 percent, and in Italy 16 percent.[7]

6. See, however, the interesting information collated in CIA, *Unemployment in the Soviet Union, Fact or Fiction?* ER 66-5 (Washington, D.C., March 1966).

7. TSU, *Narodnoe khoziaistvo SSSR v 1960 godu* (Moscow, 1961), p. 646; and Denison, p. 163.

In the case of capital, I limited my inquiry to that of a reproducible nature. Thus, productive efficiency apart, productivity may vary also because of differences in the quality and location of natural resources. Needless to say, such differences exist not only among the Western countries studied but also between the USSR and those countries. Nevertheless there are reasons to think that they could not account in any case for any large part of the observed differences in productivity, but that is a complex situation about which there is much to learn.[8]

Productivity may differ, without any corresponding variation in productive efficiency, because of differential opportunities to exploit economies of scale. Such opportunities turn on market size, which is not the same thing as size of the country, of course. Income levels, transportation costs, and access to foreign markets also matter. On the other hand, economies of scale in industry are associated to a great extent with the size of production units. When they are, they probably can be largely realized by plants of relatively modest size.[9] Such economies, nevertheless, are not always realized, but a failure to realize them, while it lowers productivity, is properly seen as reducing productive efficiency as well.[10] In any event, the USSR should not have any marked disadvantage at this point. Compared with the Western European countries studied, it may well be favored.

A country's productive capacity depends partly on available technological knowledge. Where technological knowledge differs, therefore, differences in factor productivity necessarily betoken that difference rather than variations in realization of productive possibilities and hence efficiency. Moreover technological knowledge no doubt differs to a degree among the Western countries studied. Thus technological knowledge may originate in any country, but it probably tends to do so most often in the United States, which is economically the most advanced of the countries of interest. Perhaps there are other differences in that regard among the other Western countries, especially between the relatively advanced Northwest European ones and Italy.

True, new technological discoveries are not easily monopolized. At least among countries like the ones considered in this chapter, new knowledge discovered in one seems to become available very soon to others. But to the

8. On the possible importance of disparities in resource endowment as a cause of productivity differences among countries studied, see Denison, chap. 14; and Chapter 6, this volume.

9. According to J. S. Bain, *International Differences in Industrial Structure* (New Haven, Conn., 1966), p. 65, among twenty American manufacturing industries studied, "the proportion of total industry output supplied by plants of reasonably efficient scale lay uniformly between 70 and 90 percent."

10. Ibid., pp. 55 ff., 144 ff.

extent that there is any lag, there is a reason for productivity to vary without there being a corresponding difference in efficiency.[11]

The USSR by all accounts has tended especially to be a borrower rather than a discoverer of new technologies, so its factor productivity also may have suffered to some extent without efficiency being any worse.[12]

In sum, productive efficiency is indeed not the same thing as productivity. Although the presumption is that productive efficiency varies widely even among Western countries, the Soviet performance does not seem especially distinguished. Most likely, it is matched, if not surpassed, in the West even where productive efficiency is lowest.

THE ROLE OF THE DEVELOPMENT STAGE

We are concerned with the comparative productive efficiency not merely of the USSR and the Western countries studied but also of socialism and capitalism, or at least of the variants of those social systems found in those countries. From that standpoint, must we not consider that even similar economic working arrangements may perform differently depending on historical and cultural factors? Indeed, is that not already indicated by the differences in factor productivity observed among Western countries? What, in particular, of the possibility that such differences essentially reflect differences in the stage of economic development in those countries? If so, may not the relatively low factor productivity in the USSR be due simply to the less-advanced stage of development of that country? Insofar as productive efficiency is low in the USSR, therefore, may not the cause be the less-advanced stage of development rather than any intrinsic inferiority in socialism as it exists there?

These questions are in order, but we have only five observations on factor productivity under capitalism and one on factor productivity under socialism. These hardly suffice for us to make any very firm generalizations about the relation of factor productivity and the stage of economic development. Among the Western countries studied, however, factor productivity does vary positively with one of two plausible indicators of the stage of development: capital stock per worker (Table 7.4 and Figures 7.1 and 7.2). Very possibly it also does so with the other indicator, namely, the share of

11. According to Denison, *Why Growth Rates Differ,* p. 292, "In the field I have termed 'technological knowledge,' a gap presumably exists, but I have difficulty in supposing that it is of any great importance." I wonder whether that is entirely realistic as to the rapidity of dissemination of new knowledge. For a case study that seems to corroborate Denison, however, see John E. Tilton, *International Diffusion of Technology: The Case of Semi-Conductors* (Washington, D.C., 1971).

12. On the Soviet technological lag, see also Chapter 6, this volume, n. 26.

nonfarm branches in total employment. There are, however, marked incongruities in the latter case. Thus, in terms of the share of nonfarm employment, Britain is at a very advanced stage, in fact at an even more advanced stage than the United States. Yet in factor productivity Britain ranks below the United States and is only more or less on a par with Germany and France. With labor adjusted for quality, it even appears to fall perceptibly below Germany. The same yardstick of development makes factor productivity in the United States seem incongruously high.

What of the USSR? To the extent that there is a systematic relation in Western countries of factor productivity to the development stage when the share of nonfarm employment is the yardstick, the USSR apparently fits well into that pattern. If capital stock per worker is the yardstick, however, the USSR seems not to conform to the Western pattern. The capital stock per worker of the Soviet Union is practically comparable to that of two of our three Northwest European countries—Germany and the United Kingdom—and distinctly above that of Italy. Yet, as already seen, factor productivity in the USSR is well below that in all of our Northwest European countries. Soviet factor productivity appears to fall to some extent below even that of Italy.

TABLE 7.4. Indicators of the stage of economic development and factor productivity, selected countries, 1960[1]

Country	Share of nonagricultural branches in total employment (%)	Capital stock per worker with labor		Factor productivity, with labor	
		Unadjusted for quality (USA = 100)	Adjusted for quality (USA = 100)	Unadjusted for quality (USA = 100)	Adjusted for quality (USA = 100)
United States	92.0	100	100	100	100
France	78.6	45	52	63	70
Germany	86.2	36	43	65	75
United Kingdom	95.8	35	39	64	68
Italy	68.0	25	33	47	57
USSR	61.5	34	45	41	51

[1]Capital stock per worker is calculated from reproducible fixed capital and employment in the economy generally, exclusive of selected final services as already described. Employment is adjusted for differences in hours in both variants given.

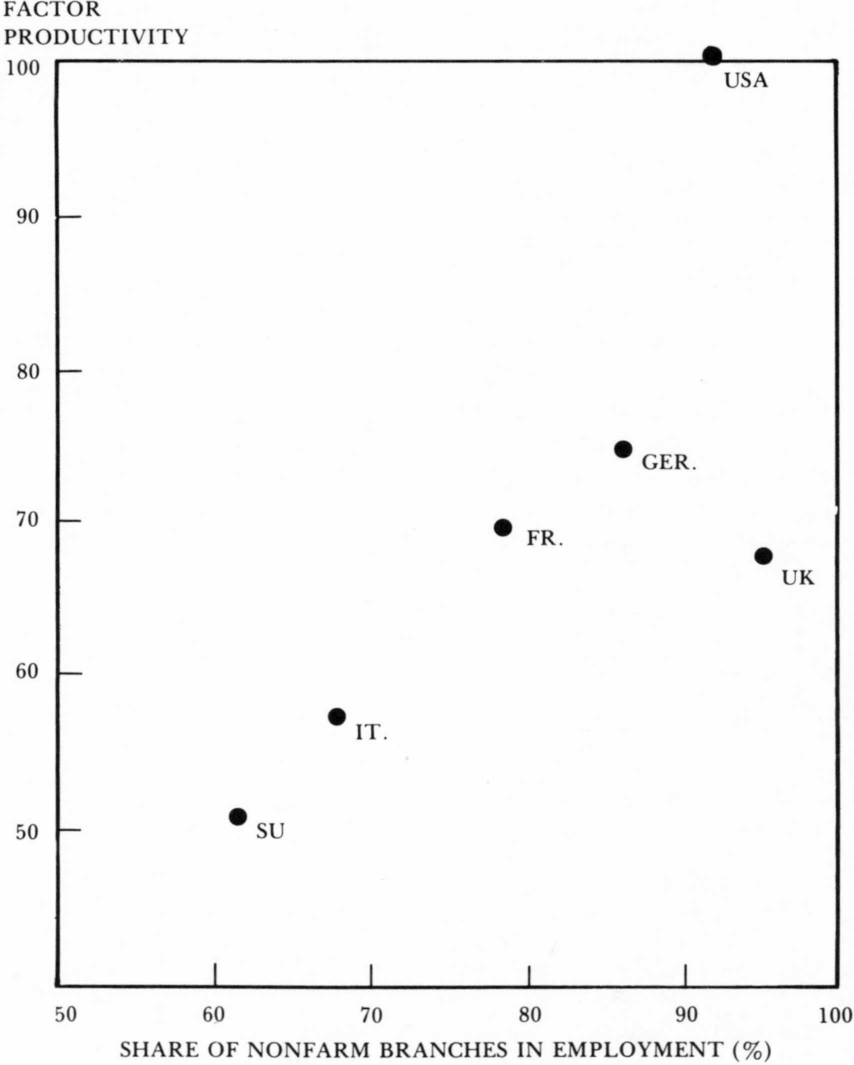

FIGURE 7.1. Nonfarm employment share and factor productivity, selected countries, 1960

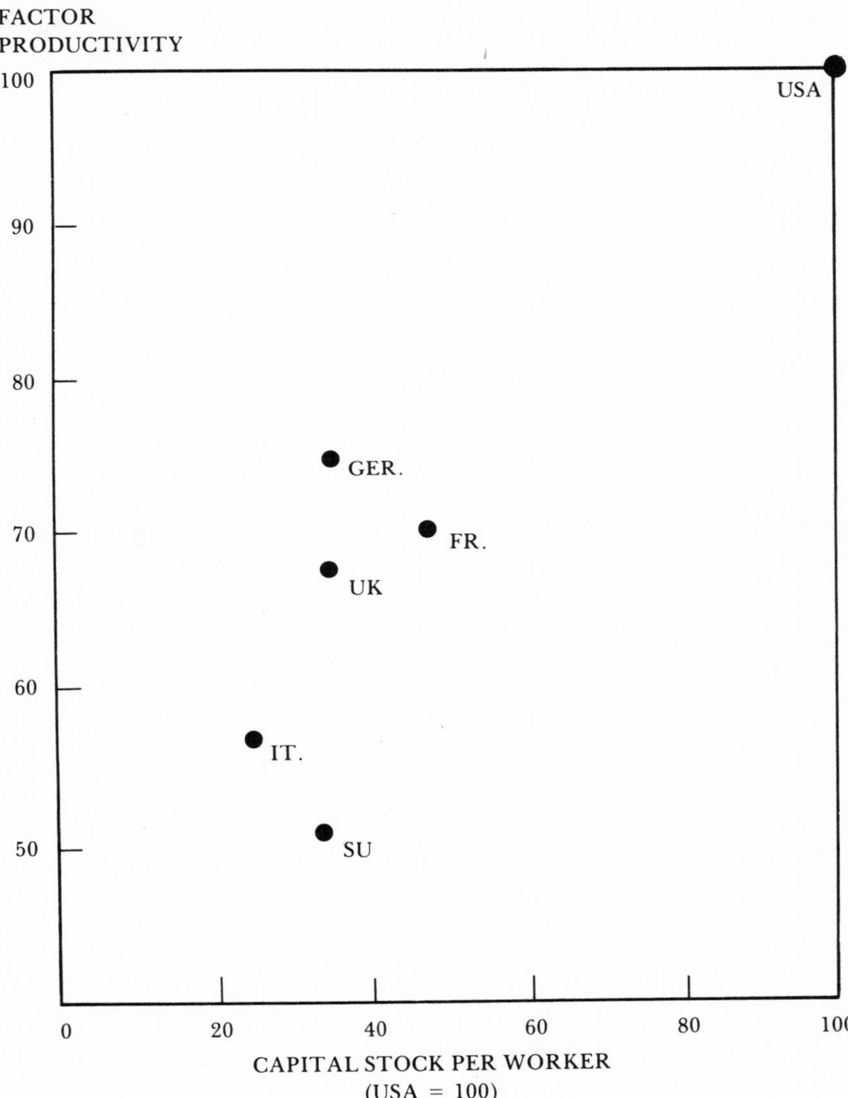

FIGURE 7.2. Capital stock per worker and factor productivity, selected countries, 1960

Of our two yardsticks of the stage of economic development, that represented by the share of nonfarm branches in total employment is more familiar. For our purposes, though, it is deficient in one important respect: the yardstick itself is apt to be affected by productive efficiency, particularly in regard to the choice of investment projects in industry. I shall have more to say in a moment about this problem, which is well known to students of economic development. The alternative yardstick of capital stock per worker is free from such defects, but the data compiled on it are especially inexact.[13]

To come, then, to the larger issue of interest, factor productivity in the USSR may well be relatively low partly because of the still not very advanced stage of economic development in that country, rather than because of any intrinsic deficiencies in Soviet socialism. Nevertheless, the low Soviet factor productivity does not seem fully explicable in such terms. The comparative productive efficiency of socialism as found in the USSR must be interpreted accordingly. Soviet performance is clearly better than it appeared initially, although it still is not at all distinguished by Western standards.

Even these tentative observations put a heavy burden on the limited and imprecise data at hand.[14] It may be useful, however, to pursue somewhat

13. Among Western countries, the figure on capital stock per worker for the United Kingdom is surprisingly low. Perhaps it is too low, but it should be noted that I refer to the economy exclusive of selective services. In at least one service sector, housing, the British capital stock per worker turns out to be relatively high. See Denison, *Why Growth Rates Differ,* p. 129. As for the USSR, regardless of all that is known about the high rate of capital investment maintained there through the years, it is striking that the country compares as favorably with the West as the data show. There seems to be no reason to think the Soviet capital stock per worker is overstated rather than understated, but to repeat, the data on capital stock per worker generally are crude.

As an indicator of the stage of economic development, capital stock per worker may be misleading here, even apart from limitations in the data from which that relation is compiled. It is well known to the technically initiated that calculation of factor productivity requires aggregation of inputs of labor and capital with weights corresponding ideally to the shares of output properly imputable to the two factors. In practice, however, ideal shares can be approximated at best. To the degree that the weights applied do diverge from them, as can readily be seen, the relation between factor productivity and capital stock per worker must be affected. The direction in which the relation would be affected would depend on the nature of divergence. Thus, if the weight for capital is too large, factor productivity should vary inversely rather than positively with capital stock per worker.

14. For the technically inclined I should explain that in formulating the foregoing findings I have sought to take into account various regression relations between factor productivity and indicators of the stage of economic development that are explained in the Technical Note. Later I will present some comparative data compiled for industry alone and will refer again in that context to the relationship of factor productivity and the stage of economic development. There, too, I will take into account regression relations described in the Technical Note.

further the intriguing question concerning the relation of factor productivity and the stage of economic development. Are there indeed reasons to think that one aspect should be related to the other? No doubt there are, but the relation can also be expected to differ frequently, as our data suggest it does, under such disparate economic working arrangements as are being considered. Thus a cardinal reason why factor productivity may vary with development stage turns on the relation of population to resources in agriculture. For historical reasons that relation may be unfavorable and so an inordinately large labor force may work in agriculture at an inordinately low productivity. By the same token, productivity in the whole economy is, on the average, also depressed. That may be so whatever the economic working arrangements, but how great the "excess" labor in agriculture is at any time must depend on how rapidly it had been absorbed into industry as development proceeded. The rate of absorption must depend, among other things, on the choice of technologies for new industrial investment projects. Should these have been unduly "capital intensive," for example, the rate of absorption of farm labor into industry would necessarily have slowed. For well-known reasons, revolving partly about the improper accounting for capital under an obsolete labor theory of value, industrial investment projects probably have been unduly capital intensive in the USSR.[15] The incongruity for the USSR between our two yardsticks of development, that is, the low share of nonfarm employment relative to the capital stock per worker, I suspect, may be due partly to that fact.

As a country becomes more advanced economically its economy also tends, by almost any reckoning, to become more complex. Interconnections multiply among an ever-increasing number of production units. The number and variety of products also tend to grow disproportionately. Very possibly factor productivity is affected, although differentially under different economic working arrangements. What the effect might be, if there should be any to speak of, under a Western market system is not very clear. Under centralist planning, such as prevails under Soviet socialism, it is commonly assumed, with good reason, that the effect is apt to be adverse. As the economy becomes more complex, the burden of decision-making on higher planning agencies becomes more onerous. That kind of pressure can hardly be favorable to productivity.[16]

15. See Abram Bergson, *The Economics of Soviet Planning* (New Haven, Conn., 1964), chap. 11.

16. The Western countries studied are all capitalist, and economic working arrangements in all of them are broadly similar but not at all the same. Divergencies in economic working arrangements must also be a source of differences in factor productivity and sometimes such differences likewise should be associated with the stage of development. Thus, among the causes of the relatively high productivity in the United States, it is often suggested, are our superior managerial practices and relatively competitive markets. It would be surprising if the

The forces affecting factor productivity that have been described should all affect productive efficiency as well. If factor productivity varies with the stage of development, therefore, so must productive efficiency, although the variation should be different under Western capitalism and socialist centralist planning. Productive efficiency in the Soviet Union must be viewed accordingly. As we saw, however, technological knowledge, too, tends to vary with the stage of development. So far as factor productivity varies correspondingly that result cannot be considered as necessarily betokening inefficiency.[17] Quality of labor is also an issue here. The failure of labor imput calculations to allow sufficiently for differences in quality affects factor productivity. Quite possibly it could cause factor productivity to vary with the stage of development. For example, workers learn not only from formal schooling but also by doing. Learning on the job, however, seems beyond the reach of the measurement of labor skill. Inasmuch as it is, there is a further reason for factor productivity to be higher in more advanced countries, but in this case the productive efficiency could not be

---

first of these two factors were not associated in one way or another with stage of development. The second, though, is not very easy to construe similarly. In more advanced countries, it has frequently been held, competition tends to decline as development proceeds.

Where economic working arrangements vary more or less independently of the development stage they may nevertheless help explain incongruities in the relation of productivity to that aspect. Thus factor productivity in Britain is perhaps not as high as would be expected for a country at its stage of development. If that is so, I wonder whether the much discussed restrictive trade-union practices of that country may not be one of the more important causes. See Denison, *Why Growth Rates Differ,* p. 292 ff., for a discussion of the possible import of divergencies in economic working arrangements for differences in factor productivity in Western countries.

Among socialist countries, economic working arrangements also vary, but among the ones that are relatively modern, the divergencies seem rarely to be both consequential and clearly related to the stage of development. Perhaps such a relation would be more pronounced were it not for the constraints on institutional innovation imposed everywhere by Soviet hegemony, but that is conjecture and so especially is any suggestion about how factor productivity could be affected at this point.

The most important difference by far is represented by the shift from centralist planning to relatively decentralized systems emphasizing markets that occurred in Yugoslavia, beginning in the early fifties, and in Hungary in January 1968. But from the standpoint of the stage of development, these two countries bracket a number of others where centralist planning is still practiced. In Czechoslovakia, one of the most advanced of all socialist countries today, a similar transformation initiated in the midsixties apparently was set back considerably by the events of August 1968.

Among countries where centralist planning is still practiced the presumption must be that, if only in degree of sophistication, procedures vary with the stage of development. The validity of that assessment remains to be explored.

17. But see Chapter 6, this volume, n. 26.

considered as varying correspondingly. Measured performance would vary because of a qualitative difference in supplies of factors, particularly labor, rather than because of any difference in effectiveness in their use.[18]

I have focused on contemporaneous differences in factor productivity in different countries. Factor productivity no doubt has also varied historically with the stage of development in any one country, but that relationship is another matter, and it is the contemporaneous variation among different countries that is now of particular concern.

Although the preceding discussion has centered on the relation of factor productivity to the development stage, the larger concern of this chapter has been to explain the apparently low Soviet productive efficiency, in particular the degree to which it is characteristic of the economic working arrangements that prevail there. But might not deficiencies in such arrangements in the USSR be culturally determined and in complex ways not necessarily related even to the stage of development? Thus, if socialism does not function too well in the USSR, what of the possibility that that system is simply not particularly appropriate for "moody" Russians, but may suit other peoples, such as the "disciplined" Germans? That suggestion is sometimes made and, despite the clichés, perhaps it is not entirely farfetched. As calculations made here for the USSR are extended to other socialist countries. I hope that we shall have a better basis than we now have to understand this interesting question.

INDUSTRIAL PRODUCTIVITY

How does productivity in the Soviet Union compare with that in the West in nonfarm branches alone? The relevance of this question is obvious, the more so if we consider that productivity in the economy is affected not only by productive efficiency within agriculture but also by the allocation of resources between agriculture and other sectors. As we have seen, that allocation is apt to be historically conditioned and hence only partly determined by prevailing economic working arrangements. By comparing productivity in nonfarm branches, we are able to observe performance apart from such historical conditioning.

Selected service branches again being omitted, the nonfarm branches include manufacturing, mining, power, construction, transport and com-

18. I referred earlier to superiority of managerial practices as a possible reason for the high level of productivity in the United States. Quality of managerial practices, however, is not easy to delineate from quality of managerial personnel. If American managerial personnnel are superior, the resultant gain in productivity represents another instance of a kind of statistical deficiency in the measurement of labor skills.

munications, and trade. I shall refer to all these sectors together as "industry," though industry is thus construed in a quite broad sense. As before, I have calculated output per worker and per composite unit of labor and capital for the gross output originating in the branches in question.

With the comparison so delineated, the United States apparently is still preeminent among Western countries (Table 7.5). Other Western countries are affected variously. Britain performs no better and perhaps somewhat worse relative to the United States than it did. Germany, France, and Italy, however, all gain on the United States, the gain being greater for France than for Germany and still greater for Italy than for France.

These are not very surprising results. Productivity in industry, it might be supposed, would tend to be higher than that in agriculture and perhaps even more so the greater the importance of agriculture in the economy. That must be so where, for historical reasons, employment in agriculture is inordinately large. With industrial productivity supplanting productivity in the economy generally as the yardstick, a country's performance relative to that of the United States should improve more or less commensurately with the comparative shares of the excluded agricultural sector in its economy and in that of the United States. That is indeed the case, as may be seen at once by juxtaposing our results with the comparative data al-

TABLE 7.5. Gross industrial product per employed worker and per unit of factor inputs, selected countries, 1960

Country	Gross industrial product per employed worker	Gross industrial product per unit of factor (labor and reproducible capital) inputs
United States	100	100
France	60	71
Germany	54	69
United Kingdom	48	61
Italy	46	60
USSR	50	58

Gross industrial product represents essentially the gross output originating in manufacturing, mining, power, construction, transport and communications, and trade. In the calculation of output per worker and per composite unit of factor inputs, reference is to employment and capital stock used in the same sectors. Valuation of output and inputs is as in Table 7.1. Employment is also adjusted for hours in the same way as in Table 7.2.

ready set forth on the share of nonfarm sectors in total employment (Table 7.4).

These results obtain whether reference is to output per worker or to output per composite unit of labor and capital. As before, though, the latter yardstick is more significant for our purposes.

What of the USSR? Its performance improves relative to that of the United States. As can be expected in view of the still very large share of agriculture in the Soviet economy, the gain is especially marked. In terms of industrial productivity, the USSR is now practically on a par with Italy and also with the United Kingdom. The United Kingdom, for the reasons just indicated, no longer enjoys any margin over Italy to speak of. The Soviet performance, however, is still somewhat less impressive in terms of factor than in terms of labor productivity.[19]

TABLE 7.6. Gross industrial product per employed worker and per unit of factor inputs (labor adjusted for quality), selected countries 1960[1]

Country	Gross industrial product per employed worker	Gross industrial product per unit of factor (labor and reproducible capital) inputs
United States	100	100
France	68	78
Germany	65	79
United Kingdom	53	66
Italy	56	70
USSR	61	68

[1]Employment adjusted throughout for differences in education and sex and age structure, as well as hours (see text).

Again, productive efficiency may diverge from factor productivity because of differences in the educational and sex structure of the population, but if we allow for such differences rather crudely, as we did before, we see that Western countries other than the United States again gain on that country (Table 7.6). So does the USSR, but it now appears to surpass Italy somewhat when output per worker is the yardstick. In terms of factor productivity, however, the USSR still only matches Italy. Once more the

19. See n. 3 above.

United Kingdom is only more or less on a par with Italy, so productivity in the USSR is comparable to that in the United Kingdom as well as Italy.

Productive efficiency may diverge from factor productivity in industry also for reasons other than differences in labor quality, but these are much the same as those making productive efficiency diverge from factor productivity in the economy generally. What I have said regarding the latter causes essentially applies here too. I conclude, therefore, that productive efficiency in industry probably varies among Western countries, though not as much as in the economy generally. As for the USSR, its productive efficiency compares more favorably with the West in industry than in the economy generally. Most likely, it still only matches the least efficient of the Western countries studied, but that now means not only Italy but also the United Kingdom. And, to repeat, the margin between the worst and the best Western performance has now narrowed.

What of the stage of economic development? As before, may not differences in that be a source of observed variations in factor productivity among Western countries? If so, may they not account as well for the still relatively low factor productivity and hence low productive efficiency in Soviet industry? By focusing on industry alone, we have excluded one important way in which the development stage can affect factor productivity, that is through a historically conditioned misallocation of resources between agriculture and industry. As we saw, however, factor productivity may vary with the development stage for other reasons, which should continue to be operative.

Yet stage of development seems most properly gauged from the capital stock per worker in industry. Among Western countries factor productivity very possibly does vary broadly with the development stage, as so viewed (Table 7.7 and Figure 7.3), but, as before, the Soviet Union does not seem to fit the Western pattern very well. Perhaps the low productivity there relative to that in the United States is partly explicable in terms of the less advanced development of the Soviet Union, but by the same token that country now seems to compare less favorably with Italy and the United Kingdom than it did earlier. As previously, there is no assurance, in any event, that factor productivity varies similarly with the development stage under socialism of the Soviet sort and capitalist mixed systems. What has been said of comparative factor productivity should hold for comparative productive efficiency as well.

CONCLUSION

Output per composite unit of factor inputs in the USSR falls at the lower end of, if not beyond, the range of experience observed in the Western countries considered. It does so for industry alone, as well as for the econ-

TABLE 7.7. Capital stock per worker and factor productivity in industry, selected countries, 1960[1]

Country	Capital stock per worker with labor		Factor productivity with labor	
	Unadjusted for quality	Adjusted for quality	Unadjusted for quality	Adjusted for quality
United States	100	100	100	100
France	49	55	71	78
Germany	37	45	69	79
United Kingdom	33	37	61	66
Italy	32	39	60	70
USSR	50	63	58	68

[1] For capital stock per worker, reference is to reproducible fixed capital and, in both variants, to employment adjusted for differences in hours.

omy generally, although Soviet performance in industry appears to be superior to that in the economy generally. Factor productivity in the USSR is found to be relatively low before and after adjustment for differences in labor quality, and the low Soviet standing does not seem to be due to a disadvantageous position in other respects considered. It seems difficult to avoid the conclusion, therefore, that Soviet standing must also be relatively low in terms of productive efficiency, for the comparative levels of factor productivity in the USSR and the West are not easy to explain otherwise.

Among Western countries, factor productivity appears to vary systematically with the stage of economic development and productive efficiency does so also. In pondering the larger import of our findings, therefore, we must consider that the USSR is still not economically very advanced relative to most of the Western countries studied. Yet the relatively low Soviet productivity does not seem to be fully explicable by that fact.

In sum, to come to the question of ultimate concern, there is further evidence of how far socialism is economically from the chaotic system critics once held it would be and from the potent mechanism that proponents have often envisaged. At least the Soviet variant of socialism seems neither colossally wasteful nor extraordinarily efficient but well within the extremes that are so familiar in polemics on socialist economics. The Soviet system, however, appears to be undistinguished by Western standards. We

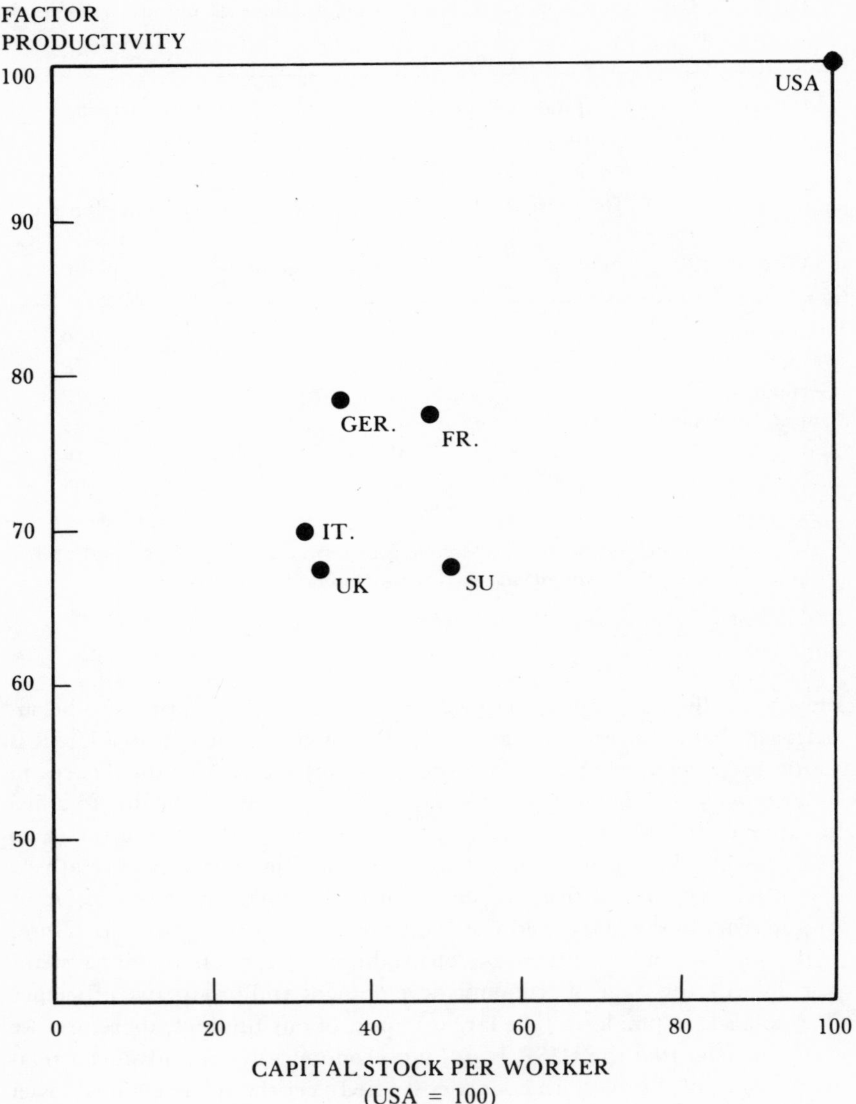

FIGURE 7.3. Capital stock per worker and factor productivity in industry, selected countries, 1960

have had to appraise the Soviet model from its performance in the USSR itself. I hope that in due course we shall also have observations on its performance elsewhere. Additional analyses on the side of capitalism should also enable us to judge better how representative the Western countries studied are of that system.

TECHNICAL NOTE[20]

I show in Table 7.8 selected data concerning various regression relations alluded to in the text. All the data pertain to relations of the form:

$$Y = aX + bS + k$$

where Y represents factor productivity, X is an indicator of the stage of economic development, and S is a dummy variable standing for the presence or absence of socialism. All regression relations were calculated from six observations on the relations of the variables in question, either in the economy generally (Table 7.4) or in industry (Table 7.7).

Rows I A-C and II A-C all relate to the economy generally. In regressions listed in rows I A-C, Y represents factor productivity where labor is unadjusted for quality. The variable X represents, in I A, the share of nonagricultural branches in total employment; in I B, the capital stock per worker; and in I-C, the capital stock per worker where labor is adjusted for quality. In rows II A-C, all relations considered are as in I A-C, except that Y represents factor productivity where labor is adjusted for quality.

Rows III A-B and IV A-B relate to industry. In III A-B, Y is factor productivity with labor unadjusted for quality. In III A, X is the capital stock per worker. In III B, it is the capital stock per worker with labor adjusted for quality. In IV A-B, all is as in III A-B except that Y represents factor productivity with labor adjusted for quality.

In the table, r stands for the coefficient of correlation. Parenthetic figures are t values.

20. I am indebted to Jonathan Eaton for assistance in carrying out the calculations summarized in this Technical Note.

TABLE 7.8. Selected data on various regressions relating to Soviet and Western productivity levels

Item	Text table	r^2	a	b	k
I	A 7.4	0.59	1.146 (1.498)	− 0.8706 (0.03424)	−28.63 (0.4415)
	B 7.4	0.96	0.6330 (6.875)	−17.81 (2.894)	37.29 (7.352)
	C 7.4	0.94	0.6937 (5.996)	−20.97 (3.039)	30.76 (4.537)
II	A 7.4	0.56	0.8780 (1.337)	− 3.140 (0.1440)	0.1429 (0.0026)
	B 7.4	0.94	0.5123 (5.732)	−15.73 (2.633)	49.31 (10.02)
	C 7.4	0.94	0.5645 (5.488)	−18.26 (2.976)	43.86 (7.277)
III	A 7.7	0.98	0.5614 (11.29)	−14.09 (4.515)	44.02 (15.71)
	B 7.7	0.99	0.6210 (14.18)	−19.04 (7.561)	37.92 (14.45)
IV	A 7.7	0.92	0.4369 (5.401)	−10.51 (2.071)	56.67 (12.43)
	B 7.7	0.94	0.4893 (6.668)	−14.42 (3.417)	51.59 (11.74)

PART THREE

GROWTH OF OUTPUT AND PRODUCTIVITY

8.

Soviet National Income, 1928-1958

The growth of Soviet national income is usefully studied by comparing the Soviet experience with that of the United States. We are interested primarily in Soviet growth during the period of the five-year plans. In 1928, when that period began, the USSR was producing a total output on the order of $170 per capita, in terms of dollar prices of the time. In the United States, we had surpassed that level in the first decade after the Civil War. In view of these circumstances it sometimes is suggested that, in contrasting Soviet growth under the five-year plans with growth in the United States, we should focus on an early period in the history of the latter. Such a comparison should be of interest, but so is one that covers a more recent period in the

Originally published in Abram Bergson and Simon Kuznets, eds., *Economic Trends in the Soviet Union* (Cambridge, Mass., 1963), this essay is reproduced with the permission of the Harvard University Press. While the stress placed on the so-called "composite index, 1937 base" still seems to have some theoretical basis, I have come to doubt on practical grounds that this measure is nearly as significant as was assumed for purposes of appraising the growth of Soviet "production potential" over the crucial period of the early five-year plans (see Chapter 9, this volume, n.21). The case for using net rather than gross product also seems less impelling than I once supposed. Despite such misgivings, the essay may be useful for the summary presentation of a great variety of statistical data on comparative Soviet and American growth. I republish it here in a highly abbreviated and somewhat revised form.

The essay was prepared initially as a report for the RAND Corporation. As explained before, "views expressed . . . are those of the author and should not be interpreted as reflecting the views of the RAND Corporation or the official opinion or policy of any of its sponsors."

United States as well as in the USSR. In any event, a comparative study of Soviet and American growth can be undertaken from different standpoints. To contrast the Soviet performance with that of the United States in both early and recent years is in order when the concern is to gain insight into the Soviet growth process.

In comparing growth of national income in the two countries, I propose to consider not only the expansion of output but also its sources, particularly the rate of growth of productivity, as represented by output per unit of factor inputs. Calculations of output per unit of inputs are familiar for the United States. In attempting to compile such data for the USSR and to compare trends with those in the Unites States, however, I tread on relatively new ground. Indeed, if one considers the difficulties involved, it is easy to feel that novelty may be about all that can be claimed for such an effort. Perhaps most important, in calculating factor productivity one ordinarily aggregates inputs by using as weights "market-determined" factor income shares. Unfortunately, the Soviet price system fails to provide us with meaningful data of that sort. By experimenting with alternative sets of "synthetic" factor income shares, I may be able to limit the range of speculation on the matter in question.

The data should be viewed in the light of diverse circumstances, particularly the fact that by the outset of the period under study the USSR generally had done little more than recover economically from the losses suffered during World War I, the 1917 Revolutions, and civil war.[1] During the early years of the interval in question, then, not only were the first important applications made of unique techniques of central planning but also an extraordinary reorganization of agriculture, with attendant extraordinary losses of capital, skill, and even lives, took place. Moreover, at a later point the USSR suffered even more cataclysmic events under the impact of another great war fought furiously on its own territory. Pertinent events at the time considered in American history are familiar and need no mention here.

I have only recently completed a substantial study of Soviet national income.[2] In good part, I summarize here results set forth in that work.

GROWTH OF SOVIET NATIONAL INCOME

For purposes of appraising trends in Soviet national income, I refer to Tables 8.1 and 8.2. Essentially, I rely here on *The Real National Income of Soviet Russia* but the computations made previously for 1928-1955 have been extrapolated to 1958. Also, in *Real SNIP* the focus is *gross* national

1. *Real SNIP,* pp. 6 ff.
2. Ibid.

product. It is now possible to compile corresponding data on *net* national product, which may be of greater interest here.

In *Real SNIP* gross national product is computed in terms of prevailing ruble prices although a partial revaluation excludes sales taxes and includes subsidies; in other words, after revaluation, output is, in effect, in terms of ruble factor cost. National income data are supposed to provide a partial basis for the appraisal of one or another or both of two abstract ultimates: production potential and welfare. The revaluation in terms of ruble factor cost, by adjusting for outstanding distortions in ruble prices, is intended primarily to make the national income data more indicative of production potential and should be interpreted accordingly. Possibly there is also a gain for appraisal of welfare, but in that case welfare probably must be evaluated from the standpoint not of "consumer utility" but of "planners' preferences." The cited figures on the Soviet net national product correspond to those compiled previously on the Soviet gross national product in terms of ruble factor cost.

In *Real SNIP* two main series were derived in terms of the latter standard. In both cases 1937 is taken as a base, but different index number formulas were applied to the two series. One series is of the conventional sort: output in all years is computed in terms of prices prevailing in the base year. The other is somewhat novel: obtained as a composite, it is intended to approximate serial data where, in the comparison of each given year with the base year, output is computed in terms of given-year prices. According to familiar theoretical reasoning, a given change in production potential may differently affect production capacity depending on the commodity structure. For example, a given change in production potential may cause a country to experience a relatively large change in capacity to produce commodity mixes that are predominantly industrial and a relatively small change in capacity to produce commodity mixes that are predominantly agricultural. Both series should provide observations about the change over a period of years in capacity to produce the commodity mix prevailing in the base year. But, while neither calculation is very reliable in that regard, the one in terms of a given-year factor cost may well be more reliable than the one in terms of base-year factor cost. Both series on gross national product have been used here to derive two corresponding series on net national product.[3]

3. Those who are familiar with the theory of national income computation probably can readily appreciate the case for using given-year (as distinct from base-year) weights to compile measures pertinent to production potential, but to my knowledge it was first elaborated by Richard Moorsteen in a talk that he gave at the RAND Corporation in the summer of 1958. Moorsteen subsequently elaborated on this question in "On Measuring Production Potential and Relative Efficiency," *Quarterly Journal of Economics,* August 1961. With special reference to Soviet circumstances, I discuss the subject in *Real SNIP,* chap. 3. I have also benefited

TABLE 8.1. USSR and United States national product, factor inputs and productivity, selected years.

USSR[1]

Item	Nature of measurement	1928	1937	1940	1950	1958
Net national product	In 1937 ruble factor cost	67.1	100.0	110.3	132.7	225.5
	As composite 1937 base	38.1	100.0	110.3	129.9	221.0
Employment	Number of workers (adjusted for nonfarm hours)	72.5	100.0	111.8	120.4	132.5
Reproducible fixed capital	In 1937 rubles	41.0	100.0	126.4	133.2	311.4
	As composite 1937 base	36.1	100.0	126.4	124.0	282.7
Farmland	Acres	83.5	100.0	101.1	98.3	131.4
Livestock herds	In 1937 rubles	147.3	100.0	117.5	108.0	139.4
		69.7		113.7	120.4	165.1
Selected inputs	With 1937 weights[2]	71.9	100.0	111.9	119.1	147.4
		70.3		113.2	119.5	163.5
Net national product per worker (adjusted for nonfarm hours)	Output in 1937 ruble factor cost	92.6	100.0	98.7	110.2	170.2
	Output as composite 1937 base	52.6	100.0	98.7	107.9	166.8
Net national product per unit of reproducible fixed capital	Output in 1937 ruble factor cost and capital in 1937 rubles	163.7	100.0	87.3	99.6	72.4
	Output and capital as composite 1937 base	105.5	100.0	87.3	104.8	78.2
		96.3		97.0	110.2	136.6
Net national product per unit of selected inputs	Output in 1937 ruble factor cost and inputs using 1937 weights[2]	93.3	100.0	98.6	111.4	153.0
		95.4		97.4	111.0	137.9
		54.7		97.0	107.9	133.9
	Output as composite 1937 base and inputs using 1937 weights[2]	53.0	100.0	98.6	109.1	149.9
		54.2		97.4	108.7	135.2

UNITED STATES[3]

Item	Nature of measurement	1869/78	1899/1908	1929	1948	1954	1957
Net national product	In 1929 dollars	11.3	43.0	100.0	—	—	—
	In 1954 dollars	—	—	100.0	162.5	—	225.3
Employment	Number of workers (adjusted for nonfarm hours)	32.5	74.2	100.0	108.5	120.3	125.8
Reproducible fixed capital	In 1929 dollars	9.8	43.9	100.0	—	—	—
	In 1947/49 dollars	—	—	100.0	105.8	131.0	146.7
Farmland	Acres	39.2	80.4	100.0	99.0	96.6	91.0
Livestock herds	In 1929 dollars	53.8	101.5	100.0	—	—	—
	In 1947/49 dollars	—	—	100.0	97.1	105.8	104.3
Selected inputs	With 1929 weights	28.2	68.4	100.0	107.7	—	129.1
	With 1954 weights	—	—	100.0	107.4	121.4	128.0
Net national product per worker (adjusted for nonfarm hours)	Output in 1929 dollars	34.8	58.0	100.0	—	—	—
	Output in 1954 dollars	—	—	100.0	150.0	—	179.1
Net national product per unit of reproducible fixed capital	Output and capital in 1929 dollars	115.3	97.9	100.0	—	—	—
	Output in 1954 dollars and capital in 1947/49 dollars	—	—	100.0	153.6	—	153.6
Net national product per unit of selected inputs	Output in 1929 dollars and inputs using 1929 weights	40.1	62.9	100.0	—	—	—
	Output in 1954 dollars and inputs using 1954 weights	—	—	100.0	151.3	—	176.0

[1]Data for 1940-1958 adjusted for territorial changes.

[2]Alternative figures correspond to different weights used in aggregating input, as given in text. Thus, for the top figures weights A were used; for the middle figures, weights B; and for the bottom figures, weights C.

[3]The entries for decade intervals are computed from annual averages for the decade.

TABLE 8.2. USSR and United States national product, factor inputs and productivity, average annual rate of growth for selected periods (percent).

USSR

Item	Nature of measurement	1928-58	1928-58 (effective years)	1928-40	1940-50	1950-58
Net national product	In 1937 ruble factor cost	4.1	4.8	4.2	1.9	6.8
	As composite 1937 base	6.0	7.0	9.3	1.7	6.8
Employment	Number of workers (adjusted for nonfarm hours)	2.0	2.3	3.7	0.7	1.2
Reproducible fixed capital	In 1937 rubles	7.0	8.1	9.8	0.5	11.2
	As composite 1937 base	7.1	8.2	11.0	−0.2	10.9
Farmland	Acres	1.5	1.8	1.6	−1.3	3.7
Livestock herds	In 1937 rubles	−0.2	−0.2	−1.9	−0.8	3.2
Selected inputs	With 1937 weights[1]	{ 2.9 2.4 2.9	{ 3.4 2.8 3.3	{ 4.2 3.8 4.1	{ 0.6 0.6 0.5	{ 4.0 2.7 4.0
Net national product per worker (adjusted for nonfarm hours)	Output in 1937 ruble factor cost	2.1	2.4	0.5	1.1	5.6
	Output as composite 1937 base	3.9	4.5	5.4	0.9	5.6
Net national product per unit of reproducible fixed capital	Output in 1937 ruble factor cost and capital in 1937 rubles	−2.7	−3.1	−5.1	1.3	−3.9
	Output and capital as composite 1937 base	−1.0	−1.1	−1.6	1.9	−3.6
Net national product per unit of selected inputs	Output in 1937 ruble factor cost and inputs using 1937 weights[1]	{ 1.2 1.7 1.2	{ 1.4 1.9 1.4	{ 0.1 0.5 0.2	{ 1.3 1.2 1.3	{ 2.7 4.0 2.8
	Output as composite 1937 base and inputs using 1937 weights[1]	{ 3.0 3.5 3.1	{ 3.5 4.1 3.6	{ 4.9 5.3 5.0	{ 1.1 1.0 1.1	{ 2.7 4.1 2.8

UNITED STATES[2]

Item	Nature of measurement	1869/78-1899/1908	1899/1908-1929	1929-57	1929-48	1948-57
Net national product	In 1929 dollars	4.6	3.4	—	—	—
	In 1954 dollars	—	—	2.9	2.6	3.7
Employment	Number of workers (adjusted for nonfarm hours)	2.8	1.2	0.8	0.4	1.7
Reproducible fixed capital	In 1929 dollars	5.1	3.3	—	—	—
	In 1947/49 dollars	—	—	1.4	0.3	3.7
Farmland	Acres	2.4	0.9	−0.3	−0.1	−0.9
Livestock herds	In 1929 dollars	2.1	0.1	—	—	—
	In 1947/49 dollars	—	—	0.2	−0.2	0.8
Selected inputs	With 1929 weights	3.0	1.5	0.9	0.4	2.0
	With 1954 weights	—	—	0.9	0.4	2.0
Net national product per worker (adjusted for nonfarm hours)	Output in 1929 dollars	1.7	2.2	—	—	—
	Output in 1954 dollars	—	—	2.1	2.2	2.0
Net national product per unit of reproducible fixed capital	Output and capital in 1929 dollars	−0.5	0.1	—	—	—
	Output in 1954 dollars and capital in 1947/49 dollars	—	—	1.5	2.3	. . .[3]
Net national product per unit of selected inputs	Output in 1929 dollars and inputs using 1929 weights	1.5	1.8	—	—	—
	Output in 1954 dollars and inputs using 1954 weights	—	—	2.0	2.2	1.7

[1] Alternative figures correspond to different weights used in aggregating input, as given in text. Thus, for the top figures, weights A were used; for the middle figures, weights B; and for the bottom figures, weights C.

[2] Where the terminal date is a decade, the rate of growth is based on an annual average centered at the middle of the decade.

[3] The symbol . . . means data are negligible.

To repeat, the revaluation of national income in terms of ruble factor cost is only partial. Moreover, as a valuation standard, ruble factor cost itself leaves something to be desired. In addition, despite substantial effort the calculations necessarily are inexact. Although the resultant errors are not likely to cumulate in any serious way, the deficiencies in valuation procedures, particularly in early years, probably give rise to something of an upward bias. The bias is only compounded (probably to a less extent than might be supposed) by the omission from national income of home processing, an activity that dwindles in relative importance as industrialization proceeds.[4]

From the *Real SNIP* figures on gross product, I derive corresponding figures on net national product by estimating depreciation charges taken from or calculated on the basis of data compiled in a forthcoming inquiry by Richard Moorsteen and Raymond Powell into the capital stock of the USSR. The charges rest on Soviet asset longevity figures, which curiously turn out to be similar to those employed by Simon Kuznets in comparable computations for the United States.[5]

---

from discussions with Moorsteen on the related question concerning the index number formula to be employed in the aggregation of inputs.

4. For the series in terms of 1937 ruble factor cost, one possible source of upward bias is eliminated. Thus, of two compilations made previously in terms of 1937 ruble factor cost use is made of the one involving extension of the revaluation within retail sales. The former series yields a slightly slower rate of growth than the latter: for 1928-1937, gross national product grew 0.7 percentage point less rapidly than with the less extended revaluation. For 1937-1948 and 1937-1954, the two series do not differ consequentially.

Ruble factor cost still includes somewhat arbitrary profit charges and omits any systematic allowance for rent and interest. Deduction of the former and inclusion of illustrative charges for the latter reduce the average annual rate of growth of gross national product 0.4 percentage point for 1928-1937. The rate also shows a slight reduction during 1937-1950 and 1950-1955. For effective years during 1928-1955 the rate of growth falls 0.3 percentage point.

The inclusion in the net national product of a significant variety of but by no means all home processing at factor cost would reduce the rate of growth of output in 1937 ruble factor cost during 1928-1937 by 0.3 percentage point. The relative decline in home processing presumably occurred primarily in these early years.

According to a recent computation by Morris Bornstein which for 1950-1955 corresponds closely to *Real SNIP*, the Soviet gross national product grew at a somewhat higher rate during 1955-1958 than during 1950-1955. According to a tentative computation in *Real SNIP*, the rate of growth during 1955-1958 was about the same as during 1950-1955. Neither calculation considers the probably significant upward bias in Soviet official data on agricultural output for recent years. Here, in extending the *Real SNIP* series for 1928-1955 to 1955, I assume that during 1955-1958 output grew somewhat less rapidly than during 1950-1955.

On the data considered in the extrapolation, see *Real SNIP*, chap. 15; and M. Bornstein, "A Comparison of Soviet and United States National Product," in JEC, *Comparisons of the United States and Soviet Economies* (Washington, D.C., 1959), pt. 2.

5. In *Real SNIP* all outlays classified in Soviet statistics as "capital repairs" (as distinct from "current repairs") are construed as "final" product and included in gross national prod-

Under the five-year plans, Soviet national income has grown at a rapid tempo, although hardly as fast as familiar Soviet official claims suggest. Thus, during the entire period 1928-1958, the Soviet net national product, in terms of 1937 ruble factor cost, apparently grew at an average rate of 4.1 percent annually. On the basis of the alternative computation obtained as a composite, the corresponding figure is 6.0 percent.[6] These figures are averages of all years in the period, including the four war years. Also of interest for present purposes are rates of growth obtained on the assumption that the entire increase in output is attributable to the twenty-six peacetime years: 4.8 and 7.0 percent, respectively. Actually the Russians did not regain their prewar level of production until 1948. The expansion of output to this level and beyond, it is true, was facilitated by reparations and by the availability for a time of partially damaged plants that could be renovated and restored to full use with limited investment. Nevertheless, the alternative rates of growth must be considered a conservative representation of the elusive aspect in question: what Soviet growth might have

---

uct. Here, before deducting depreciation, I omit from gross national product one-half of such outlays on capital repairs. The measures obtained are, I believe, more nearly comparable than they would otherwise be with the Commerce Department data for the United States after which the *Real SNIP* computations are patterned and which I use in comparing the growth of national income in the USSR and in the United States. While the share of capital repairs deducted is arbitrary, an alternative adjustment would have hardly any effect on measures that are of interest.

In their study of capital stock Moorsteen and Powell give data on the volume of outlays for capital repairs in terms of 1937 ruble prices. With the aid of deflators for fixed capital investment implied in *Real SNIP,* I have derived corresponding figures in prices of other years that are needed to adjust the *Real SNIP* data on gross national product to given-year values. As with depreciation, the fact that the data are prevailing ruble prices poses no problems.

To return to depreciation, from the Moorsteen-Powell computations alternative series on depreciation are or may be compiled. I use here a series representing depreciation on basic assets excluding capital repairs. Since some capital repairs are treated here as a final product, some allowance should properly be made for their depreciation, but it did not seem advisable to use a second Moorsteen-Powell series where depreciation is computed in a manner that conforms to Soviet accounting theory, which yields total charges twice those given by the series I employ. Essentially, for the second series, depreciation is charged both on basic investments and on capital repairs. Moreover, in the case of capital repairs the charge is related not to actual outlays on capital repairs but to outlays dictated by Soviet accounting norms. Since outlays in accord with such norms are presupposed by the Soviet asset longevity figures, theoretically there is something to be said for this approach, but I hesitate to rely on the Soviet norms. In any event, this approach would yield depreciation charges less comparable than those actually relied upon with the depreciation data for the United States, which is of concern here.

Reference here and elsewhere to unpublished calculations of Moorsteen and Powell is with the kind permission of the authors and the RAND Corporation.

6. These rates of growth and others cited below, where in order, have been adjusted for changes in Soviet boundaries that occurred in the period studied, chiefly in 1939 and 1940. As

been if there had been no war. Following Gregory Grossman, I will refer to measures that impute to nonwar years Soviet growth for periods spanning the war as rates of growth for "effective years."

While growth is generally swift, the rate fluctuates. The tempo also depends on the formula. Thus, during 1928-1940, with valuation at 1937 ruble factor cost, output grew 4.2 percent annually. With valuation at ruble factor cost of the given year the rate was more than twice as great: 9.2 percent. As explained, particularly for the early years my calculations are inexact and probably subject to an upward bias. Nevertheless output clearly grew rapidly. For 1940-1950, an interval spanning the war, the rate of growth sharply declined according to both formulas, although the drop is greater in terms of ruble factor cost of the given year. During 1950-1958 the tempo was again relatively high: 6.8 percent annually, according to both measures. By implication, the rate of growth during this interval exceeded that during 1928-1940 when valuation is at 1937 ruble factor cost. When valuation is at ruble factor cost of the given year, it equaled or fell short of the corresponding tempo for 1928-1940. Thus, the answer to the interesting question of whether growth is tending to accelerate, proceed without change, or slow down awkwardly depends on the formula used in the calculations.

SOVIET COMPARED WITH AMERICAN NATIONAL INCOME GROWTH

For the national income of the United States, one necessarily turns to the computations of Simon Kuznets and the U.S. Department of Commerce. Accordingly, for comparison with the Soviet data, in Tables 8.1 and 8.2 I present corresponding figures for the United States compiled from those computations. For years before 1929, I use Professor Kuznets's calculations of the United States net national product in terms of 1929 dollar prices.

---

in *Real SNIP* (chap. 13), I assume that the territories incorporated in the USSR in 1939 and later add 10 percent to the total output produced within the pre-1939 boundaries. For the various factor inputs in the USSR to which I will refer later I assume that the relation of new territories to those within the pre-1939 boundaries is the same as that for total output. The territorial acquisitions therefore do not affect the relation of output to the different inputs. For reproducible fixed capital, this adjustment simply reverses the one made in compiling the unadjusted series from which I start. Or rather, that is the case for 1940, but there is no reason to proceed differently for 1950-1955. For inputs other than fixed capital (employment, farmland, and livestock herds), the stated assumption is rather arbitrary, but the resultant errors in my calculations cannot be significant. See *Real SNIP,* chap. 13; Abram Bergson and Hans Heymann, Jr., *Soviet National Income and Product 1940-48* (New York, 1953), p. 233; and TSU, *Narodnoe khoziaistvo SSSR v 1958 godu* (Moscow, 1959) pp. 386-387, 445-446.

Since the calculations for the USSR were patterned after those of the U.S. Department of Commerce, net national product has essentially the same meaning here as in the Commerce Department calculations. As is well known, Kuznets defines net national product somewhat differently than the Commerce Department, but his data are used only for selected years and for these years the comparisons, I believe, are not consequentially affected by that feature. While Kuznets's calculations generally are in terms of 1929 dollar prices, because of the nature of the computation they may sometimes significantly reflect dollar prices of the given year. For reasons that will become evident, that characteristic is not undesirable for my purposes. But as Kuznets makes clear, his computations are often crude. In early years, particularly, there may be some tendency toward an upward bias.[7]

For years since 1929, I use national income data published by the Department of Commerce. These data, which have been revised recently, are in terms of 1954 dollar prices. Although hardly devoid of error, the Commerce Department calculations must be statistically among the most reliable available on national income. The Commerce Department publishes

7. I refer to data compiled in Simon Kuznets, *Capital in the American Economy: Its Formation and Financing* (Princeton, N.J., 1961), and use variant III, the one statistically most comparable with Commerce Department calculations. On the nature and import of the difference in scope between Kuznets's and the Commerce Department's concepts of net national product, see Simon Kuznets, "Long Term Changes in National Income of the United States of America Since 1870," in Simon Kuznets, ed., *Income and Wealth of the United States* (Cambridge, 1952), pp. 29 ff. Reasons for thinking that Kuznets's computations may materially reflect given-year prices are detailed in *Real SNIP,* chaps. 7 and 14. As was explained, my real national income data, particularly for early years, may be subject to something of an upward bias for various reasons, among them the undervaluation of farm labor services and omission of home processing. Although Kuznets is not explicit on the matter, his measures of real national income must also reflect an underevaluation of farm labor services, especially for early years. He makes clear his measures are also affected by the omission of home processing.

In addition Kuznets considers as sources of bias the "increase in the extent of hauling, distribution, and other services" and "higher costs in cities." For present purposes, the concern being production potential, I doubt that such activities are properly interpreted that way, although there is much to be said for Kuznets's approach if the subject is welfare. As he acknowledges, the adjustment he suggests for the bias in question, together with the one caused by the deletion of home processing and entailing an increase in household consumption in 1869/78 of 50 percent, represent "a rather generous allowance" (see ibid., p. 60). Nevertheless, if we adjust consumption for 1869/78 in this way and increase consumption for 1899/1908 correspondingly by, say, 25 percent, the annual rate of growth of net national product over the interval falls only 0.5 percentage point.

In Table 8.1 I incorporate in the index for 1869/78 an allowance for a 5 percent undercoverage, which Kuznets indicates is probable. That is quite apart from the elimination of home processing.

figures in constant prices only on gross national product, but corresponding data on net national product can be derived, chiefly from Kuznets's data in terms of replacement cost.[8]

In order to gauge comparative trends in output, either of our two series for the USSR may be used. For the United States only one series is at hand for any given interval. Conceivably, however, additional measures for each country could be derived. In fact, as will appear, something is known about further alternatives. Which sorts of data should be compared in the two countries? Although the pertinent methodological issue is rarely explored, I think there will be no dissent if I observe certain principles set forth in *Real SNIP*. Essentially, comparisons may be useful where the measures for each country are (as here) in local prices. Preferably the same index number formula should be applied in the two countries, although the effect of a change in formula is of interest as well. If possible, the data for each country should also be in terms of prices that are more or less contemporaneous with the period in question. Furthermore the base years for the two countries might well be similarly located in the intervals under study, although it is desirable, too, to know the effect on the results of a shift in the base year.

The data permit us to compare the Soviet performance under the five-year plans with that of the United States in early and recent times. I direct the reader's attention to two intervals in the United States, namely, 1929-1957 and 1869/78-1899/1908. Let us compare first the Soviet performance with that of the United States in the recent period. The net national product of the USSR grew during 1928-1958 at an average annual rate of 4.1 percent if output is valued at 1937 ruble factor cost and 6.0 percent if output is valued at ruble factor cost of the given year. The corresponding figures for effective years are 4.8 and 7.0 percent. In contrast, the net national product of the United States valued at 1954 prices, grew during 1929-1957 at an average annual rate of only 2.9 percent. For comparison with the Soviet series in 1937 ruble factor costs, according to the methodological principles indicated, one may want to consider data for the United States in terms of prices of, say, the late thirties. Similarly, for comparison

8. The figures on gross national product since 1929 in dollar prices of 1954 are from U.S. Department of Commerce, *U.S. Income and Output* (Washington, D.C., 1958), pp. 118-119. In the same prices, depreciation is estimated to have been $22.6 billion in 1954 and $48.4 billion in 1957.

For depreciation in 1929 and 1948 I use Kuznets's estimates of depreciation on nonwar goods, excluding depletion. From depreciation in terms of current replacement cost, corresponding figures in terms of 1954 replacement cost are obtained by use of the inflators for private investment in fixed capital implied in the Commerce Department national income calculations in terms of 1954 prices. Kuznets's estimates of depreciation are available only up to 1955, but the corresponding figure in 1954 dollars can be extrapolated to 1957.

with the Soviet series in ruble factor cost of the given year, it would be preferable to use United States data compiled according to a corresponding formula. Each of those recomputations probably would raise the rate of growth of American output only a fraction of a percentage point.[9] The conclusion must be that Soviet output has tended systematically to grow more rapidly than ours. The Russians outpaced us if measures for both countries are in appropriate base-year values and even more so if measures are in appropriate given-year values.

Turning now to the comparison of the Soviet performance under the five-year plans with that of the United States during 1869/78-1899/1908, the pertinent Soviet measures are as before, but in the United States, output grew at an average annual rate of 4.6 percent. American output is calculated in terms of 1929 dollars, but depending on the measures used for the USSR, reference should properly be made either to data in terms of dollar prices of, say, the late 1880s or to data in terms of dollar prices of given years. The effect of each of these two recomputations is conjectural. Measures in appropriate base-year values for both countries probably would show that neither country markedly surpassed the other. With measures for both countries in appropriate given-year values, the outcome is especially speculative, although I wonder whether the American tempo could match that of the USSR. Thus the shift in base year for the United States, even over a long interval, to a relatively early date might not have had as large an impact on real national income as that observed for the USSR when the base year is shifted from 1937 to 1928. Nevertheless, the facts in this matter are still unsettled, for the effect of a shift in base year on American national income measures still has to be systematically investigated.

In view of the terminal dates selected and the use of decade average as the terminal figures in the early intervals, the growth rates calculated for the United States probably reflect (as is desirable here) secular trends rather than the fluctuations due to business cycles.

TRENDS IN SOVIET FACTOR PRODUCTIVITY

The results of the attempt to relate trends in output to trends in major inputs taken together for the USSR are shown in Tables 8.1 and 8.2. In compiling those measures, I consider the two series on net national product but in each case compare output with an aggregate of the following inputs.

Employment. A calculation made previously for 1928-1955 has been extended to 1958. Essentially, employment is the sum of: (1) average employ-

9. *Real SNIP,* chap. 14, pp. 265 ff.

ment during the year in nonfarm, civilian occupations as determined chiefly from Warren Eason's computations; (2) agricultural employment in terms of "full-time" equivalents as estimated for 1928 from a Soviet official calculation and for 1937 and later years from data compiled by Nancy Nimitz; (3) the penal labor force, which was negligible in 1928, and is assumed to have totaled 3.5 million in 1940 and 1950 and 2 million in 1958; and (4) the armed forces as determined from diverse information, including data released by Khrushchev in his speech to the Supreme Soviet on January 14, 1960. The data on agricultural employment almost inevitably are rather crude. The figures on penal labor are also quite arbitrary, but at least in respect to trends for the entire period 1928-1958, an error at this point should not be very significant. While the precise form of measurement varies somewhat among sectors, employment is more or less in terms of man-years. In the tables the figures cited also allow for changes in hours in the case of civilian, nonfarm workers, as indicated by trends in industry alone. Information at hand on trends in the agricultural workday under the five-year plans is conflicting: possibly there was no change to speak of; possibly as a result of collectivization, hours declined.[10] In this initial inquiry, it seemed best not to attempt to adjust employment for changes in labor quality, although measures of factor productivity with such an adjustment are certainly of interest.

Reproducible fixed capital. This figure includes producers' durables and building and structures of all kinds. I rely here on computations by Moorsteen and Powell, who measure the fixed capital stock both gross and net of depreciation. The latter aspect is more appropriate here, although the two series move close together and for practical purposes the choice of one over the other is of little import. The data are also compiled in terms of ruble prices for different years. For the moment, emphasis is on those valued at 1937 ruble prices, but later I shall refer to an alternative composite 1937 base series similar to the one compiled for national income.

10. For the underlying data on employment in man-years for 1928-1955, before adjustment for changes in nonfarm hours and in boundaries, see *Real SNIP,* app. K. The 1958 figure is 93.6 million man-years, constituted as follows: civilian nonfarm, 50.1 million; farm, 37.9; military, 3.6; and penal, 2.0.

Civilian nonfarm and farm employment data are primarily from TSU, *Narodnoe khoziaistvo 1958,* pp. 655-659; and from TSU, *Sel'skoe khoziaistvo SSSR* (Moscow, 1960), p. 450. For the armed forces data, see *Pravda,* January 15, 1960. Perhaps wrongly, no allowance is made for a further decline in penal labor below the assumed 1955 level. The employment equivalent of changes in nonfarm hours for 1928-1955 is determined from date in *Real SNIP,* app. H. Normal working hours for 1958 are taken to be 113 percent of those prevailing in 1937 (see TSU, *Narodnoe khoziaistvo 1958,* p. 665).

The composite 1937 base series is derived from the Moorsteen-Powell computations in terms of the prices of different years.

The volume of net fixed capital assets at any date is the sum of the stock of fixed capital, net of depreciation, on hand on January 1, 1928, and the total net investment in fixed capital from that time to the date in question. Because of limitations on Soviet data underlying the net stock of fixed capital on hand on January 1, 1928, this item may be overstated as much as 30 percent. As the share of the initial stock in the total on hand at any date dwindles in the course of time, the rate of growth necessarily is affected, particularly in early years.[11]

Gross fixed capital investment in the period since January 1, 1928, was determined from a computation much the same as that made in *Real SNIP:* for producers' durables, outlays in current prices computed from Soviet data are deflated by price indexes compiled by Moorsteen; for construction, outlays in constant prices are assumed to vary with the physical volume of material inputs into construction computed by Powell. Depreciation is deducted as already indicated. As a result of the war, the Russians are supposed to have lost one-third of the fixed capital on hand at the time of the German attack. While that is a rather arbitrary figure, under alternative assumptions that the losses totaled 15 percent and 50 percent of the prewar stock, the assets on hand on Janury 1, 1950, vary only 8 percent from the amount calculated initially.[12]

This is not the place to discuss the thorny question of the theoretical basis for the measurement of "real" capital stock, but it should be observed that in 1937 Soviet fixed capital goods were subject only to an inconsequential degree, directly or indirectly, to the famous "turnover tax" and, as a result of a price reform of the previous year, subsidies were no longer the major feature that they had been in this area. By implication, capital goods prices in 1937 probably conform more or less to the ruble factor cost

11. For intervals considered in the tables, the rates of growth of the fixed capital stock in 1937 prices based on a January 1, 1928, stock reduced 30 percent are as follows: 1928-1958, 8.3 percent; 1928-1958 (effective years), 9.6 percent; 1928-1940, 12.6 percent; 1940-1950, 0.9 percent; and 1950-1958, 11.5 percent.

12. As already explained, fixed capital stock excludes capital repairs and is net of depreciation. Since I have classified as "final" product one-half of expenditures on capital repairs, it might have been preferable to use a series in which capital repairs to this extent are included with basic assets in the stock of fixed capital after an allowance for depreciation. For present purposes, however, I believe the series actually used is more appropriate than either of two others that Moorsteen and Powell offer. In both cases all outlays on capital repairs are included, but in one the charge for depreciation is doubled while it is increased 50 percent in the other. On the rationale of the former calculation, see n. 5; the latter is simply an arbitrary variant. By appropriate averaging, Moorsteen-Powell data for January 1 have been centered on July 1.

standard in terms of which national income has been valued. Broadly speaking, capital goods prices also tend to conform to ruble factor cost in years for which such prices enter into my composite 1937 base series.

The data on Soviet fixed capital evidently represent *capacity*. While a computation of factor productivity on that basis is of interest, one may also want to allow for variations in intensity of use. Because of the increase in shift work, intensity probably has increased over the years studied.

Farmland. Soviet farmland is taken to mean the total sown area given by Soviet official statistics. Although on the eve of the five-year plans vast areas of the USSR were still uncultivated, in terms of climate, soil, or both, much of this land was either inferior or entirely unsuitable for agriculture. By the same token, the expansion of the sown area since 1928 undoubtedly has been associated with a significant decline in quality. While a decline in quality pervaded the whole period, it is especially characteristic of the years since 1954, during which the sown area has sharply increased under Khrushchev's New Lands Program.[13] No account can be taken of this qualitative deterioration.

Livestock. Herd sizes of different kinds of livestock (cows, other cattle, hogs, sheep and goats, and horses) given by Soviet official data are aggregated in terms of the average ruble prices realized on the farm in 1937. Estimates of the latter were compiled for *Real SNIP* by George Karcz. Changes in animal weights and productivity, which have been ignored, declined markedly in the thirties, but by the end of the period studied probably were as high as or higher than they had been on the eve of the five-year plans.[14]

So much for inputs that are aggregated. In summing them I use as weights three sets of "synthetic" factor income shares (Table 8.3). Thus, I assign to employment in all three cases a measure of importance corresponding to the total wages and other labor income earned in the USSR in 1937 (in the case of farm households some of the earnings may be more properly classified as agricultural rent). For reproducible fixed capital with weights A and C, I allow for a net return of 20.0 percent annually of the stock on hand on July 1, 1937. With weights B the rate of return is reduced to 8 percent. In the United States in 1929 private capital (excluding agricultural land) generally earned an average net return of 6.9 percent. Because of the relatively limited capital stock in the USSR in 1937, even

13. TSU, *Narodnoe khoziaistvo 1958,* pp. 386-387.

14. For the underlying herd figures, see ibid., pp. 445-446. Livestock prices in 1937 can be found in *Real SNIP,* app. G.

TABLE 8.3. Weights used in aggregating Soviet factor inputs

Item	Weights A		Weights B		Weights C	
	Rubles (bil.)	Percent	Rubles (bil.)	Percent	Rubles (bil.)	Percent
Employment	179.9	70.4	179.9	80.5	179.9	67.5
Reproducible fixed capital	46.2	18.1	18.5	8.3	46.2	17.3
Farmland	22.4	8.8	22.4	10.0	33.6	12.6
Livestock herds	7.0	2.7	2.8	1.3	7.0	2.6
All	*255.5*	*100.0*	*223.6*	*100.0*	*266.7*	*100.0*

assuming a rate of 20 percent, the total income accruing to reproducible fixed capital amounted to but 26 percent of all Soviet labor income in the same year. This is the same percentage as the corresponding relation that prevailed in the United States in 1929. Going back to relatively early dates in American history, however, there is hardly any evidence of a sharp increase in the net return to capital above the 1929 level. Although that fact could mean different things, it may be wrong to suppose (as it is tempting to do) that the relative shortage of capital in the USSR calls for the imputation of a notably high return to it.

For farmland in the case of weights A and B, the assumed weight means that the agricultural rent equaled 40 percent of Soviet farm labor income in 1937. Weights C assume that agricultural rent was 60 percent of Soviet farm labor income that year. The former relation is about the same as that for the United States in 1929. Compared with farm labor income, agricultural rent in the United States tended to be greater in earlier than in recent years. For livestock herds, I allow in all cases the same net return as for reproducible fixed capital.[15]

15. The total wage and other labor income earned in the USSR in 1937 is the sum of "total net income, currently earned," exclusive of "imputed rent," of all Soviet households in 1937, and of Soviet employers' contributions to social insurance, as given in Abram Bergson, Hans Heymann, Jr., and Oleg Hoeffding, *Soviet National Income and Product, 1928-48: Revised Data,* RM-2544 (Santa Monica, Calif.: RAND Corporation, March 1, 1960). According to the Moorsteen-Powell calculations, the Soviet stock of reproducible fixed capital net of depreciation on July 1, 1937, totaled 231.1 billion rubles in 1937 prices. The weights assigned reproducible fixed capital are calculated from this magnitude and the assumed rate of return. The weight assigned farmland is calculated from the assumed relation to farm labor income and

While the factor income shares used as weights in aggregating inputs are "synthetic," they refer to circumstances prevailing in the USSR in 1937. By the same token, all three input series may be considered to be in terms of base-year weights. When output is measured in terms of values for the given year, it may be more appropriate to aggregate inputs in terms of given-year weights. According to a computation based on given-year weights, however, the overall trends of output per unit of inputs would not change consequentially although the rate of increase for early years may diminish somewhat and that for later years may increase somewhat. In the computation, weights A for inputs are imputed to the given year in each comparison with 1937. Evidently the recalculation illustrates the effect of the use of given-year weights for inputs on the assumption that relative factor prices vary inversely with relative inputs.[16]

In calculating output per unit of inputs, I consider four factor inputs, of which three (labor, reproducible fixed capital, and farmland) are major, but those considered are not exhaustive of factor inputs in the USSR. More to the point, the distinction between items treated as factor inputs and items treated as sources of change in factor productivity is necessarily somewhat conventional, but it may be desirable to include in aggregate factor inputs at least one other item: inventories. Nevertheless, when this

---

its magnitude (56.0 billion rubles) as shown in Bergson et al., *Soviet National Income Revised.*

The relative earnings of different factor inputs in the United States in 1929 and pertinent trends in earnings over time are considered later in this chapter.

The comparative relations between the stock of reproducible fixed capital and labor income for the two countries may be of interest. So may the farmland-man ratios that may be derived from the data on factor inputs:

	Reproducible fixed capital/ labor income, all sectors, local prices	Acres of farmland per "man-year" employed
USSR, 1937	1.28	8.9
United States, 1929	3.77	47.5

16. The results of the recomputation of the average annual rate of growth of net national product per unit of input follow, together with the figures obtained originally by use of weights for the base year. In both calculations, output is the composite 1937 base series: with weights A imputed to 1937, 1928-1958 = 3.0 percent, 1928-1958 (effective years) = 3.5 percent, 1928-1940 = 4.9 percent, 1940-1950 = 1.1 percent, and 1950-1958 = 2.7 percent; with weights A imputed to given year, 1928-1958 = 3.1 percent, 1928-1958 (effective years) = 3.6 percent, 1928-1940 = 4.0 percent, 1940-1950 = 1.2 percent, and 1950-1958 = 4.0 percent. In the recomputations, the composite 1937 base series for fixed capital is used instead of the one in terms of 1937 prices.

In the calculations employing base-year weights, I aggregate inputs arithmetically in terms

inquiry was being organized, it was felt that the inclusion of inventories could not materially affect the results, and it is indeed the case if we may rely on the new estimates of Soviet inventories that Raymond Powell made available to me recently. Thus, if inventories are included with factor inputs, output per unit of inputs grows at an annual rate that is 0.1 to 0.3 percent lower than the tempos previously computed.

Among the items reckoned here in total factor inputs is farmland. Some inquiries into factor productivity attempt to treat as inputs all natural resources, including not only farmland but also extractive wealth and urban land, but such an extension of the inputs aggregated was not possible. Consequently extractive wealth and urban land must be viewed as sources of change in factor productivity.

To come finally to the results: if output is valued at 1937 ruble factor cost, during 1928-1958 net national product per unit of inputs grew at an average annual rate of 1.2 to 1.7 percent. With output valued at ruble factor cost of the given year, net national product per unit of inputs grew at an average annual rate of 3.0 to 3.5 percent. For "effective years" during 1928-1958, the corresponding figures are 1.4 to 1.9 and 3.5 to 4.1 percent, respectively. Although these computations leave much to be desired, I conclude that under the five-year plans output has tended systematically to grow more rapidly than input. This finding is true for either measure of output, but the margin between output and inputs is larger when output is in terms of ruble factor cost of the given year.[17]

As for national income, so for factor productivity the tempo varies in different intervals. For 1928-1940, at 1937 ruble factor cost, net national product per unit of input grew at an average annual rate of 0.1 to 0.5 per-

---

of those weights. According to familiar theoretical reasoning, it may be preferable to aggregate input geometrically. The following alternative series illustrate the effect of such a recomputation on the average annual rate of growth of net national product at 1937 ruble factor cost per unit of input aggregated according to weights A: with inputs aggregated arithmetically, 1928-1958 = 1.2 percent, 1928-1958 (effective years) = 1.4 percent, 1928-1940 = 0.1 percent, 1940-1950 = 1.3 percent, and 1950-1958 = 2.7 percent; with inputs aggregrated geometrically, 1928-1958 = 1.3 percent, 1928-1958 (effective years) = 1.5 percent, 1928-1940 (negligible), 1940-1950 = 1.3 percent, and 1950-1958 = 3.5 percent. Use of the geometric aggregation thus reduces the rate of growth of output per unit of input for early years and increases it for recent years, but the effect throughout is limited.

17. With respect to national income per unit of inputs, it is difficult to appraise the allowance for the effects of the war reflected in the average rate of growth for effective years during 1928-1958. In 1950 output per unit of inputs was still just 11.2 to 13.6 percent above the corresponding figure for 1940 (with inputs aggregated according to weights A) and this increase was probably realized during the reconstruction period. By implication, output per unit of inputs hardly increased during the war and might have declined.

cent. With the alternative valuation of output, the corresponding figures are far greater: 4.9 to 5.3 percent. If we consider the crudity of my calculations for these early years, we must conclude that with the former sort of measure net national product per unit of input grew little, if at all, and may even have decreased. For output valued at given-year ruble factor cost, however, a markedly rapid growth rate was achieved.

During 1940-1950 either measure of net national product per unit of inputs grew 1.0, or somewhat more than 1.0, percent annually. This finding suggests that despite the war, output grew somewhat more rapidly than inputs. For 1950-1958 the two measures are again in essential accord: with output valued at 1937 ruble factor cost net national product per unit of inputs grew 2.7 to 4.0 percent annually; with output valued at given-year ruble factor cost, the corresponding figures are 2.7 to 4.1 percent. Thus, in either case growth was relatively rapid, but the answer to the interesting question of whether, compared with prewar years, productivity growth accelerated or slowed down depends on the computation. Output at 1937 ruble factor cost suggests that growth accelerated. With output at given-year factor cost, the tempo was either broadly the same as in prewar years or declined somewhat.

The role of different productive inputs in the growth of aggregate output is difficult to gauge because of the need here to employ rather arbitrary weights. Nevertheless it is of interest that for 1928-1958 as a whole aggregate inputs by any computation grew more rapidly than labor, the input with the predominant weight. That phenomenon is due solely to the notable expansion of reproducible fixed capital, which grew more than three times as rapidly as employment. Of the two remaining inputs considered, farmland tended to grow somewhat more slowly than employment, while livestock herds actually declined. By implication, the growth of reproducible fixed capital more than offset these two lagging inputs, so far as aggregate inputs are concerned.

During 1928-1940 and again during 1950-1958, the pattern of structural change was broadly similar to that for 1928-1958, but the divergence between reproducible fixed capital and employment in the first interval was smaller and in the second was much greater than during the entire period 1928-1958. Also land and livestock lagged even further behind employment during 1928-1940 than they did during 1928-1958, whereas after 1950 they both finally outpaced employment. During 1940-1950, all inputs either increased little or declined, but employment very likely increased as much as, if not more than, the rest.

From the data compiled, one may compute not only output per unit of input generally but also output per unit of one input or another. Of the different calculations of the latter type, however, only two are of particular interest: in one case output is related to employment, in the other to reproducible fixed capital. Trends in output per unit of employment under the five-year plans are discussed in *Real SNIP,* and trends in output related to fixed capital are being considered by Moorsteen and Powell. Furthermore what could be said in either regard is more or less implied in my discussion of trends in output per unit of input generally and in the structure of inputs. Accordingly the data on output per worker and on output per unit of reproducible fixed capital (Tables 8.1 and 8.2) are presented only for reference purposes. Interesting as those topics are, I do not attempt to explore them here.[18]

SOVIET COMPARED WITH UNITED STATES FACTOR PRODUCTIVITY TRENDS

Although output per unit of inputs has been computed previously for the United States, in order to compare it with the data for the USSR, it seemed best to make a fresh calculation. The results appear in Tables 8.1 and 8.2. In calculating output per unit of inputs, the two series on the net national product of the United States, one for 1929 and earlier years in terms of 1929 dollars and the other for 1929 and later years in terms of 1954 dollars, are related to two series of inputs. Both sets of inputs are aggregates corresponding to those used for the USSR, and they differ chiefly in the weights employed, although some of the series for individual inputs also vary somewhat. The following-input series were used:

Employment. In both input series, I rely mainly on a compilation made in *Real SNIP.* For years up to 1929, employment is the sum of: (1) the

18. The data may help us, however, to understand an outstanding feature: the sharp decline under the five-year plans in output per unit of reproducible fixed capital. In theoretical discussions of economic growth it sometimes is assumed that the capital coefficient—that is, the volume of reproducible fixed capital per unit of output—is fairly stable as growth proceeds. To my knowledge, the validity of this supposition has yet to be investigated in any systematic way empirically, but if the sharp increase in the capital coefficient observed for the USSR under the five-year plans turns out to be unique, it is not difficult to understand why. In the course of economic development, capital stock ordinarily grows more rapidly than the labor force. By the same token, there must be a tendency toward diminishing returns to capital. Ordinarily, technological progress may offset that aspect to a large degree, if not entirely. For the USSR, however, since the capital stock increases radically in relation to the labor force, the tendency toward diminishing returns is correspondingly accentuated and technological progress, although probably marked, is only a partial offset.

Data set forth below on output per unit of reproducible fixed capital in the United States fail to show any precise constancy, but the variation over long periods is relatively limited, at least in comparison to the Soviet experience. Moreover, capital stock grows in relation to the labor force much less in the United States than in the USSR. By implication, diminishing returns to capital should have been less pronounced in the United States and hence more easily offset by technological progress than has been so for the USSR.

labor force in nonagricultural branches after allowance for unemployment and (2) the number of farmers, together with the number of agricultural employees in terms of their assumed full-time equivalent. In both categories I use Jacob Schmookler's adaptation of the basic Solomon Fabricant data. For 1929 and later years, calculations by Kuznets and the Commerce Department yield employment in all sectors in terms of its full-time equivalent. To allow for changes in the hours of nonfarm workers, I rely on data compiled by Dewhurst and his associates.[19] In accord with the procedure followed for the USSR, changes in the farm working day are ignored; farm hours tended to decline systematically during periods considered here. As for the USSR, qualitative changes in employment are omitted from the calculations.

Reproducible fixed capital. Two related compilations are used, one in which total inputs are compared with output in 1929 dollars and another in which total inputs are compared with output in 1954 dollars. In the case of the former I rely chiefly on Raymond Goldsmith's perpetual inventory data in terms of 1929 dollars. By summing Goldsmith's "structures" and "producers' durables," net of depreciation, I believe I obtain figures comparable in scope with those for Soviet reproducible fixed capital. Because of limitations in the underlying data and calculations, Goldsmith feels that his estimate of reproducible wealth for any particular date may err by as much as 10 to 20 percent or even more, but the margin of error is probably smaller in comparisons made over long intervals. Goldsmith's data are available only for years since 1896. To obtain a corresponding estimate for 1869/78, like Goldsmith I link his measures with similar data of a census type compiled by Kuznets. The Kuznets data differ somewhat in scope from Goldsmith's.[20]

19. The employment data before adjustment for nonfarm hours, are: 1869/78 = 12.4 million, 1899/1908 = 29.1 million, 1929 = 44.9 million, 1948 = 54.0 million, 1954 = 61.6 million, and 1957 = 64.5 million. After adjustment for nonfarm hours, they are: 1869/78 = 14.6 million, 1899/1908 = 33.3 million, 1929 = 44.9 million, 1948 = 48.7 million, 1954 = 54.0 million, and 1957 = 56.5 million. All figures are either taken from or derived by use of sources and methods described in *Real SNIP,* chap. 14. Data for 1954 are needed because 1954 is a weight year in the aggregation of inputs.

20. The absolute figures on reproducible fixed capital in terms of 1929 dollars are (in billions): 1869/78 = 22.4, 1899/1908 = 100.6, and 1929 = 228.9. In Raymond W. Goldsmith, *A Study of Saving in the United States* (Princeton, N.J., 1956), vol. 3, p. 20, end-of-the-year data are given for the American stock of structures and producers' durables in 1929 dollars. The 1929 figure used here is the total of the assets in those two categories recentered on July 1. For 1899/1908, the figure is the average of the end-of-year totals of assets in the two categories. The figure for 1869/78 actually pertains to the midpoint of that interval (that is, the end of 1873) and is extrapolated from an estimate of 30.5 billion in 1929 prices for reproduc-

For comparison of total inputs with output in 1954 dollars, I again rely on data on reproducible fixed capital compiled by Goldsmith's perpetual inventory method. These are the results of a forthcoming computation that is, for the most part, in terms of 1947/49 dollars, although for 1929-1945 the figures are obtained through a partial recomputation of data in 1929 dollars. As before, I use the sum of Goldsmith's structures and producers' durables, net of depreciation.[21] The data on fixed capital for the United States, like those for the USSR, refer to stocks rather than employment.

Farmland. For both total input measures, I use "farm cropland" as given in the U.S. census returns. Figures for terminal dates not coincident with or near a census date are obtained by extrapolation or interpolation. Because the census returns on farm cropland begin with 1879, the estimate for 1869/78 had to be extrapolated. As with the data for the USSR, those for the United States are in physical units and are not adjusted for changes in quality. In the United States quality may have deteriorated materially in early years when the acreage was expanding rapidly. Since 1929, however, farm cropland has tended to contract somewhat, and quality should have improved.[22]

Livestock. Most of the data are those compiled by Goldsmith. As in the case of reproducible fixed capital, for comparison with output in 1929

---

ible fixed capital in 1980. The latter figure is obtained by linking to Goldsmith's calculations corresponding data he has compiled for earlier years from data of Kuznets. See Raymond W. Goldsmith, "The Growth of Reproducible Wealth of the United States of America from 1805 to 1950," in Kuznets, ed., *Income and Wealth in the United States,* pp. 306-307. To obtain totals comparable to those for later years, I sum the following Goldsmith-Kuznets asset categories: nonfarm residences, agricultural structures and equipment, nonagricultural business structures and equipment, and government structures and equipment.

21. The absolute figures on reproducible fixed capital in 1947/49 dollars are (in billions): 1929 = 474.3, 1948 = 501.8, 1954 = 621.5, and 1957 = 695.7. With Goldsmith's kind permission, I cite a mimeographed work issued in July 1960 that is an appendix in his forthcoming *National Wealth of the United States in the Postwar Period.* The figures given there pertain to the end of the year and have been recentered here on July 1. Also the figure for 1929 is adjusted for the 1945 break in Goldsmith's series.

22. Farm cropland for the end of 1873 (the midpoint of 1869/78) is taken as 14 to 15 percent below the total given for 1879 in U.S. Department of Commerce, *Historical Statistics of the United States, 1789-1945* (Washington, D.C., 1949), p. 121. Farm cropland for the end of 1903 (the midpoint of 1899/1908) and for 1929-1954 is either taken or interpolated from data given in ibid., p. 121; U.S. Department of Commerce, *Statistical Abstract of the United States, 1958* (Washington, D.C., 1958), p. 612; and *Statistical Abstract of the United States, 1959* (Washington, D.C., 1959), p. 614. The corresponding figure for 1957 is based on the change from 1954 to 1957 in "harvested crops—acreage used for specified purposes," given in ibid., p. 653.

dollars, Goldsmith's data in 1929 dollars are used. Comparison with the output in 1954 dollars is based on his figures in 1947/49 dollars. The underlying calculations take into account changes in the size of different herds but not changes in quality. While this was also the rule for the data on the USSR, no doubt livestock quality has tended to improve more in the United States than in the USSR.[23]

Two sets of weights are used to aggregate inputs. A set based on 1929 factor incomes is used in the derivation of a series on total inputs to be related to net national product in 1929 dollars. The other set, based on 1954 factor incomes, gives a corresponding series to be related to net national product in 1954 dollars. The weights are given in Table 8.4. The figures represent the results of an attempt to determine from U.S. Department of Commerce tabulations of national income the earnings attributable to the factors in question. Thus employment figures are intended to include, in addition to actual compensation of employees, the returns of entrepreneurs imputable to their labor services. The latter are determined with the help of calculations by D. Gale Johnson. For each year reproducible fixed capital is credited essentially with the average return earned in that year on capital generally, exclusive of various items, among them agricultural land. Data on capital stock again come from Goldsmith. Agricultural rent computations were done by Johnson. Livestock herds are arbitrarily credited with the same rate of return as reproducible fixed capital.[24]

23. The average annual value of livestock herds in 1929 prices for 1899/1908 and a corresponding figure for July 1, 1929, are computed from end-of-year figures in Goldsmith, *A Study of Saving,* vol. 3, p. 21. The value of livestock for the end of 1873 (midpoint of the interval 1868/78) is extrapolated from a Goldsmith-Kuznets figure for 1880 in Goldsmith, "The Growth of Reproducible Wealth," in Kuznets, ed., *Income and Wealth in the United States,* p. 307. For data in 1947/49 dollars for July 1, 1929, 1948, 1954, and 1957, I recentered end-of-year figures in Goldsmith, *National Wealth of the United States in the Postwar Period.*

24. The weight for employment in 1929 is the sum of: (1) compensation of nonfarm employees, from data in U.S. Department of Commerce, *U.S. Income and Output,* pp. 126-127, 220, and U.S. Department of Commerce, *National Income, 1954* (Washington, D.C., 1954), p. 178, calculated at $49.79 billion; (2) agricultural labor income, including imputed labor income of farm entrepreneurs, which, according to D. Gale Johnson, "Allocation of Agricultural Income," *Journal of Farm Economics,* November 1948, p. 728, amounted to $5.19 billion; and (3) imputed labor income of nonfarm entrepreneurs, $5.71 billion following D. Gale Johnson, "Functional Distribution of Income in the United States," *Review of Economics and Statistics,* May 1954, p. 177. I impute to labor services 65 percent of the earnings of nonfarm entrepreneurs, which, according to U.S. Department of Commerce, *U.S. Income and Output,* pp. 126-127, amounted to $8.79 billion.

The total stock of reproducible fixed capital in the United States on July 1, 1929, calculated from Goldsmith's data, was $228.9 billion at current prices. The figure for the income of this factor, therefore, implies an average return of 6.89 percent. The rate of return is calculated

TABLE 8.4. Weights used in aggregating American factor inputs

Item	Calculated factor incomes, 1929		Calculated factor incomes, 1954	
	Dollars (bil.)	Percent	Dollars (bil.)	Percent
Employment	60.69	77.0	234.2	84.8
Reproducible fixed capital	15.77	20.0	38.1	13.8
Farmland	1.89	2.4	3.2	1.2
Livestock herds	0.45	0.6	0.6	0.2
All	*78.80*	*100.0*	*276.1*	*100.0*

The year 1954 saw a recession in the United States, but the growth of total inputs during 1929-1957 hardly changed if, instead of 1954, 1929 serves as the weight year (compare Tables 8.1 and 8.2).[25]

For the United States, as for the USSR, the factor inputs considered are not all-inclusive and, among other items, omits inventories. But for the period 1929-1957, inclusion of this minor input would have no perceptible effect on the growth of output per unit of inputs.

---

by relating these two aspects: (1) all property income earned—excluding agricultural rent—estimated to be $23.53 billion mainly on the basis of data in U.S. Department of Commerce, *U.S. Income and Output,* pp. 126-127, and (2) the total "national wealth"—excluding consumer durables, monetary gold and silver, and agricultural and public land—which, from Goldsmith's data, totaled $341.5 billion in current values on July 1, 1929.

Agricultural rent, including earnings of farm structures, in 1929 is given in Johnson, *Journal of Farm Economics,* November 1948, p. 728. Considering the comparative shares of land and structures in total farm real estate value before the war, I take agricultural rent, exclusive of earnings of farm structures, to be $1.89 billion. According to Goldsmith's data, American livestock herds were worth $6.5 billion at current prices in 1929 and I allow here the rate of return imputed to reproducible fixed capital.

The weights for 1954 are derived by essentially the same methods and sources. However, the average rate of return on "national wealth," excluding consumer durables, monetary gold and silver, and agricultural and public land, is 4.99 percent.

25. Data on total inputs cited in the tables are obtained by arithmetic aggregation, but geometric aggregation has even less effect on output per unit of inputs in the United States than in the USSR. Thus, during 1929-1957 the rate of growth of output per unit of inputs (based on 1954 weights) is unchanged at 2.0 percent a year. During 1869/78-1899/1908, the rate of growth declined 0.1 percent (based on 1929 weights).

In constrasting trends in output per unit of inputs in the USSR and the United States, we again must decide what data can properly be compared. I try to observe the guiding principles concerning output that I outlined earlier. We might like to consider input data in terms of the base year and formula employed for output, although this approach only compounds the difficulties that inhibit proceeding in a methodologically impeccable manner. As was done for total output, we compare the Soviet performance under the five-year plans with that of the United States during each of two intervals, 1929-1957 and 1869/78-1899/1908.

We consider first the comparison with American performance during 1929-1957. In the USSR with output valued at 1937 ruble factor cost, the net national product per unit of input grew during 1928-1958 at an average annual rate of 1.2 to 1.7 percent and for effective years at an average rate of 1.4 to 1.9 percent. With output valued at ruble factor cost of the given year, the corresponding figures are 3.0 to 3.5 percent and 3.5 to 4.1 percent. In the former case, inputs are aggregated as is appropriate in terms of weights pertaining to 1937. In the latter instance, use is made again of these weights, but if (as may be desired) weights pertaining to the given year were substituted, the results probably would not be seriously affected. In the United States the net national product per unit of input grew during 1929-1957 at an average annual rate of 2.0 percent if output is valued at dollar prices of 1954 and inputs are aggregated in terms of 1954 weights. As we have seen, however, revaluations of output appropriate for comparison with the two Soviet measures would have little effect, and I believe the same is true of the corresponding input revaluations that are in order.[26]

I conclude that when measures are in appropriate base-year values neither country much outpaced the other, although the United States may have some margin of superiority. When the measures are in appropriate given-year values, however, output per unit of input may well have grown more rapidly in the USSR than in the United States.

I turn to the comparison with American performance during 1869/78-1899/1908. United States net national product per unit of inputs increased at an average annual rate of 1.5 percent with output valued at dollar prices of 1929 and inputs aggregated in terms of 1929 weights. I have already commented on the possible effect on the rate of growth of the net national product of changes in base year and formula. As to the effect of corresponding changes for inputs, a further computation may be illuminating. If inputs are reaggregated with weights pertaining to the near-end of the

26. On this aspect, I refer to the comparative results obtained in aggregating American inputs in terms of 1929 and 1954 weights (Tables 8.1 and 8.2).

1880s net national product per unit of inputs grew annually during 1869/78-1899/1908 0.1 percentage point less than was computed initially.[27]

While the comparative trends are indeed uncertain when measures are in appropriate base-year values, the presumption is that neither country outpaced the other very decidedly. When measures are in appropriate given-year values, there may well be a margin in favor of the Russians, although that is speculative.

From the data compiled, we may also contrast trends in input volume and structure in the two countries. As implied, the USSR during 1928-1958 experienced a decidedly more rapid increase in inputs generally than the United States during 1927-1957. The relative rates for different inputs, however, varied markedly. The USSR experienced a decline and the United States an increase in livestock herds; for land, the situation was the reverse. Considering effective years, employment in the USSR increased three times as fast as in the United States; the rate of growth of reproducible fixed capital in the Soviet Union was more than five times ours. If reference for the USSR is to 1928-1958 and for the USA to 1869/78-1899/1908, total inputs in the two countries probably increased at about the same rate. Moreover the tempos were likewise not very disparate for employment and farmland. Yet the growth of livestock herds in the USSR lagged behind that in the United States. Reproducible fixed capital growth in the Soviet Union was markedly above that in the United States, but our rate of expansion was also high and it has not been equaled by us during a more recent lengthy interval.

CONCLUSION

The attempt to measure the rate and sources of Soviet national output growth over the period of the five-year plans is beset with formidable difficulties, which seem only to be compounded when the data are compared with contemporaneous and earlier American experience. Not only are the needed statistical data often inexact, but Soviet performance, especially

27. The weights, which are intended to represent factor shares in terms of 1890 prices and quantities of 1884-1893 or end of 1888 and derive from data in diverse sources, are: employment, $7.24 billion (75.2 percent); reproducible fixed capital, $1.69 billion (17.6 percent); farmland, $.52 billion (5.4 percent); livestock, $.17 billion (1.8 percent); all, $9.63 billion (100.0 percent).

Reaggregation of inputs in terms of the foregoing weights required data on input for the base date. As determined by use of the sources and methods employed in deriving American inputs for other years, the figures are (percent of 1929): employment, adjusted for nonfarm hours, 1884-1893 = 53.5; reproducible fixed capital, end of 1888 (in 1929 dollars) = 24.3; farmland, end of 1888 (in acres) = 59.3; livestock herds, end of 1888 (in 1929 dollars) = 93.8.

under the early plans, is notably sensitive to the choice of one of two index number formulas for the measurement of output growth: (1) a formula of a conventional sort in which output is valued in prices of a single base year, 1937, or (2) a more novel computation in which 1937 is a base year but changes in output from that year are measured in terms of given-year prices.

Given such index number relativity, it may be desirable for purposes of comparison to refer to measures of American output indicated by corresponding formulas, and, indeed, in terms of base years that are located, more or less like 1937, in the Soviet interval considered (1928-1958)—base years, that is, that are at intermediate points in the periods investigated for the United States (1869/78-1899/1908 and 1929-1957). Such measures are not at hand; what their magnitudes may be has to be inferred from other related computations.

Soviet net national product nevertheless is found to have grown at an average rate of 4.8 percent yearly over the period 1928-1958 with output valued at base-year prices. With valuation at given-year prices, the corresponding tempo was 7.0 percent.[28] In terms of either computation, the USSR appears to have outpaced the United States when for the latter reference is to 1929-1957. When reference is to 1869/78-1899/1908 in the United States, however, probably neither country much excels the other. At least that is so if for both countries output is valued at base-year prices. In terms of given-year prices, the comparative tempos are especially conjectural.

If output growth depends on the index number formula, so must the growth of factor productivity. Thus Soviet net national product per unit of factor input grew over the period 1928-1958 by 1.4 to 1.9 percent yearly with output valued at base-year prices and by 3.5 to 4.1 percent yearly with output valued at given-year prices. The United States during 1929-1957 must have nearly matched the foregoing Soviet performance with valuation for both countries in base-year prices. With valuation for both countries in given-year prices, the USSR must have appreciably surpassed us. Consider now the period 1869/78-1899/1908 in the United States. With output in both countries valued at base-year prices, we should have at least matched the Soviet 1928-1958 rate. With output in both countries in given-year prices, the Russians during 1928-1958 may possibly have outdistanced us.

As implied, aggregate inputs tended to grow much more rapidly in the USSR under the plans than they did in the United States contemporaneously. The more rapid growth of Soviet inputs thus contributed signifi-

28. Here and later I cite average rates of growth for "effective years" in the USSR.

cantly to the growth of Soviet output relative to ours. In the United States during 1869/78-1899/1908, however, aggregate inputs grew fully as rapidly as they did in the USSR during 1928-1958. There does not seem, therefore, to be a divergence at this point that could affect comparative output growth.

The USSR outpaced us contemporaneously with respect to growth of both of two principal factors in question: labor and reproducible fixed capital. The Soviet stock of reproducible fixed capital during 1928-1958 actually grew five times as fast as ours did during 1929-1957. During 1869/78-1899/1908, our labor growth rate exceeded the 1928-1958 Soviet rate. While our stock of reproducible fixed capital also grew rapidly, it still fell short of the Soviet 1928-1958 tempo.

Data have been compiled for the two countries on growth not only over the indicated periods but also during subperiods. On the important question as to how Soviet growth lately compares with that in prewar years, the answer regrettably must be that it depends on the formula. With output in base-year prices, growth of output and factor productivity accelerates. With output in given-year prices, the trend is the reverse.

I alluded at the outset to a theoretical application of national income data such as have been compiled: appraisal of production potential. The data, especially for the USSR are often remote from statistics such as are prescribed by theory for that application, but so far as they bear on that aspect, both types of computations that have been made for that country are illuminating. Possibly, however, the computations with output valued in given-year prices are nearer the mark, at least for appraisal of growth in capacity to produce the base-year output mix.

Indefinite as they often are, the results discussed here may provide further insight into the nature of the Soviet growth process under the five-year plans. They can also be read for their bearing on the comparative merit, for purposes of generating growth, of the two economic systems that are contrasted, Soviet socialist planning, on the one hand, and the American mixed-enterprise system, on the other. The data are of interest from that standpoint, but if they are so viewed, it should be considered that the comparative trends discerned in factor productivity reflect not only relative "technological progress" in the two countries but also other aspects, perhaps the most important of which is variation in labor quality. In addition, with regard to technological progress, the Russians under the five-year plans have been favored by the opportunity to borrow technologies wholesale from more advanced countries. We too must have enjoyed a similar "advantage of backwardness" in the post-Civil War decades, but I wonder whether the resulting gains could have been nearly as consequential. In terms of growth, each of the periods studied is rather special, for reasons that in the case of USSR have already been noted; for the United States the reasons are sufficiently evident not to need laboring.

Further research, it may be hoped, will better enable us to appraise the important question addressed here. Meantime Soviet socialist planning does not seem quite as potent in generating growth as proponents have often held, but that system no doubt has also been underrated by many Western critics.

9. Productivity in Soviet Postwar Economic Development

The evolution of Soviet Russia's economy has long been followed with fascination in the West. Western interest, it is true, has often centered on the expansion of Soviet economic and military potential in reflection of the Cold War, which seems now to be subsiding. Another, more persistent concern has been to gain insight into the development process under a novel social system and so to gauge more clearly the comparative economic merit of that system. In this chapter and the next I view Soviet economic development in the latter, more academic perspective. Such an inquiry has been undertaken more than once for the USSR, but a fresh survey of more recent trends can take account of further thoughts and additional results of ongoing Western research and can also pay more attention to unduly neglected aspects.

These studies memorialize a great economist. My subject is perhaps a fitting one in view of the wide range of Knut Wicksell's political and social, as well as economic, interests. It is intriguing to recall too that, like Karl Marx, he spent some time in the British museum.

This chapter and Chapter 10 were originally prepared for delivery as lectures in memory of Knut Wicksell, at the Stockholm School of Economics, April 22 and 25, 1974. They were published in Stockholm in 1974 in their complete text, and, with the permission of the Wicksell Society, they are republished here in that form after some editing. I also publish explanatory notes.

While that parallel is hardly to be pressed, Wicksell reportedly did at one time invite Russia to annex Sweden. That was before the October Revolution, however, and avowedly in belief that tsarism would then be reformed in the Swedish image. If only the invitation had been accepted and the reform had materialized!

SOME METHODOLOGICAL CONSIDERATIONS

Economic development is a many-sided process, but what can be achieved anywhere above all turns on what is achieved in one particular sphere: productivity. I propose to turn first to this cardinal aspect. In my inquiry I will apply a very conventional yardstick: the growth of output per worker.

It is rudimentary that a social system may affect the growth of output per worker through its impact on diverse conditioning factors: (1) the increase in the stock of reproducible capital (plant and machinery and other facilities) that is available to collaborate with labor; (2) improvement in the quality of labor, as manifest in worker attitudes and skills; and (3) technological progress, including both innovations in productive technologies and gains in productive efficiency due to redesign of the specific working arrangements (institutions, policies, and practices) by which the economy is organized.

The comparative roles of these different factors are not immaterial. Thus an increase in the capital stock, at least if it is at all widespread, requires the allocation of some part of the national income or output to investment and so necessarily entails a cost in the form of a sacrifice of other uses of that income, mainly consumption. The bigger the increase in the capital stock, the bigger the cost. Both labor quality improvement and technological progress, to be sure, are also apt to entail costs, one in the form of "investment in human capital" and the other in the form of outlays for research and development. But, relative to the gain in productivity, such costs should often not be at all comparable to those represented by an increase in investment in physical capital. That should be true especially in the case of technological progress. It may commonly be true for improvement of labor quality.

Moreover in the case of labor quality improvement, particularly where it results from additional education, the costs may also be compensated for by political and social values of a well-known sort. Such values, however, are sometimes said to be generated too by investments in physical capital: such as a modern investment project that is held to enhance national prestige.

In assessing economic merit, then, we must consider not only the growth in output per worker but also the comparative roles of different conditioning factors. Of particular interest is the relative importance of capital investment, on the one hand, and labor quality improvement and technological progress, on the other. The influence of the latter two factors relative to each other is also of concern.

An inquiry into the economic merit of a social system must be comparative. In the case of Soviet socialism, we want to compare performance with that in so-called capitalist countries. Which of these countries should we consider? While the growth of output per worker depends on the social system, it is also affected by diverse forces more or less beyond the reach of the social system. Ideally, therefore, we would like to consider capitalist countries where such external forces are the same as those operating in the USSR. That approach, needless to say, is hardly feasible. One need ponder only a moment the nature of the diverse forces that might be in question in order to be aware of that.

Yet in comparative inquiries into Soviet growth, a contrast very often has been drawn with the experience of the United States. That practice has frequently reflected the preoccupation with the Cold War to which I referred earlier. Among the forces affecting productivity growth that are beyond the reach of the social system, however, are the natural resource endowment and the related factor of the size of the country, both of which affect opportunities for exploitation of economies of scale and dependence on foreign trade. Consequently a comparison of Soviet performance with that of the United States is not without interest for our purposes, for both countries are of continental dimensions and relatively well-endowed with natural resources.

On the other hand, despite the many Soviet five-year plans that have by now been implemented, the United States has continued to produce a far larger output per worker than the Soviet Union. At least among Western countries in postwar years, performance with respect to productivity growth appears to vary inversely with the stage of economic development as represented by the level of productivity. Broadly speaking, the lower the level of productivity, the faster productivity grows and conversely.[1] Such an inverse relation could not have been predicted with any certainty, but it is not very surprising in view of well-known "advantages of backwardness" that a less advanced country may exploit to promote productivity growth once its economy has gathered momentum. I refer, for example, to the possibility of borrowing modern technology wholesale from more advanced countries. For the economy generally, though not necessarily for a limited sector, productivity growth may also be speeded if a relatively large and not too well-employed agricultural population is available for transfer to more productive use in industry. That, of course, is commonly the case in less advanced countries.

1. See Chapter 11, this volume.

In short, productivity growth is in a degree historically conditioned, and while the social system presumably enters into the equation that expresses such conditioning, we must recognize here too that there are apt to be forces external to the system that affect its performance, at least during any observed period. It also follows that we should compare the Soviet Union with not only the United States but also capitalist countries that are less advanced than the United States. Accordingly I propose to discuss also France, Germany (the Federal Republic, of course), the United Kingdom, Italy, and Japan. In 1960, an intermediate year in the postwar period that I shall consider, output per worker was higher in France, Germany and the United Kingdom than in the Soviet Union but not nearly as high as in the United States (Table 9.1). In Italy output per worker was approximately at the Soviet level. Comparison of the Soviet Union with Italy, therefore, seems especially in order, as is true of Japan, although output per worker there in 1960 was somewhat below that of the USSR.

While the countries in question are usually called "capitalist," they are, of course, all decidedly mixed and quite remote from the pure laissez-faire

TABLE 9.1. Real national income per employed worker and employment share of nonfarm branches, selected countries, 1960[1]

Country	(1) Real national income per employed worker (U.S. = 100)	(2) Share of nonfarm branches in total employment (%)
United States	100	92.0
France	58	78.6
Germany	58	86.2
United Kingdom	56	96.0
Italy	40	67.7
Japan	27	69.8
USSR	39	61.2

[1]In comparisons of Western countries with the United States, output is represented by gross domestic product, and is valued at United States factor cost of 1960 or, in the case of Japan, at United States factor cost of 1965. In the comparison of the USSR with the United States reference is to gross national product valued at American market prices of 1960. Nonagricultural branches exclude for Western countries and include for the USSR forestry and fishing. On sources and methods for this table and others in this chapter, see the Preface.

system of textbooks. Perhaps I should simply call all of them, including Japan, "Western countries." Among them, however, some economic working arrangements differ markedly, but how such differences may have affected their performance relative to each other is an intriguing question that I cannot really pursue here.

An inquiry into economic development almost inevitably tends to be quantitative, and this one can be no exception to that rule. I should explain that for Western countries I draw heavily on data compiled by the Organization for Economic Cooperation and Development (OECD). For the USSR, I use some Soviet official data, but much of Soviet data are superseded by the results of Western research. Though largely based on exhaustive inquiries, the Western calculations have their limitations, but there are many reasons to think that, at least for purposes of comparison of the USSR with Western countries, they are nearer the mark than the Soviet official data. That contention appears especially true in the important sphere of aggregate output for the economy generally and major sectors. In compiling such aggregative measures Western scholars necessarily draw on detailed Soviet official data for particular products and the like, but they have sought systematically to collate those data in conformity with Western methodology and statistical practice. Soviet official aggregative output measures are often compiled rather differently or by procedures that are not too clear. Because of their manifest deficiencies, official Soviet data have sometimes been rejected even by Soviet economists.[2]

OUTPUT PER WORKER IN THE ECONOMY GENERALLY

In studying productivity growth, I have focused on the fifteen-year period between 1955 and 1970 and on the experience in the economy generally

2. For this inquiry I have revised somewhat Stanley Cohn's well-known calculations on Soviet real national income. Among other things, Cohn aggregates indices of the physical volume of output of different sectors by reference to weights that are supposed to represent the gross product in individual sectors in 1959, including hypothetical charges for interest and agricultural rent. While such weights are appealing in principle, the particular charges made for interest and agricultural rent are inevitably rather arbitrary. Questions arise too from Cohn's application of his hypothetical 8 percent interest rate to gross rather than net capital stocks in the different sectors and from his valuation of farm labor income in kind at retail prices. I use as weights the gross product originating in the different sectors in 1959, but value the output, unlike Cohn, essentially in terms of the actual ruble factor charges incurred. Needless to say, such valuation also has limitations.

Some of my sectorial weights differ appreciably from Cohn's. Most important, agriculture accounts here for just 25 percent of the Soviet gross product in 1959 instead of the 29 percent Cohn postulates. The chief beneficiary of the reduction in agriculture's share is industry. The difference is perhaps worth stressing since Cohn has been criticized especially for overvaluing agricultural relative to industrial factor inputs. But the impact of the change in weights, to-

and in industry. To begin with the economy generally, among Western countries the growth of output per worker apparently (Table 9.2) conforms broadly to the pattern already referred to, that is, the tempo is more rapid the less advanced the country is economically, as measured by the level of real national income per worker. Thus, as everyone knows, Japan has been a stellar performer in the international growth league for some years. Its prowess is evident here, although it is hardly explicable simply by reference to her not very advanced stage of development. Among the Western countries considered, Japan is, in fact, economically the least advanced; or at least it was in 1960, the year for which I have compared levels of real national income per worker. Productivity also has grown notably rapidly in Italy, though not as rapidly as in Japan, and next to Japan Italy is the least advanced country on our list.

Our three Northwest European countries—France, Germany, and the United Kingdom—are all practically on a par in terms of their degree of economic advance, and on that scale all outrank Italy as well as Japan. In all three countries, output per worker has grown less rapidly than in Italy. The differential, however, is much less pronounced for France and Germany than for the United Kingdom. Finally, there is the United States,

---

gether with some limited revisions made in Cohn's sectorial indices of physical volume, on the rate of growth of Soviet real national income is very limited: for the period 1955-1969, Soviet output, according to Cohn's calculations, grew 5.5 percent yearly; according to my calculations it increased 5.6 percent yearly.

Revaluation of output at ruble factor cost fixes output per worker in agriculture in 1960 at 48.0 percent of that in industry. The corresponding figures for Italy and Japan in 1960 are 37.6 and 40.2 percent. Perhaps even at ruble factor cost Soviet agricultural factor inputs are overvalued by Western standards, although that is not the only possible interpretation of the cited percentages.

The revision of the Cohn series is explained further in a separate appendix to which I refer in the Preface to this volume and in which I detail sources and methods for my main data and calculations, especially those in Tables 9.1 and 9.2-9.6.

To return to official Soviet statistics, one feature of such data on real national income that is often criticized is the omission from the calculation of a variety of services. While the official data are not reliable, for present purposes the exclusion of many services from the community's real output has its point. Moreover, if allowance is made for the restricted scope of the official series, for two periods on which I shall focus here the resultant tempos of growth do not differ nearly as much from those indicated by Western calculations as often has been the situation in the past. Yet the difference is by no means inconsequential. Thus, with the exclusion of services such as are omitted from the official series, according to the calculations to be used here Soviet real national income grew during 1955-1970 6.3 percent yearly and during 1960-1970 it grew 5.9 percent per year. The corresponding rates indicated by the official Soviet national income series are 7.8 and 7.1 percent. On the subjects of official Soviet national income data and the Soviet official statistics generally, see V. G. Treml and J. P. Hardt, eds., *Soviet Economic Statistics* (Durham, N.C., 1972).

economically the most advanced but with a productivity growth that is the slowest of all the countries considered.

I have assembled data on productivity growth in the economy generally in two variants. In one, I refer simply to the growth of real national income per employed worker. In the other, I exclude output originating in diverse service branches and the corresponding numbers of workers employed. The service branches omitted are chiefly defense, public administration, education, health care, and housing. While less familiar than real national income per worker, real material product per worker as a yardstick is conceptually no less interesting. For most of the services omitted, measurement of productivity growth is very difficult. Indeed, according to conventional national income accounting practice, the output of such branches is often measured simply by the corresponding input, principally labor, so in effect, productivity in these branches does not grow at all. It is of much in-

TABLE 9.2. Average annual rate of growth of real national income and real material product per employed worker, selected countries, 1955-1970 (percent)[1]

Country	(1) Real national income per employed worker	(2) Real material product per employed worker
United States	2.1	2.5
France	5.0	5.4
Germany	4.8	5.2
United Kingdom	2.6	3.0
Italy	5.9	6.8
Japan	8.8	—
USSR	4.2	4.9

[1]Real national income is represented by real gross domestic product and real material product by real gross domestic product excluding the output originating in selected services, chiefly defense, public administration, education, health care, and housing. Output originating in cultural and recreational activities and diverse other sources is also omitted. In the calculation of output per worker, employment essentially corresponds in scope to output, although, in the case of real material product per worker, workers engaged in providing housing services are included.

For Western countries, output is valued either at "constant" market prices or "constant" factor cost. For the USSR, valuation is at "constant" factor cost. Employment is adjusted for changes in hours in industry, but not proportionately.

terest, therefore, to see how output per worker varies when such services are excluded from the calculations.[3]

The inverse relation of productivity growth to the stage of development that I have described is observed among Western countries whether reference is to real national income or real material product per worker. Tempos are uniformly higher, though, for real material product than for real national income. That finding was to be expected inasmuch as real material product per worker excludes a number of service branches in which, by convention, productivity does not grow at all. For Japan, I could obtain data only on real national income per worker, but real material product per worker no doubt would show a higher tempo there just as it does for other countries.

To come to the USSR, whichever the yardstick, productivity growth there evidently falls well within the range of that among Western countries.[4] Nevertheless, as we saw, the stage of development of the USSR is most comparable with that of Japan and Italy, our two least advanced Western countries. It is noteworthy, therefore, with regard to productivity growth, that the Soviet Union is outpaced by both these countries. Our data are too imprecise to allow us to accord much credibility to slight discrepancies in growth rate, but the USSR is also at least matched, if not surpassed, by France and Germany, two Western countries that are more advanced economically than it is. The USSR surpasses only two of the Western countries considered: the United Kingdom and the United States. Both of these countries, however, especially the United States, are economically more advanced than the USSR.

While Soviet productivity growth seems unimpressive when compared to that in our Western countries, as in those countries, the rate of increase is higher for real material product than for real national income per worker. Such a result was statistically inevitable for the USSR no less than for other countries.

Use of real national income per worker as a yardstick, it has sometimes been assumed, may tend to distort comparative data on productivity growth in the USSR and the West. While productivity growth in diverse

3. One of the excluded branches—housing services—is not among those for which in national income accounting output is measured by inputs, but such services are still rather special and best left, I think, for separate inquiry. The available data seemed to allow the omission of housing services only from output without excluding from employment the workers engaged in providing such services.

4. Here and elsewhere I take into account the results of a number of calculations of a conventional statistical kind bearing on the nature and reliability of the comparative relationship between different measures of performance and the stage of development for the USSR and the West, as indicated by various criteria, including the level of real national income per worker. See the Technical Note appended to Chapter 10.

services is discounted by such data for all countries alike, the resulting bias, it has been held, could vary because of differences between the USSR and the West in the volume and tempos of growth of the services affected. There are such differences, which regrettably we can consider only in passing, but with the use of real material product per worker as an alternative yardstick of productivity growth, the comparative Soviet performance is evidently much as before.[5]

SOURCES OF PRODUCTIVITY GROWTH

By inquiring into the comparative growth of output per worker in the USSR and the West, I hope to provide insight into the relative merit of alternative social systems in the area of economic growth. As we saw, however, any given tempo of growth of output per worker can be more or less costly in terms of the capital required to achieve it, and the more costly it is, presumably the less meritorious it is.

Soviet growth does not compare too favorably with that in the West in that regard, if relevant data at hand are at all indicative. To begin with, I have calculated for each country considered the share of national income that had to be invested in order to achieve whatever productivity growth was realized. By relating that share to the corresponding rate of growth of output per worker, we obtain, in effect, a measure of how expensive it was in terms of capital investment to increase productivity by one percentage point (Table 9.3).

Among Western countries, the share of national income invested evidently varies widely but, when related to the rate of growth of output per worker, also rather systematically. Thus the capital investment cost of productivity growth tends to be higher the more advanced the country and lower the less advanced the country. While the relation is imperfect, the pattern here again is not very surprising because it has been observed for Western countries more generally.

5. In the calculation of real national income, no allowance is made for changes in productivity in particular categories of selected services. For selected services taken as a group, output per worker may still rise because of the upgrading of labor, that is, its shift from low- to high-valued services. Furthermore, output per worker in selected services has in fact risen markedly in several of the Western countries studied, particularly France, Germany, and Italy. On the other hand, it has risen only to a limited extent in the USSR. Perhaps there was actually relatively little upgrading of labor in selected services in the USSR over the period in question, but such improvement might have been understated because of the sometimes rather crude methods by which real output has been calculated for selected services in the USSR. Any error at this point, however, could not be very significant. On the underlying trends in output and employment in selected services and in other sectors, see Appendix Table 19.

TABLE 9.3. Share of gross investment in real national income and ratio of investment share to rate of growth of real national income per worker, selected countries, 1955-1969[1]

Country	Gross investment/real national income (%)		Investment share/rate of growth of real national income per worker	
	(1) For fixed capital investment	(2) For all investment	(3) For fixed capital investment	(4) For all investment
United States	17.9	18.7	8.5	8.9
France	22.8	24.9	4.6	5.0
Germany	25.0	26.7	5.2	5.6
United Kingdom	17.0	18.0	6.5	6.9
Italy	20.6	21.6	3.5	3.7
Japan	31.6	35.7	3.6	4.1
USSR	24.1	27.6	5.7	6.6

[1]For investment shares, gross domestic investment is compared with gross domestic product, except for Japan, for which reference is to gross national product. In the case of Western countries output is valued at 1963 national prices and in the case of the USSR at 1963 ruble factor cost. Rates of growth of real national income per worker are from Table 9.2.

As for the USSR, in terms of the share of national income invested, it is comparable only with Western countries that have invested relatively heavily. Even so, its capital investment cost of productivity growth is by no means unparalleled in the West, but it is high relative to that in Italy and Japan, the two Western countries that, to repeat, are most comparable to the USSR in development stage. The capital investment cost of productivity growth in the USSR also appears to be higher than that in France and Germany, though the latter countries are relatively advanced economically.

Actually one may wonder that the Soviet capital investment costs do not turn out to be even higher. By all accounts has not the share of Soviet national income invested in fact been higher than anywhere in the West? Such is often suggested, but, as Kuznets has pointed out, Soviet development has been distinguished not so much by the size of its capital investment share as by the rapidity with which the share has increased.[6] Still the Soviet investment share, even as recorded here, is notably high in light of the fact that the government has been able to superimpose that allocation of output upon defense expenditures that, to say the least, are also sizable. In the West, the only two countries that match or surpass the USSR in regard to investment share are Germany and Japan. Over the years in question, defense outlays have been minimal in Germany and quite inconsequential in Japan.

Although my comparative data on the relation of the investment share to productivity growth are illuminating, they do have limitations. Most important, what counts for the growth of output per worker is the rate at which the stock of capital that the average worker is equipped with is being expanded. The share of national income invested in a country is related to the tempo of growth of its capital stock, but it is not the same as that growth, and still less does the investment share indicate the tempo of growth of the country's capital stock per worker.[7] What of that aspect?

The capital stock per worker of the USSR has increased at an average annual rate of 7.8 percent (Table 9.4). In the West, that tempo is exceeded only in Japan and is much above the corresponding rate in any other Western country, including Germany, France, and Italy. Comparative data on the growth of capital stock per worker are apt to be inexact, and those I have been able to compile are no exception to that rule. But juxtaposing the indicated tempos with those already considered for the growth of real national income per worker again shows clearly that such growth in the USSR has been relatively expensive in terms of capital.

That finding, moreover, seems to become more evident if we carry our calculations further and adjust, for each country considered, the rate of growth of its real national income per worker in order to discount for the contribution to that growth due to the increase in capital stock per worker. The adjusted tempo supposedly represents the increase in productivity that

6. S. Kuznets, "A Comparative Appraisal," in A. Bergson and S. Kuznets, eds., *Economic Trends in the Soviet Union* (Cambridge, Mass., 1963), pp. 353-354.

7. Our data on investment shares relate to gross investment. The relation between the rate of growth of a country's capital stock and the share of gross investment in national income is defined by this formula, which is well-known to the initiated:

$$r_k = (I - D)/K = (I/Y)/(K/Y) - (D/K)$$

Here r_k is the rate of growth of the capital stock, I gross investment, D depreciation, K the capital stock, and Y national income. Whatever the investment share (I/Y), evidently the rate of capital stock growth depends on the "capital output ratio" (K/Y) and also on the rate at which the capital stock depreciates (D/K).

TABLE 9.4. Average annual rate of growth, enterprise fixed capital stock per employed worker and real national income per employed worker, adjusted, selected countries, 1955-1970 (percent)[1]

Country	(1) Enterprise fixed capital stock per employed worker	(2) Real national income per employed worker, adjusted for capital stock growth
United States	2.5	1.6
France	4.9	3.9
Germany	5.8	3.4
United Kingdom	4.2	1.8
Italy	5.9	4.4
Japan	9.4	5.9
USSR	7.8	2.4

[1] Enterprise fixed capital comprises essentially structures and equipment of business firms, exclusive of housing, although some fixed assets of private, nonprofit institutions may be included. For the USSR, reference is to nonresidential reproducible fixed assets generally, including those in public and social agencies. For all countries, reference is to employment in the economy generally.

might have been realized apart from the mere quantitative expansion of capital stock per worker.

Whereas such a calculation has lately become very fashionable in economics, probably no one will be surprised to learn that it has limitations. For somewhat technical reasons, the resulting inaccuracy must be greater for an economy like that of the USSR, where there is no capital market to provide us with observations on the rate of return on capital and hence on the contribution of capital to output. But it still seems illuminating that, after discounting for the increase in capital, productivity growth in the USSR compares even less favorably with that in the West than it did before (Table 9.4). Thus the USSR continues to be outmatched by Italy and Japan, and by a relatively wider margin than before. It is also surpassed more clearly than before by France and Germany. It continues to outpace the United States and England but only by a very modest and perhaps statistically doubtful margin.[8]

8. To repeat, my data on capital stocks refer particularly to enterprise fixed capital and are generally inexact. For the present purposes what counts is the volume of capital "services." Following E. F. Denison, *Why Growth Rates Differ* (Washington, D. C., 1967), pp. 139 ff., I

If Soviet productivity growth has not been especially great by Western standards and at the same time has been notably costly in terms of capital, may we also conclude that other sources of productivity growth have been relatively weak? Is that true particularly of labor quality improvement and technological progress? Even in a summary account, we must consider that productivity growth depends on additional causal factors, perhaps chiefly the natural resource endowment. In the West, resource limitations usually are compensated for, at least in part, through foreign trade. If that has not always been so for the Soviet Union, a principal reason has been

---

assume that such services vary with an average of two index numbers, one representing enterprise fixed capital net of depreciation and the other representing such capital gross of depreciation. For Italy and Japan serial data were available or could be compiled of only one kind. Thus such data were available only for net enterprise fixed capital in Italy and only for gross enterprise fixed capital in Japan. Italian net enterprise fixed capital grew at an average annual rate of 5.9 percent during 1955-1970, a tempo that is within the range of other Western experience. Probably no serious error has been made in gauging the tempo of the corresponding gross stock from that experience.

For Japan, however, the gross stock of enterprise fixed capital grew at an average yearly rate of 9.8 percent during 1955-1970. This tempo is quite disparate from other Western experience, so I felt it best to gauge the growth of the net stock by assuming that the net stock was 0.60 of the gross stock in 1955. That is approximately the relation that prevailed in Germany at the time (0.61) and not too different from the corresponding concurrent data for France (0.54) and the United Kingdom (0.54). For 1970, I take the ratio of the net to gross stock to be 0.80, or somewhat more than the ratio prevailing in the USSR in the late sixties (0.74). The high Soviet ratio, of course, reflects the very rapid growth of the Soviet capital stock. For the Soviet gross stock the yearly average rate of increase is 9.4 percent, which is nearly as high as the Japanese tempo.

Interestingly, however, in the USSR the net stock grew 9.5 percent yearly, practically at the same rate as the gross stock, so the ratio of net to gross fixed capital there was already quite high (0.73) in 1955. That relation probably reflects the net resultant of complex circumstances that did not always have a close parallel in Japan. Most important, while both countries suffered heavily from the war's destruction, Soviet fixed capital was growing at superrates even before the war and did so again once peace had been restored. Very possibly, then, Japanese capital stock, while just as "youthful" as that of the USSR in 1970, was, as I have assumed, decidedly "older" than the latter in 1955.

Nevertheless, the index of the Japanese net enterprise fixed capital that I obtain shows an average annual increase of 12.0 percent and seems, if anything, likely to be too high. I have accordingly been reluctant to accept an even higher index, which gives an average rate of increase of 16.8 percent, based on an admittedly preliminary collation of diverse estimates in an unpublished study of Raymond Goldsmith. While reference is to reproducible fixed assets generally, rather than to enterprise fixed capital alone, that difference in scope should not be too material. Substituting the Goldsmith index for mine, however, would raise the yearly rate of increase in enterprise fixed capital per worker during 1955-1970 from 9.4 (Table 9.4) to 12.4 percent. The corresponding tempo for output per worker, adjusted for capital stock, would fall from 5.9 (Table 9.4) to 5.0.

I have discussed estimates of Italian gross and Japanese net enterprise fixed capital only for 1955-1970. Corresponding data for the period 1960-1970 were obtained similarly.

In the text I mention the problem posed here by the absence in the USSR of a capital mar-

that country's own economic working arrangements, particularly the policy of limiting economic dependence on the West. Lately in the process of erosion, that policy nevertheless had an impact during the period in question, though Western strategic controls have no doubt also been costly. The Soviet policy of self-sufficiency and such controls apart, however, the USSR may sometimes have been at a disadvantage regarding natural resources, especially in agriculture. But there are reasons to think that that disadvantage does not explain much of the Soviet underperformance in terms of productivity growth in the economy generally.[9]

---

ket that could provide information on the rate of return on capital in that country. In Table 9.4, to adjust the growth of output per worker in the USSR for the growth of the capital stock per worker, I impute to Soviet capital a rate of return of 12 percent. The resulting share of capital (including depreciation) in the gross domestic product—23 percent—does not seem implausible in the light of corresponding Western shares and related considerations (see Chapter 6 and Appendix Table 22).

Assuming a 16 percent rate of return on capital lowers the adjusted growth rate for the USSR in Table 9.4 from 2.4 to 2.1 percent. A rate of return of 8 percent raises the adjusted growth rate for the USSR to 2.8 percent.

As the technically initiated reader has probably surmised, in adjusting productivity growth for the increase in the capital stock per worker, I assume a so-called Cobb-Douglas "production function" relating the economy's output to factor inputs. That formula, with its "elasticity of substitution" (σ) equal to unity, also leaves something to be desired, but use instead of a so-called CES production function with σ equal to, say, 0.6, hardly affects results of interest. Thus the rate of growth of output per worker with adjustment on that basis rises by 0.1 percentage point for the USSR and by 0.2 and 0.4 percentage point for Italy and Japan. For other Western countries the corresponding change is either negligible or negative, but in no case is it more than 0.2 percentage point.

I compare here Cobb-Douglas and CES results as they would be if labor and enterprise capital were the only factor inputs employed. The limited and diversely signed differences may be puzzling; I continue as before, however, to use weights dated at an intermediate point in the period considered. Therefore, as is not difficult to see, use of the CES function instead of Cobb-Douglas must tend to have more or less offsetting effects for the two subintervals produced. My results should be viewed in that light.

9. Given a so-called Cobb-Douglas production function (see n. 8), any factor input other than labor makes a contribution to the rate of growth of output per worker that corresponds quantitatively to the product of the share of output imputable to the factor in question and the rate of growth of its supply per employed worker. It is in accord with this principle that the rate of growth of output per worker has been adjusted for the expansion in the stock of capital per worker. It also follows that after the adjustment productivity growth depends on the variation, relative to employment, in inputs of other factors, including agricultural land. But in an economy that is at all modern, the variation in that factor is not apt to be very consequential, inasmuch as the share of output attributable to farmland must be relatively limited. On the possible share of output imputable to agricultural land in the USSR and the West, see Chapter 8 and Denison, *Why Growth Rates Differ,* p. 38.

If the Russians have been at any disadvantage regarding farmland, it is due to limitations in the quality rather than in the quantity of the available supply. See D. G. Johnson, "Agricultural Production," in Bergson and Kuznets, eds., *Economic Trends in the Soviet Union,* pp. 224-227.

By implication, labor quality improvement and technological progress seem to have proceeded at only a modest pace in the USSR. I refer, however, to the impact on productivity growth of labor quality improvement and technological progress taken together, and we also want to know the comparative roles of those two factors taken separately. That may properly be the subject of a study in itself, but a principal source of labor quality improvement is education, and the Soviet commitment of resources to such activities, it is well known, has been large. If only on that account, it would be surprising if the USSR should not have excelled in the area of labor quality improvement, and further evidence points to the same result. By the same token, we may conclude that any Soviet underperformance with respect to productivity growth must be due primarily, if not entirely, to relatively slow technological progress.[10]

PRODUCTIVITY GROWTH IN INDUSTRY

Industry is construed here in a very broad sense to include not only manufacturing, mining, and power but also construction, transport, communications, trade, and finance—in effect, all branches of the economy except agriculture and the diverse service branches referred to previously. How does Soviet productivity growth in industry as so understood compare with productivity growth in the West? Among Western countries, tempos of growth of output per worker differ much as they did before; that is, the less advanced the country economically the higher the tempo (Tables 9.2 and 9.5). It may seem odd, though, that productivity in industry alone grows less rapidly than in non-service branches generally, including agriculture. Thus, the tempo of growth practically everywhere is lower for industrial than for real material output per worker.

As we saw, real material output per worker relates to industry and agriculture together. Should not the tempo for industry alone rather have been

10. For comparative outlays on education in the USSR and the West, see Appendix Tables 14 and 17. It is illuminating that the improvement in "educational quality" during 1950-1962 has been calculated as equivalent to these average yearly percentage increases in output per worker: in the United States, 0.72; in France, 0.46; in Germany, 0.18; in the United Kingdom 0.45; and in Italy, 0.69 (see Denison, *Why Growth Rates Differ,* p. 89). The corresponding figure for Japan during 1958-1968 is 0.26 (see H. Kanamori, "What Accounts for Japan's High Rate of Growth," *Review of Income and Wealth,* June 1972, Supplement, p. 56). By a similar calculation, but evaluating Soviet educational attainment according to "earning weights" for Italy, I find that the annual percentage increase in Soviet output per worker indicated by the improvement in educational quality during 1959-1970 was no less than 1.40! For the Italian earnings weights applied, see Denison, p. 85. The calculation also requires data on the distribution of the Soviet labor force by degree of educational attainment; see TSU, *Itogi vsesoiuznoĭ perepici naseleniia 1970 goda* (Moscow, 1972), p. 408.

TABLE 9.5. Average annual rate of growth, selected industrial indicators and countries, 1955-1970 (percent)[1]

Country	(1) Output per employed worker	(2) Enterprise fixed capital per employed worker	(3) Output per employed worker adjusted for capital stock growth
United States	2.1	2.9	1.5
France	4.6	3.8	3.6
Germany	4.6	5.3	3.2
United Kingdom	2.9	4.6	1.8
Italy	5.4	4.0	4.2
Japan	—	—	—
USSR	4.2	6.2	2.2

[1]Industry essentially comprises the economy generally, exclusive of the selected service branches referred to in Table 9.2. It also excludes agriculture. For output per worker, reference is to the gross domestic product originating in industry valued as in Table 9.2 and the corresponding employment, though workers in housing are included. Employment is adjusted for changes in hours but not proportionately. Enterprise fixed capital is as in Table 9.4, except that stocks in agriculture are excluded. For Germany, reference is to all enterprise fixed capital, including stocks in agriculture, and for the USSR to nonresidential, nonfarm, reproducible fixed assets, including those in social and public agencies. In the calculation of enterprise fixed capital per worker, employment is that in industry.

the higher one? To assume so would be to underestimate greatly the progress of Western agriculture. While we are concerned primarily with industry, I should record that with respect to the growth of output per worker in the period in question, agriculture systematically outpaced industry, often markedly so.[11] But industry also must commonly grow less rapidly than real material output per worker because of a related phenomenon referred to previously: the transfer to industry of relatively unproductive agricul-

11. Compare the rates of growth of industrial output per worker with these corresponding percentage tempos for agriculture: United States, 6.2; France, 6.0; Germany, 5.7; United Kingdom, 5.5; and Italy, 7.6. For the underlying data, see Appendix Table 19. For Japan corresponding data are lacking, but see K. Ohkawa and H. Rosovsky, "Postwar Japanese Growth in Historical Perspective: A Second Look," in L. Klein and K. Ohkawa, eds., *Economic Growth: The Japanese Experience Since the Meiji Era* (Homewood, Ill., 1968), p. 16.

tural workers. This change raises the output of such workers and hence productivity in the economy generally, but not in industry alone.[12]

The transfer of agricultural labor to industry should tend to be more potent in holding back the rate of industrial productivity growth relative to nonservice branches generally the larger the farm sector is in the economy as a whole. As measured by the share of agriculture in total employment, the relative size of the farm sector varies closely with the stage of economic development as indicated by the level of real national income per worker. Or rather that is so for the complementary relation, the share of nonfarm branches in total employment (Table 9.1). Indeed, the latter share is itself often taken as a criterion of development stage. Not surprisingly, therefore, among Western countries the shortfall of the growth of industrial output per worker relative to that of real material output per worker apparently tends to be somewhat greater the less advanced the country is economically.

To all this, however, the United Kingdom is an outstanding exception, but one that proves the rule. In that country, industrial productivity grows at essentially the same rate as real material output per worker. That is an odd result because the United Kingdom is not too highly advanced in terms of the level of real national income per worker. But it is not at all odd if we consider that for the United Kingdom we obtain a quite different calibration of development stage in terms of our alternative criterion, the share of nonfarm branches in total employment. In fact, in terms of that indicator, the United Kingdom rates as more advanced than the United States (Table 9.1).

Again we must recall statistical limitations. Particularly we must not stress too much the small differences among Western countries in the margin between tempos of industrial and real material output per worker. For the same reason, comparison of that margin for the USSR (to come to that country) to the corresponding margins for Western countries is also treacherous. Still the USSR falls, with Italy and Japan, at the bottom of our list with respect to the stage of economic development whether the criterion is the level of real national income per worker or the share of agriculture in total employment. It is interesting, therefore, that in the USSR, too, industrial output grows distinctly less rapidly than real material output per worker.

The margin in favor of real material output per worker nevertheless seems modest by Western standards, but especially for the USSR one may wonder that there is any margin at all. In that country, real material

12. On the possible significance of labor transfers like the ones in question for productivity growth in Western countries during the period considered, see Denison, *Why Growth Rates Differ,* chap. 16.

product per worker comprehends the experience of the notorious Soviet collective farm system along with that of industry. If only on that account, at least in the USSR, should not the tempo of growth be higher for industrial output per worker than for real material output per worker? Soviet collectivized agriculture has certainly had its vicissitudes, and, to be sure, there is no counterpart here of the dazzling performance of agriculture in the West regarding the growth of output per worker, but over the period considered that sector was by no means moribund. Indeed, it fully matched industry in productivity growth.[13]

That fact, of course, does not explain why growth of industrial productivity should be less rapid than that of real material product per worker, but at least a limited margin in favor of the latter was assured by the phenomenon that in the USSR, as in the West, accompanied the rise in agriculture productivity: transfers to more productive work in industry of relatively underutilized agricultural workers. In the USSR, however, such transfers have been notably modest considering the relatively large numbers of agricultural workers available (Table 9.1).[14] Why they have been so is an intriguing question, on which comment is best deferred.

How many agricultural workers are available at any time depends on their rate of transfer to industry. It also depends on their number at earlier stages, and that, as was indicated, is necessarily a historically conditioned circumstance more or less beyond the reach of social systems. Let me explain, then, that I have singled out industry for special consideration partly in order to exclude the effects of this factor and so to allow us to see how the two systems perform apart from it. Industry, however, is interesting itself, and how the two systems compare in that sphere warrants attention in any event.

In fact, in industry, as for the economy generally, Soviet performance falls well within the range of that of Western countries but seems undistinguished in terms of stage of development. Thus industrial output per worker in the USSR has grown more rapidly than in the United States and the United Kingdom, at about the same rate as in France and Germany, and less rapidly than in Italy. With available data, I could not calculate the rate of growth of industrial output per worker for Japan, but it is obviously far above that for the USSR.[15]

13. During 1955-1970, output per worker in Soviet agriculture grew at an average annual rate of 4.3 percent, or at practically the same tempo as prevailed in industry. See Appendix Table 19.

14. See Appendix Table 19 for relevant data for 1955 and 1970.

15. If in relation to the rate of growth of real national income per worker the rate of growth of industrial output per worker in Japan were the same as for Italy, it would be 8.1 percent. For manufacturing, mining, and electric power, output per worker in Japan grew at an average annual rate of 10.5 percent during 1954-1961. The corresponding tempo for

So much for the growth of industrial output per worker. What of the sources of that growth? Fixed capital per worker in industry apparently varies among Western countries and between the USSR and these countries broadly as it did before, as does output per worker after adjustment for such variation (Table 9.5).[16] Here too, moreover, the USSR might well have matched if not surpassed other countries with respect to the improvement in labor quality, so the presumption is that technological progress there must have been modest by Western standards. That seems so even though, as before, productivity growth must reflect still other forces. Here, however, limitations in agricultural resources should no longer be consequential.

In sum, relative to that in the West, technological progress in industry in the USSR seems no more rapid than in the economy generally. All things considered that is not an implausible state of affairs, although it is rather surprising.

THE TIME PERIOD

A word concerning the fifteen-year period under investigation. By 1955 World War II was a decade in the past, and all the countries studied, even those greatly ravaged by war, were producing a real national income that, relative to population, was about as high as or higher than that of prewar years.[17] Nevertheless the pace of recovery varied, and here and there in the most war-torn countries some war damage remained. Curiously, that condition might have been favorable, rather than unfavorable, to subsequent productivity growth. At least the growth could be economical of capital so far as partially damaged works could sometimes be restored to full effectiveness with limited investment.

But the shocks and dislocations of a great war are hardly limited to physical damage alone, and even after such damage has been largely made good, economic life may still be affected in diverse ways that are significant for productivity growth. Nevertheless, the impact should be favorable

---

manufacturing alone for 1961-1964 was 8.1 percent. Serial data underlying these tempos are five-year moving averages. See Ohkawa and Rosovsky, in Klein and Ohkawa, eds., *Economic Growth,* p. 14.

16. For Italy, in relation to the rate of growth of fixed capital per worker in the economy generally (Table 9.4), the rate of growth of fixed capital per worker in industry is comparatively low (Table 9.5). The incongruity is due at least partly to the rapid increase in Italy of employment in industry relative to that in the economy generally. See Appendix Table 19.

17. See Chapter 11, this volume; A. Maddison, *Economic Growth in the West* (New York, 1964), pp. 200, 202, 205-206; and A. Maddison, *Economic Growth in Japan and the USSR* (New York, 1969), pp. 154-157, 159.

rather than unfavorable. Because of a war-related postponement of innovations, for example, subsequent technological progress may, if anything, be accelerated. That is more likely insofar as new technologies may be borrowed from countries less affected by the war.

Distant as the years 1955-1970 are from the war, then, our comparative data on productivity growth may still bear its imprint. How consequential might the resulting distortions be? Not very, at least not favorably to the West, if we may judge from other data compiled for a period still further removed from the war (Table 9.6). Thus real national income per worker grew in different countries during 1960-1970 at much the same rates as during 1955-1970. In some Western countries, especially Italy and Japan, growth accelerated somewhat, while in the USSR there apparently was some retardation.

Tempos of growth of fixed capital per worker also were much as before, as were those of real national income per worker after adjustment for the growth in capital stock. The contrasting experience, however, of Italy and

TABLE 9.6. Average annual rate of growth of selected indicators and countries, 1955-1970 and 1960-1970 (percent)[1]

	Real national income per employed worker		Enterprise fixed capital per employed worker		Real national income per employed worker, adjusted for capital stock growth	
Country	(1) 1955-1970	(2) 1960-1970	(3) 1955-1970	(4) 1960-1970	(5) 1955-1970	(6) 1960-1970
United States	2.1	2.4	2.5	2.6	1.6	1.9
France	5.0`	5.1	4.9	5.5	3.9	3.9
Germany	4.8	4.7	5.8	5.9	3.4	3.2
United Kingdom	2.6	2.8	4.2	4.5	1.8	1.9
Italy	5.9	6.7	5.9	6.9	4.4	5.0
Japan	8.8	9.8	9.4	11.2	5.9	6.3
USSR	4.2	3.5	7.8	6.7	2.4	2.0

[1]The indicators are understood as in Tables 9.2 and 9.4.

Japan, on the one hand, and the USSR, on the other, with respect to the variation over time in the rate of growth of real national income per worker is probably due in part, though not entirely, to concomitant shifts in tempos of growth of fixed capital per worker.

The more recent tempos are illuminating, but the well-known fact remains that postwar rates of productivity growth in more or less advanced Western countries, including those we are considering, have again and again been high by the long-term historic standards of the countries in question.[18] Has the war had an impact beyond the legacy of disruptions such as those I have mentioned? What of the possibility that prewar events, particularly the Great Depression, contributed to dislocations from which recovery is still in progress? To what extent, in any case, are the often high tempos of recent years likely to prove transient rather than persistent?

The foregoing questions began to be posed soon after the relatively high postwar tempos first became evident and by now are the subject of a considerable literature.[19] I cannot add much to that literature here. Suffice it to say that where tempos have been high they have generally persisted longer than many supposed they would. On the other hand, among the countries in question, as we have seen, the postwar growth rates have tended to be higher the less advanced the country. To what extent that relation prevailed historically and to what extent it is peculiarly a feature of postwar years seems not yet to have been sufficiently explored. Whatever its historical antecedents, the relation perhaps already signals that less advanced countries may experience some retardation in the future as they gain on the more advanced ones.[20]

How does Soviet productivity growth in postwar years compare to that over protracted earlier periods? In 1928, when the first five-year plan was launched, the Soviet economy had just recovered from the combined blows of World War I, revolution and civil war. Since that date, it has evolved under the impact not only of the five-year plans but also of collectivization and its attendant wholesale destruction of agricultural capital and skills, the great Stalinian purges of the late thirties, and World War II. Under the circumstances, it is difficult to prepare and to interpret measures of long-term productivity growth such as we have been considering. But for

18. See Maddison, *Economic Growth in the West,* chaps. 2 and 3; Maddison, *Economic Growth in Japan and the USSR,* pp. xv ff., 50 ff.; and S. Kuznets, *Postwar Economic Growth* (Cambridge, Mass., 1964), chap. 4.

19. See the works cited above, n. 18.

20. Note that the postwar acceleration in productivity growth is most clearly evident in output per worker. To what extent it is manifest in that yardstick after adjustment for capital stock growth still remains to be determined, I believe.

what it is worth, for the USSR, too, postwar tempos appear to be high relative to those of earlier intervals.[21]

As we have seen, though, in contrast to the West, in the USSR there appears to have been some retardation in productivity growth lately. Perhaps, therefore, the rapid postwar growth will more likely prove to be a transient phenomenon in the USSR than in the West. We must not, however, give too much weight to modest variations in tempos observed over relatively limited periods such as the ones in question. The rates could be, for example, somewhat affected by the particular terminal dates chosen for this inquiry.

It should be observed, though, that among Western countries, only the United States experienced during the two periods studied a recession entailing any significant year-to-year drop in output. In the United States there was only one such episode, in 1970, and it was hardly favorable to that country in our comparisons. Contrary to a view sometimes encountered, the Soviet economy does not appear to be subject to business cycles such as we know in the West, but levels of economic activity do fluctuate, chiefly due to variations in the harvest. The years 1955, 1960, and 1970, however, were all relatively good years in Soviet agriculture, so our comparisons should not be subject to any consequential distortions at this point.

CONCLUSION

The growth of Soviet productivity has been explored previously, but by examining the more recent experience of the USSR in some depth, I hope to have shown more clearly than was possible before that the USSR has enjoyed certain advantages in the generation of productivity growth. These, however, have probably not been nearly as decisive as has often been as-

21. I am in effect discounting here the very high rates of growth of output per worker that are found to have prevailed in the USSR in the thirties when output is valued in preplan prices. As is well known, with such valuation, output and hence output per worker grew notably fast, for preplan prices were especially high for many industrial goods, including machinery, production of which expanded particularly fast. Valuation in terms of these prices necessarily means assigning a relatively heavy weight in the calculation to such goods.

Preplan prices, however, seem rather special when it is considered that they relate to a quite early stage of Soviet industrialization. It is for that reason that they are so high for many industrial goods. Also, as Kuznets pointed out long ago in a conference discussion, the prices of such goods were often all the higher because the Soviet policy of autarky was already substantially in effect even before the first five-year plan was initiated. Many industrial goods that otherwise might have been imported, therefore, were instead being supplied domestically at high cost. On early trends in output per worker, with output valued in both preplan and later prices, see Chapter 8, this volume.

sumed. The Soviet government has been able to mobilize substantial resources for capital investment and might well have managed, through large-scale allocations of resources to education, to assure gains in labor quality comparing quite favorably with those in the West. But technological progress appears to have been limited, so much so that, despite substantial commitments to capital investment and education, output per worker apparently has grown at only moderate tempos relative to those in the West. True, the rate of growth of output per worker falls well within the range of Western experience, but the Soviet tempo still seems substandard when we compare it to the rates achieved in Western countries at more or less comparable levels of productivity. Such a comparison is in order since in the West output per worker appears to grow more rapidly the lower its level. Contrary to a rather widely held opinion, Soviet performance in regard to productivity growth compares little, if at all, more favorably to that of the West in industry than in the economy generally.

Technological progress in the USSR has been gauged here from comparative data on the rates and sources of growth of output per worker, but an undistinguished Soviet performance in the sphere of technological progress is not entirely surprising in view of the nature of the relevant economic working arrangements. Under the system of centralist planning that prevails in the USSR, among the outstanding features of those arrangements, as illuminated by much Western research, are the relatively meager and often distorted incentives for innovation and the extraordinarily complex and seemingly stultifying bureaucratic process through which such activity takes place.[22]

Productivity expansion is central to economic development, but it is not the only interesting facet of that process. I turn in the next chapter to comparative Soviet performance in a realm that is closely related to productivity growth and, perhaps because of that relationship, tends to be neglected in writings on economic growth. It nevertheless merits attention for its own sake. I refer to trends in consumption.

22. On the nature and functioning of economic working arrangements concerned with innovation in the USSR, see the sources cited in A. Bergson, *Planning and Productivity under Soviet Socialism* (New York, 1967), p. 83, n. 7; and R. Aman, R. J. Berry, and R. W. Davies, *Science and Industry in the USSR* (Paris (?), n.d.).

10. Consumption in Soviet Postwar Economic Development

In evaluating Soviet postwar accomplishments in the sphere of consumption, I employ the comparative approach that I used in Chapter 9. Indeed I consider the same Western countries as before: the United States, France, Germany, the United Kingdom, Italy, and Japan.

The measure that is ordinarily used to gauge performance in consumption is the growth of consumption per capita. I certainly must apply that yardstick here, but a related one bearing on the material reward to effort is also of interest, namely, the growth of consumption per worker. And in considering that aspect it is necessary also to pay some attention to variations in working hours and leisure.

As is usually so in the study of development, consumption here is an aggregate of consumer goods generally, valued at so-called "constant" prices. Whether the aggregate represents "real" consumption per capita or per worker, a deeper concern is generally consumer welfare, an elusive, indeed ultimately philosophical matter that I can hardly hope to quantify with any exactitude. Perhaps it can be assessed better by looking at trends not only in aggregate consumption but also, if only broadly, in underlying consumption structure. As the primers teach, a measure of aggregate "real" consumption, if properly compiled, should reflect variations in structure as they affect the satisfaction of consumer wants, at least as such wants are expressed in the market. In practice one may wonder whether the reflection of structural variations is always very faithful, but our aggregative measures should not err too consequentially at this point, at least not favorably to the West.[1]

In a study of comparative economic merit, however, structural trends have an interest of their own. They may illuminate more clearly than aggregative measures can the relative responsiveness of different systems to consumer wants and, to a degree, the nature of the wants themselves. By now, no one will be shocked to read that, if the much-heralded socialist transformation of man has occurred at all in the USSR, it probably has not been especially marked in the sphere of consumption. But just how consumer demand in the USSR compares with that in the West is still an intriguing question, especially since, according to a widely broadcast critique, consumer welfare in the West suffers particularly because of the dubiety of the very wants that are satisfied.

Expression of consumer demand in the market, of course, occurs in the USSR as well as in the West. Although centralist planning prevails generally in the Soviet Union, the government has found it expedient to distribute the bulk of consumer goods among households as they are distributed in the West, through an open market. As in the West too, however, some supplies are distributed as communal goods in an extramarket way, either free or at relatively nominal charge. Not too surprisingly, the chief such goods in the USSR, as in the West, are education and health care. In fact, in the Soviet Union education and health care are distributed practically in their entirety as communal goods.

In comparing trends in aggregate consumption, therefore, we must, where possible, take account of such goods. In exploring related structural trends, however, I shall focus chiefly on goods that in both the USSR and the West are supplied to households primarily or exclusively through the market. As already indicated, Soviet outlays for education have been notably large, and that appears to be so also for health care, although Japanese outlays for health care, I believe, have been relatively large as well. Perhaps, therefore, the Soviet model is to be considered as scoring well at this point, but, that, needless to say, is a complex issue that is not to be decided simply by comparing magnitudes of outlays in different countries. It is also an issue that I cannot really pursue here.[2]

In the study of economic development, productivity growth, the theme of Chapter 9, has tended to overshadow the theme of this one, consump-

1. See below, n. 6.

2. On comparative outlays on education and health care in the USSR and the West, see Chapter 9, n. 10. In accord with conventional usage, consumption is understood here to include military subsistence.

tion trends. That is understandable, for productivity growth is the more basic aspect and trends in it predetermine those in consumption to some extent. But from the standpoint of economic merit, consumption trends are of concern for their own sake and are properly the subject of a separate inquiry.

CONSUMPTION PER CAPITA AND PER WORKER

In exploring trends in consumption per capita and per worker, I focus primarily, as I did in considering productivity growth, on the period 1955-1970. In the case of consumption per worker, the relation of consumption trends to productivity growth must be especially close, of course, at least if the yardstick of productivity growth is real national income per worker. On the other hand, consumption per capita necessarily tends to vary with real national income per capita. As a preliminary to consideration of trends in consumption per capita and per worker, therefore, it is advisable to consider briefly the variation in real national income per capita as it is related to trends already examined in real national income per worker. For present purposes, I refer to real national income per worker without any adjustment for changing hours, which are to be considered separately.

Among Western countries, as may be expected, the rate of growth of real national income per capita tends to be more or less comparable to that of real national income per worker (Table 10.1). The tempos given by the two yardsticks nevertheless do diverge. The deviations, first in one direction and then in the other, reflect to some extent the vagaries of population age structure, particularly the number of people of working age in relation to the population generally. A further factor, however, is the rate of participation of persons of working age in gainful employment. That coefficient sometimes varies little if at all, but in the case of Italy a sharp decline in the participation rate explains much of the marked reduction in tempo that is observed when the yardstick of output per capita supplants that of output per worker. Such a decline in the participation rate in the course of industrialization may seem odd, but it is understandable, especially for a country still at a not very advanced stage. As workers shift from small-scale production and agriculture and as educational opportunities increase, the relative numbers of young people and possibly women who are gainfully engaged often tend to fall. Not surprisingly, then, Japan, a country at a similar stage, also experienced a marked decline in participation in gainful employment by persons of working age. But in that country curiously there was a more-than-offsetting increase in persons of working age relative to the population generally. Hence, in the case of Japan, real national income per capita grew more rather than less rapidly than real national income per worker.

TABLE 10.1. Average annual rate of growth of real national income and consumption per capita and per worker, selected countries, 1955-1970 and 1960-1970 (percent)[1]

	Real national income		Consumption	
Country	(1) Per capita	(2) Per employed worker	(3) Per capita	(4) Per employed worker
		1955-1970		
United States	2.0	1.9	2.3 (2.5)	2.2 (2.4)
France	4.3	4.9	4.0	4.6
Germany	4.2	4.5	4.5	4.8
United Kingdom	2.0	2.3	1.9 (2.0)	2.2 (2.3)
Italy	4.8	5.7	4.7	5.6
Japan	9.3	8.8	7.6	7.1
USSR	4.3	3.9	3.8 (3.9)	3.4 (3.5)
		1960-1970		
United States	2.8	2.2	2.9 (3.1)	2.3 (2.5)
France	4.7	5.0	4.6	5.0
Germany	3.9	4.4	4.1	4.6
United Kingdom	2.0	2.5	1.7 (1.8)	2.2 (2.3)
Italy	4.6	6.2	5.2	6.7
Japan	9.9	9.6	7.9	7.6
USSR	4.2	3.3	3.8 (3.9)	2.9 (3.0)

[1]Real national income and employment are as in Tables 9.2 and 9.6, except that employment is unadjusted for changes in hours. Consumption is in "constant" prices. Figures outside parentheses relate to private consumption only. Those inside parentheses include publicly supported education and health care. On sources and methods for this table and Tables 10.2-10.5, see the Preface.

Turning to the USSR, real national income per capita there too grew somewhat more rapidly than real national income per worker; moreover it did so despite a slight reduction in the persons of working age in relation to the population. That is to say that in the case of the USSR, the rate of participation in gainful employment by persons of working age has increased appreciably. Since the USSR is at a similar economic stage to Italy and Japan and especially since in the USSR the rate of participation has been relatively high during the period in question, though perhaps not quite so high as sometimes assumed, the growth of the labor force is noteworthy.[3] It underlines a familiar aspect of Soviet development—one quite complementary to the high investment rates—that I discussed previously, namely, the intensive mobilization of human resources for economic pursuits. To achieve such mobilization, so far as feasible, was the government's policy from the earliest five-year plans. That policy is apparently still in effect.

As we have seen, the growth of output per worker in the Soviet Union appears undistinguished by Western standards. The USSR has been able, however, to enhance that performance to a degree by relatively intensive employment of its working-age population. Chiefly on that account, it often compares somewhat more favorably with the West in terms of the alternative yardstick of growth of output per capita, although the comparison is evidently also affected by shifts in age structure.[4]

With respect to trends in consumption, that activity necessarily competes for output with nonconsumption, principally defense and public administration, on the one hand, and investment, on the other. Of these two sorts of nonconsumption, investment is usually the distinctly larger claimant. It is also decidedly the more interesting one in an inquiry into economic development. In trying to understand the comparative trends that we observe in consumption and output per capita, therefore, it is helpful to

3. See below, n. 4.

4. How participation rates have varied in different countries may be seen from these percentage rates of increase of employment and population of working age (15 to 64 years) during 1955-1970. For each country I cite first the rate of employment increase: United States, 1.5, 1.4; France, 0.50, 0.87; Germany, 1.2, 0.90; United Kingdom, 0.22, 0.29; Italy, (−) 0.03, 0.64; Japan 1.5, 1.9; USSR, 1.8, 1.2.

The corresponding ratios of employment to population of working age at any one time are probably not fully comparable between countries, but these percentage ratios for 1960 may broadly indicate relative participation rates such as I alluded to above: United States, 63.3; France 69.0; Germany, 69.8; United Kingdom, 72.4; Italy, 62.4; Japan, 74.5; USSR, 73.4.

Statistical incomparabilities apart, participation rates such as the foregoing are, of course, of a rather gross nature, and for purposes of analysis one may want to distinguish participation in the labor force from the degree of its employment. Also, participation in the labor force is properly seen in terms of age- and sex-specific rates. I must leave for a separate inquiry consideration of comparative Soviet and Western participation along these lines, but relative participation in the USSR I suspect, would appear distinctly greater if allowance were made, for example, for the comparatively large number of females among persons of working age there.

Employment data underlying the cited rates of increase in employment and ratios of employment to population of working age are from Appendix Table 19. On the population of working age, I draw essentially on OECD sources for Western countries. For the USSR, see U.S. Department of Commerce, *Estimates and Projections of the Population of the USSR by Age and Sex: 1950 to 2000, International Population Reports,* series p-91, no. 23 (Washington, D.C., 1973).

consider the concomitant trends in the share of nonconsumption in output, particularly the share of investment.

Trends in the rate of investment, as that share is usually designated, are already foreshadowed by variations in the capital stock and output and hence in the so-called capital-output ratio that are more or less implied in data presented previously on the growth of output and capital stock per worker (see especially Table 9.6). That variations in the rate of investment are related to variations in capital stock and output becomes evident even to the uninitiated after reflection on the so-called "balanced-growth" path of growth economics. That is a path in which, among other things, the capital-output ratio is constant, that is, one in which capital stock and output grow at the same constant rate. A corollary is that the volume of investment must also grow proportionately with output. Hence the rate of investment, which is the relation of the volume of investment to output, must also be constant.

On the other hand, it follows that, the rate of investment should ordinarily vary with departures from balanced growth. Thus the investment rate can be expected to rise or fall, depending on whether capital stock grows more or less rapidly than output. Also variations in the investment rate can easily become the more pronounced should growth of the capital stock be accelerating or decelerating, though how output is varying matters as well. It is worth noting that such acceleration and deceleration effects are transitory. Thus the variations in the investment rate that they occasion necessarily cease if and when capital stock and output settle down at the new higher or lower tempos toward which they are moving.

The data on capital stock that we considered previously refer only to so-called "enterprise" assets and hence to only a portion of the capital to which investment contributes. But taken together with our data on output, they do suggest patterns that are broadly consistent with known investment rates. Among the Western countries considered, none appears to be on a balanced-growth path in any exact sense, yet the departures from such a path must often be limited, or alternatively offsetting, as where the capital stock grows more rapidly than output but is decelerating. As a result, the investment rate frequently did not vary too much over the period in question. We must see in this light the fact that in a number of countries consumption per capita and output per capita are found to have moved more or less together (Table 10.1). However, some stability in the output share of nonconsumption generally, including defense, is indicated as well.

Nevertheless consumption and output per capita do diverge, and in one country—Japan—the extent is marked. But that case too is understandable if we consider that among Western countries Japan is notable for the degree of departure from a balanced-growth path. Thus our data on the capital stock of Japan are especially inexact. Apparently that stock has grown somewhat more rapidly than output. At the same time its growth appreciably accelerated. The rate of investment consequently rose more than commensurately with the capital-output ratio, so consumption per capita necessarily grew distinctly less rapidly than output per capita. Note that for Japan, investment has been quite the predominant claimant in nonconsumption, for defense outlays have been inconsequential.

Comparative trends in consumption and output per capita in the USSR are to be approached similarly. If our data are at all indicative, that country, like Japan, departed appreciably from balanced growth. In the Soviet Union, however, capital stock grew much more rapidly than output but tended to decelerate to some extent. The investment rate thus rose less than commensurately with the capital-output ratio, but it certainly rose. As a result, consumption per capita almost inevitably grew less than output per capita (Table 10.1). In the case of the USSR, of course, nonconsumption also includes sizable defense outlays.[5]

As expected, then, the USSR compares with Western countries regarding the growth of consumption per capita much as it did regarding growth of output per capita. Relative performance, however, is often downgraded by the shift in yardstick. While that may be due partly to factors—chiefly

5. For the examination of the interrelationship of the growth of capital stock and output, on the one hand, and the rate of investment on the other, my point of departure was data on capital stock and real national income underlying the calculations (Tables 9.2, 9.4, 9.6) on the growth of capital stock and real national income per worker. It may be appropriate to record summarily the percentage rates of growth of capital stock and output that were used. Figures outside parentheses apply to 1955-1970 and those inside parentheses to 1960-1970. I cite first the capital stock growth rates: United States, 3.9 (4.2), 3.4 (4.1); France, 5.4 (6.1), 5.4 (5.8); Germany, 6.7 (6.0), 5.7 (4.8); United Kingdom, 4.2 (4.4), 2.6 (2.6); Italy, 5.6, (5.7), 5.6 (5.5); Japan, 11.0 (12.5), 10.4 (11.1); USSR, 9.4 (8.8), 5.7 (5.5). These are average rates of growth for the two periods on which I have focused in Chapters 9 and 10. However, comparable data compiled for briefer intervals sometimes seemed further to clarify variations in tempos.

The data on capital stock growth refer to enterprise "assets," strictly speaking, those of a fixed sort. On the scope of these assets see the notes to Table 9.4. In judging the impact of trends in such assets on reproducible capital stock more generally, it was sometimes possible to consider related data on assets other than enterprise fixed capital.

In growth economics, a balanced-growth path is usually defined as one in which the *net* capital stock and *net* output (e.g., "net domestic product") grow at one and the same constant rate. The corollary is that the rate of *net* investment is constant. Since I have been discussing gross output (i.e., the "gross domestic product"), I have focused on the rate of gross investment. Moreover the rate of growth of capital stock, so far as that stock is represented by enterprise fixed capital, has been obtained from an average of two index numbers, one relating to net and the other to gross assets. Despite these departures from convention, the data compiled here still seem usable, as I have used them, to distinguish balanced from unbalanced growth. Thus if an economy were on a balanced-growth path as usually understood (i.e., with net capital stock and net output growing at the same constant rate), it is not difficult to see that

defense outlays—that are more or less external to the growth process, the USSR in effect paid a two-fold price for capital—costly and technologically not too progressive a way of achieving productivity growth. On the one hand, output per worker and hence output per capita did not grow as rapidly as they might have otherwise. On the other hand, consumption per capita grew less rapidly than it might have relative to output per capita.

The finding that growth under the Soviet model in the USSR has been unbalanced will hardly come as a surprise. The imbalance became manifest at the beginning of the five-year plans and has prevailed ever since. The analysis here, however, may have clarified the nature and extent of the imbalance, as well as its implications for consumption. Some may wonder, though, that the shortfall in growth of consumption per capita relative to that of output per capita lately has not been greater than I have found it to be. Very possibly the shortfall has been understated to some extent by my imperfect data.[6] But, to repeat, consumption per capita has in fact been favored somewhat since, as indicated, the government has lately acquiesced in a limited retardation in growth of capital stock. That development, I think, is properly taken as epitomizing an often noted shift in priorities, which is not as pronounced as sometimes suggested but is nevertheless quite definite.

---

gross capital stock and gross output would grow at much the same rate, provided only that the longevity structure of gross assets and the average annual depreciation charge on them were fairly stable. It follows that the economy would also be on a more-or-less-balanced-growth path in terms of capital stock, as given by an average of indices of net and gross assets and gross output. The converse evidently should also hold.

Note that, as the analysis requires, I focus on investment in constant prices. Pertinent trends were determined by reference to sources and methods set forth in the appendix referred to in the Preface to this volume.

6. Our data on consumption, like those on real national income, are imperfect. They could err in either direction, but I alluded at the outset to limitations in the mode of aggregating consumption for the USSR. Thus the aggregation is in terms of ruble prices paid by consumers in 1968. Although such prices must often diverge from theoretical norms, the resulting errors probably offset each other frequently. A considerable volume of substandard and otherwise unappealing varieties of goods is produced in the USSR, however, probably especially among nonfoods, so the volume of products affected must have grown more rapidly than consumption generally (see Table 10.3). Since prices of seconds and the like in the Soviet sellers' market must be fairly comparable to those of more favored varieties, our measures of aggregate consumption for the USSR could be upwardly biased.

Also troubling is the apparent inclusion in the measure of aggregate consumption of components whose growth is given by Soviet official index numbers of the kind that in other contexts have been found to be inflated. Since housing has increased less rapidly than consumption generally, still another source of upward bias in aggregate consumption calculations is the inclusion of such services at the almost nominal rental rates prevailing in the USSR. Curiously, though, valuation of housing at rentals as much as six times those charged in the USSR

The imbalance in Soviet growth is familiar, but it may be something of a surprise that Japanese growth, too, has been notably disproportionate. Indeed the shortfall of the growth of consumption below that of output is greater in Japan than in the USSR. We are primarily concerned with the USSR rather than Japan, yet it should be observed that the incongruity between consumption and output growth could easily be overstressed in the case of Japan. The capital stock of Japan, it is true, has increased even more rapidly than that of the USSR, but Japan has also appreciably outpaced the USSR in terms of technological progress and productivity growth. As a result, consumption per capita has grown far more rapidly in Japan than in the USSR, despite the greater lag of consumption behind output in Japan. That lag has lately been magnified in Japan and reduced in the USSR by variation in the rate of growth of capital stock—an acceleration in the case of Japan and a deceleration in the case of the USSR. As explained, such acceleration and deceleration effects on the relation of consumption to output are apt to prove transitory.

Italy also has outpaced the USSR in consumption per capita, apparently by a wider margin than in output per capita. That at least in part reflects the comparative stability of the capital-output ratio in Italy, as well as the superior Italian technological progress.

All that has been said about the growth of consumption per capita relative to that of output per capita evidently must apply as well to my alternative consumption yardstick, growth of consumption per worker relative to output per worker. For the growth of consumption per worker, therefore, I shall do no more than draw attention to my results (Table 10.1) and note that that yardstick, as was to be expected, is less favorable to the USSR than the growth of consumption per capita. That follows from the relationship between the growth of output per worker and output per capita. Comparisons in terms of the two consumption yardsticks necessarily parallel those in terms of growth of output per worker and output per capita.

In Chapter 9 my inquiry into the growth of output per worker considered 1960-1970 in addition to 1955-1970. Tempos for 1960-1970 may be compiled also for output per capita and for consumption per worker and per capita. As with the tempos for output per worker, these diverge somewhat

---

(and thus accounting for 9.1 percent of household consumption in 1960) decreases the rate of growth of per capita consumption (inclusive of health care and education) by only 0.1 percentage point in 1955-1970 and in 1960-1970.

Finally, it should be noted that according to an alternative, admittedly crude calculation, which excludes all nonconsumption from real national income, consumption increases somewhat more slowly than indicated: in per-capita terms, at an annual percentage rate during 1955-1970 of 3.5 rather than 3.9 (Table 10.1).

in both directions from the tempos for 1955-1970 (Table 10.1). But the reasons for and import of these variations, I think, should be sufficiently evident by now not to need explication.

WORKING HOURS AND LEISURE

In a study of consumption trends, changes in working hours could be treated in more than one way. It will suffice here simply to adjust appropriately the comparative data on the growth of consumption per worker. Specifically, the data are recalculated to allow employment to vary proportionately with hours as well as numbers. Account could be taken of changes in hours only for nonfarm workers and use had to be made of data on working time of very uneven quality, but the results are more or less as expected, with rates of growth generally rising by perceptible though somewhat varying amounts (Table 10.2).[7]

Such a gain occurred for the USSR as well as for Western countries. Indeed for 1955-1970, though not for 1960-1970, the Soviet gain was relatively more pronounced. That reflects a major reform in hours initiated by the government in 1956 and largely completed by the end of 1960, a reform that finally gave Soviet workers practically a forty-hour week. At the time, a forty-hour week was unusually short even by the standards of relatively advanced Western countries, and one may wonder that the same government that was seeking to mobilize labor resources so intensively also found it appropriate to cut working time to that extent. In the absence of any very illuminating Soviet explanation, we can only speculate that a major concern was to honor a long-standing ideological commitment to an advanced working week, a commitment that, in fact, the government had honored during the early five-year plans but broke in 1940, on the eve of the German attack, and deferred honoring again for more than a decade and a half thereafter. The government no doubt was also aware, perhaps from the earlier Soviet experience as well as the experience of Western countries, that especially if hours are at all long, their curtailment need not mean a commensurate fall in productivity.[8]

In exploring working hours it is desirable ultimately to gauge leisure, but

7. Since allowance is made only for changes in nonfarm hours, the comparative weight of nonfarm and farm employment and hence the adjusted tempos of growth are affected only slightly by the decision to take 1955, rather than (as might also have been done) 1960 or 1970, as the "base" year in the calculation, in which employment is adjusted for changes in hours from that period. The fact that in the case of services no allowance was made initially for the impact of changing hours on the volume of consumption may raise questions, but here, too, the resulting distortion must be very small.

8. See E. F. Denison, *Why Growth Rates Differ* (Washington, D.C., 1967), pp. 59 ff.

TABLE 10.2. Average annual rate of growth of consumption per worker, selected countries, 1955-1970 and 1960-1970 (percent)[1]

Country	(1) Consumption per employed worker	(2) Consumption per employed worker, adjusted for hours
	1955-1970	
United States	2.2 (2.4)	2.7 (2.8)
France	4.6	4.9
Germany	4.8	5.7
United Kingdom	2.2 (2.3)	2.7 (2.8)
Italy	5.6	6.3
Japan	7.1	7.3
USSR	3.4 (3.5)	4.2 (4.3)
	1960-1970	
United States	2.3 (2.5)	2.8 (2.9)
France	5.0	5.3
Germany	4.6	5.3
United Kingdom	2.2 (2.3)	2.6 (2.7)
Italy	6.7	7.9
Japan	7.6	8.2
USSR	2.9 (3.0)	3.4 (3.5)

[1] Consumption is as in Table 10.1, with parenthetic data inclusive of publicly supplied education and health care. Employment in col. (1) is as in Tables 9.2 and 9.6 except that the adjustment for hours is omitted. Adjustment for hours in col. (2) is for nonfarm workers only and (in contrast to the adjustment in Tables 9.2 and 9.6) is proportional to the change in hours.

demands on leisure are made not only by employment of the gainful sort on which we focus but also by other activities, principally housework, shopping, and commuting. Some, to be sure, consider such activities pleasurable, but, at least in these days of Women's Liberation, probably few would hold them to be entirely so. Hence an inquiry into consumption could properly be extended still further to embrace not only working hours but also time devoted to housework, shopping, and commuting. The data that are needed for such a study are unavailable, but, as is fairly familiar, in seeking to intensify mobilization of labor the Soviet government has heeded the corollary that it must appropriately expand the supply of public dining facilities. One surmises, therefore, that in the USSR time devoted to housework might have diminished somewhat more rapidly than is usual for a country at the Soviet stage.[9] Or rather that it might have done so in the cities. The relatively slow decline in employment in agriculture to which I have already referred must have been an offset, for housework must be especially heavy in that sector.

In Soviet experience shopping time probably has been less favorable, for there are reasons to think that time devoted to shopping in the USSR may be inordinately great.[10] It would not be very surprising in view of well-known facts about the Soviet consumer goods market, facts that to some extent will be adumbrated in our discussion of consumption structure.

CONSUMPTION STRUCTURE

To begin the examination of trends in consumption structure, we should look at some comparative data that I have compiled on a particular coefficient (Table 10.3). For any category of consumption, what I shall call the "consumption elasticity" represents for a country and period considered the ratio of the percentage increase in real outlays in that consumption category to the percentage increase in real outlays in consumption generally. Reference is, in other words, to the number of percentage points by which real outlays on the consumption category increase for each percentage point increase in real outlays in consumption generally. In the United States during 1960-1970, for example, the coefficient for clothing is 0.93, which means that real outlays in that category increased somewhat less than proportionately to real consumption outlays generally, the percentage increase in the former being only 0.93 of that in the latter.

Among Western countries, the magnitude of the consumption elasticity varies between countries and consumption categories but nevertheless conforms to a rather clear pattern. Thus the elasticity for food is everywhere distinctly less than unity, though never below 0.50. That characteristic holds for both intervals considered. Similarly the elasticity for clothing is generally close to unity, indeed remarkably so, and here, too, the results are much the same whether reference is to 1955-1970 or to 1960-1970.

Durables here include automobiles as well as furniture, radios, and the like. For these goods, the elasticity is everywhere greater than unity and

9. On public dining facilities in the USSR, see Gur Ofer, *The Service Sector in Soviet Economic Growth* (Cambridge, Mass., 1973), pp. 123 ff.

10. Ibid., pp. 114 ff.

TABLE 10.3. Consumption elasticities for selected commodity categories and countries, 1955-1970 and 1960-1970[1]

Country	Elasticity (1) Food	(2) Clothing	(3) Durables	(4) Housing (rent)
		1955-1970		
United States	0.61	0.93	1.06	1.23
France	0.67	0.97	1.50	1.06
Germany	0.73[2]	0.96	—	1.19
United Kingdom	0.54	1.10	1.96	1.07
Italy	0.85	0.98	1.35	0.57
Japan	0.74	0.96	—	0.92
USSR	0.77	1.12	1.83	0.75
		1960-1970		
United States	0.56	0.92	1.40	1.13
France	0.64	0.97	1.49	1.05
Germany	0.68	0.95	—	1.18
United Kingdom	0.50	0.92	1.57	1.20
Italy	0.83	1.01	1.48	0.55
Japan	0.70	0.81	—	0.90
USSR	0.72	1.04	1.79	0.70

[1]For any consumption category, a consumption elasticity for a given period represents the ratio of the percentage increase over the period in real outlays on that category to the percentage increase over the period in real outlays on all private consumption. The base of the percentage in each case is the arithmetic mean of the initial and final real outlays.

[2]1958-1970.

usually markedly so. Among the few countries for which we have been able to measure the elasticity for durables, the coefficient is also strikingly uniform for 1960-1970 but varies widely for 1955-1970. Our data relate to the volume of durables currently acquired rather than to the services from inventories of durables currently available. In any case, one inevitably wonders whether, to some extent, we are not observing here the uneven response in different countries to accumulated wartime production deficiencies. The period 1955-1970 would, of course, have been affected more than the period 1960-1970 by such a phenomenon. For the United States, the notably low coefficient for 1955-1970 seems clearly rather special because it reflects a great boom in auto purchases at the beginning of that interval.[11]

Among the categories given in Table 10.3, housing is relatively difficult to characterize summarily in terms of the consumption elasticity, for the coefficient for housing varies from somewhat above to well below unity. Housing must have been especially affected by the war, so the coefficient may vary among countries on that account, though curiously, in contrast to the case of durables, the variation for 1960-1970 is little less than for 1955-1970. We may also be observing for housing a phenomenon that perhaps might have been expected to prevail for consumption categories generally, although, if it does, it is not often very discernable. I refer to a possible variation of the elasticity with the level of income per capita. In the case of housing, I wonder, for example, whether the relatively low coefficients for Japan and Italy may not be explicable in such terms.[12]

I must remind the reader again of statistical limitations. Also tastes for different consumer goods presumably differ to some extent among countries, and the comparative variation in consumption in different categories in relation to consumption generally must likewise be affected by differences in price structure among countries. We must view in light of these facts the comparative elasticities for one or another category in different countries. Under the circumstances we may wonder that among different countries the elasticities are as uniform as they are.

As the technically initiated will recognize, my consumption elasticities are closely related to, though not quite the same thing as, the expenditure elasticities familiar in consumer demand theory. It is interesting to note, therefore, that from household budget data the expenditure elasticity for food has been found, like my consumption elasticity for that category, generally to be significantly less than unity. In fact, such a result has been designated, in honor of its discoverer, Engel's law. It represents one of the most systematic regularities of economics.[13] More generally, our coeffi-

11. Household real outlays for "autos and parts" in 1955 were not surpassed until 1963. See *National Income, 1966,* pp. 48-49.

12. Calculations for consumption elasticities similar to those previously mentioned (Chapter 9, n. 4) concerning the comparative relation, for the USSR and the West, between productivity growth and related aspects and development stage, seem generally to support the impression that there is no systematic relation between the consumption elasticity for one category or another and development stage. Likewise, usually no interesting difference emerges between the USSR and the West at this point. However, there are exceptions. Thus, for food and housing, the relation between the consumption elasticity and development stage appears to be relatively significant. Curiously, though, it is so primarily when the development stage is given by the employment share of nonfarm branches rather than by the level of real national income per worker.

13. H. S. Houthakker, "An International Comparison of Household Expenditure Patterns," *Econometrica,* October 1957, pp. 540 ff.

cients seem broadly consistent with expenditure elasticities observed from budgetary data. Admittedly, however, the expenditure elasticities themselves often vary in ways that remain to be analyzed.

In the USSR, too, if our data are at all indicative, Engel's law holds. Indeed the consumption elasticity for food fits quite well with the corresponding magnitudes for Western countries. That is also true for clothing. Although the Soviet elasticity for that category is perhaps somewhat high compared with the Western magnitudes, it is nevertheless distinctly higher than the elasticity for food as in the West.

For durables the Soviet coefficient tends to be relatively high too, but again not very markedly so, and as in the West, the elasticity is distinctly greater than that for clothing. Regarding Soviet durables, we must reckon with accumulated deficiencies not only of wartime but, by all accounts, of the earlier Stalinian years of peace. To what extent inventories in 1955 or 1960 were low compared with those in, say, Italy or Japan is not so clear, however. Certainly it was true of autos, Soviet stocks of which are relatively minute even today. Yet if we may judge from comparative holdings in more recent years (Table 10.4), Soviet stocks of other durables in 1955 and 1960, while limited, might not have compared too unfavorably with those

TABLE 10.4. Inventories of selected durables for specified countries and years (per 1000 persons)

Country	(1) Passenger cars[1]	(2) Radios	(3) TV sets	(4) Refrigerators	(5) Washing machines
United States (1970)	439	1416	413	265[2]	223
France (1970)	242	314[3]	201[3]	—	—
Germany (1970)	241	468[4]	262[3]	—	—
United Kingdom (1970)	212	324[3]	284[3]	—	—
Italy (1970)	190	213[3]	170[3]	—	—
Japan (1970)	85	255[4]	214[5]	—	—
USSR (1955)	2	66	4	4	1
(1960)	3	129	22	10	13
(1970)	7	199	143	89	148

[1] Includes enterprise and governmental as well as household car registrations.
[2] Does not include stock in excess of one unit per family.
[3] License issued 1969.
[4] 1968.
[5] 1969.

in Italy and Japan. In any event, we must not suppose that the high Soviet consumption elasticity merely reflects an increase in current acquisitions from inordinately low levels. According to rather crude data, outlays on durables in 1955 in the USSR must have been of a similar order to those in Italy (Table 10.5).

For housing, the Soviet consumption elasticity is among the lower coefficients for that category, but even so it falls squarely between those of Italy and Japan, the two countries nearest to the USSR with respect to the level of income per capita. Like durables, housing suffered proverbially in the USSR under Stalin in peacetime as well as during the war, and whether the volume of such services available per capita in the USSR in 1955 could really have been fully comparable to that in Italy, as it has been calculated to be (Table 10.5), seems doubtful. But we must not rush to conclude that the Soviet consumption elasticity compares as it does to those in the West merely because of the inordinately low initial level of outlays.

TABLE 10.5. Consumption per capita by commodity category, selected countries, 1955, in American prices of 1955 (dollars)[1]

Country	(1) All	(2) Food	(3) Clothing	(4) Housing	(5) Durables	(6) Other
United States	1510	391	144	132	150	692
France	885	309	69	69	23	415
Germany	858	325	65	71	43	354
United Kingdom	992	316	78	107	39	449
Italy	527	217	38	32	4	236
USSR	498	194	29	32	10	235

[1]Valuation is at United States "factor cost." Discrepancies between sums of indicated items and indicated totals are due to rounding.

It was not possible to compile comparative consumption coefficients for the diverse so-called "private" services: entertainment and recreation, personal care, repair work, and the like. Many such activities have been in notoriously short supply in the USSR, but just how the consumption elasticity for private services there might compare to the corresponding coefficient in the West is uncertain.[14] Services of trade are nominally included in other consumption categories already considered. It should be noted, how-

14. On private services in the USSR, see D. W. Bronson and B. S. Severin, "Soviet Consumer Welfare: The Brezhnev Era," in JEC, *Soviet Economic Prospects for the Seventies* (Washington, D.C., 1973), pp. 31 ff.

ever, that here too supply appears to have been inordinately limited,[15] but how its relative variation compares with that in the West is conjectural.

What is to be concluded from these facts on consumption structure? Our comparative data are open to more than one interpretation, but two implications seem especially plausible. For one, at least among the broad consumption categories considered, the tastes of Soviet consumers probably are similar to those of consumers in the West. For another, in expanding consumption generally over the years in question the Soviet government must have sought seriously to gratify those tastes.

Neither conclusion is very surprising, for the fact that the Soviet government has lately been more or less attentive to wants broadly similar to those in the West is suggested almost by each day's news. But to create a New Man has avowedly been a cardinal Soviet goal ever since the Revolution. It is illuminating to see quantitatively that after more than a half-century, at least in the sphere of consumption, the New Man cannot be very different from the old one, or at least his contemporary Western counterpart.[16] Moreover the government, far from contending against the wants of the old man has been responding to them quite positively. It has been doing so even though at the present stage it entails the relatively rapid expansion of products, particularly durables, usually thought of as epitomizing Western "Consumerism."

To come to our larger theme, from the standpoint of comparative economic merit there would seem to be little difference between the two systems at this point. Thus far, however, I have considered only broad consumption categories. It is difficult to do much more here, but I should explain that when we consider consumption in more detail the situation changes. Very possibly consumer tastes in the USSR are still broadly similar to those in the West, but, whether they are or not, the consumption structure must very often diverge from such tastes. That would seem to be the import of all that we know of the principles and procedures by which Soviet economic working arrangements operate in the sphere in question. Sometimes the divergence between consumption structure and household tastes is apparently due to the supercession, often hypothesized in Western theory of socialism, of household tastes by politically determined planners' preferences. But probably more commonly planners as well as households are simply frustrated by deficiencies in the extraordinarily intricate bureaucratic mechanism that governs economic life under Soviet centralist planning. That is so generally and is especially so with respect to the quali-

15. Ofer, *The Service Sector in Soviet Economic Growth,* chaps. 6, 7.

16. On what has been achieved in respect to the creation of New Man more generally, see J. J. Schwartz, "Molding Communist Youth," *Problems of Communism,* September-October 1973.

ties and assortment of particular products. Structural distortions in these respects are proverbial in the USSR. They have also been widely reported in the West and so need not be elaborated here.[17]

In a study of economic development, we are more concerned with trends over time than with circumstances at any one time. It should be observed, therefore, that divergencies between consumption structure and household tastes are by no means new. They emerged under the early five-year plans under Stalin. I wonder, however, if they have not lately become more consequential for consumers. While the government has sought to improve the economic working arrangements, its task has become more difficult as the economy itself has become more complex. Also consumers themselves have become more choosy as consumption standards generally have risen.

I have been discussing the consumption structure in terms of different kinds of goods. Even in a summary account, we must also consider that, while "Consumerism" in general has lately come under attack even in the West, even its defenders must sometimes have misgivings about an outstanding feature of that phenomenon: the incessant introduction of new models and varieties of goods. New products obviously have often been a major source of increase in consumer welfare in the West, but such innovations surely can be carried to excess. Some may feel that that is often unavoidable so long as demand can be artificially stimulated by advertising. Yet even those who are sympathetically inclined to that much maligned activity must agree that validation of new products by the market is necessarily flawed if it fails to consider the loss of welfare to holders of newly outmoded old products. Indeed that must be a partial explanation of the oft-noted lag of welfare, reported by the consumer himself, behind per capita consumption as conventionally measured.[18]

It should be observed, therefore, that as far as new products are concerned circumstances in the USSR have been quite otherwise than in the West. Advertising is by no means unknown in the USSR and actually appears to be on the increase, but by Western standards it is still limited and muted, though perhaps not always the colorless information that critics of advertising in the West might be willing to endorse.[19] More important, comparative statistics on new products are not at hand for the USSR, but varieties of goods reportedly are still relatively quite limited and so apparently is the frequency of introduction of style and model changes

17. A. Bergson, *The Economics of Soviet Planning* (New Haven, Conn., 1964), chap. 12.

18. R. Easterlin, *Does Economic Growth Improve the Human Lot?* (Mimeographed, Philadelphia, June 1972).

19. M. I. Goldman, "Product Differentiation and Advertising: Some Lessons from Soviet Experience," *Journal of Political Economy*, August 1960; and M. I. Goldman, *Soviet Marketing* (Glencoe, Ill., 1963), especially pp. 160 ff., 195 ff.

and, in fact, new products generally. That, I suspect, reflects the government's concern not so much for the loss of welfare that new goods occasion to consumers of old ones as for the economies of continued serial production of products of fixed specifications. The fact remains, however, that, at least in this important sphere, Soviet central planning may have an advantage over the Western market. On the other hand, stability can be carried to excess no less than change. In the area of new product introduction may not Soviet central planning sometimes be at fault?

The neglect by the market of welfare losses imposed on consumers of old products by consumers of new ones is evidently just one example of a larger feature that has lately come to the fore, though usually in very different manifestations. I refer to the failure of commercial calculations in the West to take account of the broader social consequences, or, as the economist calls them, "externalities," of business and household behavior. Externalities are a large theme and properly warrant a separate inquiry, but I should record that, while externalities in principle can be "goods," we are today especially preoccupied with the "bads" in the form of pollution, congestion, and the like. As the daily news often reminds us, such bads are by no means absent in the USSR. Very possibly they are nevertheless not as prevalent as in Western countries at a comparable stage, but if so the reasons probably are found chiefly in two government policies already implied: that of limiting, through use of relatively capital-intensive technologies in industry, transfers of agriculture workers to the city and so impeding the pace of urbanization associated with industrialization, and the even more specific policy of delaying massive introduction of the automobile. These policies, in turn, have diverse sources, but it is more than doubtful that in either case the desire to avoid pollution, congestion, and the like have been among the more weighty of them. Paradoxically, economic calculation under Soviet socialism seems again and again just as narrowly commercial as that under Western capitalism.[20]

20. On externalities in Soviet planning, see M. I. Goldman, "The Convergence of Environmental Disruption," *Science,* October 1970. Of the two policies referred to, that of limiting urbanization has no doubt been motivated especially by a desire to economize on urban housing and other infrastructure. Lately housing, as indicated, has grown at a respectable tempo, but the government still limits transfer of labor from agriculture to industry. In that way, it has been able to assure a more rapid increase in urban housing space per capita than otherwise would have been possible, an understandable desideratum in view of the acute intitial scarcity. Soviet urbanization policy is the subject of a study now in progress by Gur Ofer. As for Soviet policy on the automobile, I surmise that it reflects chiefly a preoccupation with the comparative costs of automobiles and other means of transportation, the comparison being made with due regard, in the case of the automobile, to the cost of highways.

CONCLUSION

In exploring postwar economic development in the USSR, I have sought to gain insight into the process of growth in that country and into the economic merit of its novel social system. In the previous chapter I considered economic merit manifested in the growth of output per worker and found that Soviet performance, while not unimpressive, does not compare very favorably with that of Western countries. The government has been able to mobilize notable amounts of capital for development and also to promote a rapid increase in workers' educational attainment, but such forces making for productivity increase have tended to be offset by the relatively modest pace of technological progress.

In this chapter we saw that the Soviet performance has also been undistinguished in the realm of consumption. Given the primacy of productivity growth, that was not a very surprising finding, but it is instructive, I think, to see that in the USSR consumption growth relative to that in the West has suffered for two reasons: because of the slow pace of Soviet technological progress and because of the costly increase in capital input per unit of output, that is, the increase in the capital-output ratio. Particularly striking is the contrast with the experience of Italy and Japan, two countries at a stage of development that is similar to that of the USSR. Both countries surpass the USSR with respect to consumption, in the case of Japan to a marked degree. In both countries, the superior performance is due chiefly to more rapid technological progress, but Italy has also avoided any consequential increase in capital-output ratio and Japan probably has been able to avoid an increase comparable to that in the USSR, as well. The Japanese consumer has suffered somewhat lately, however, because of the acceleration of capital stock.

Growth of consumption per capita in the USSR has been speeded to some extent by an increase in labor participation rates. These testify to the government's capacity to mobilize resources intensively. Structural trends suggest that, contrary to some claims, consumer tastes in the USSR have not evolved in any unique way, meritorious or otherwise. In this important sphere, the decisive factor presumably is not so much the social system as the progress of industrialization. A notable feature, one that is perhaps more of a virtue sometimes than a vice, is the slow pace of product (including style and model) change in the USSR relative to that in the West.

The novel social system that prevails in the USSR, of course, is the Soviet variant of socialism with its famous system of centralist planning and its related development strategy, which stresses growth and limited economic dependence on the West.[21] The so-called Soviet model of economic growth

21. See Chapter 1, this volume.

certainly works, but, at least in the postwar years studied, probably not as well as often supposed.

Are there not still other yardsticks to apply in judging economic merit with respect to development? What, in particular, of the equity of income distribution? Does not the USSR compare favorably with the West at least at this point? Indeed, may not the greater equity, through adverse effects on incentives, be a reason for the undistinguished Soviet productivity growth and consumption? The questions are in order, and no doubt other, similar ones could be raised, so this inquiry is hardly exhaustive of economic merit in development and is even less comprehensive as far as economic merit generally is concerned. But it may facilitate appraisal of such merit to know that in the important spheres of productivity growth and consumption the Soviet model, although effective, is not especially imposing from a comparative perspective.

TECHNICAL NOTE

Results of regression computations referred to in Chapter 9, note 4, are set forth in Table 10.6. The computations are of three types, depending on which of three formulas is applied:

$$X = aY + cS + k$$
$$X = bE + cS + k$$
$$X = aY + bE + cS + k$$

Here Y stands for real national income per worker in 1960, E for the employment share of nonfarm branches, and S for Soviet socialism, a "dummy" variable. The terms a, b, c, and k are constants. Observations on X, Y, E, and S are drawn from Table 9.1 and other tables indicated in Table 10.6. In that table, r stands for the corrected coefficient of correlation and parenthetic figures represent the probability relating to the nul hypothesis. Note that while there are usually seven observations on the variables in question, there are only six where reference is to Table 9.2, column (2); Table 9.5, column (1); and Table 9.5, column (3). In the case of Table 10.1 columns (3) and (4), reference is to data outside parentheses.

TABLE 10.6 Selected data on various regressions relating to Soviet and Western growth

Observations on dependent variable (X)	Independent variable(s)	r^2	a	b	c	k
Table 9.2, col. (1)	Y	0.57	-0.0830 (0.034)	—	-2.1187 (0.264)	9.555
	E	0.64	—	-0.1812 (0.024)	-4.3853 (0.069)	19.68
	Y,E	0.72	-0.0446 (0.238)	-0.1139 (0.175)	-3.7828 (0.102)	16.69
Table 9.2, col. (2)	Y	0.34	-0.0622 (0.122)	—	-1.1362 (0.524)	8.463
	E	0.77	—	-0.0147 (0.023)	-3.0565 (0.076)	16.98
	Y,E	0.84	-0.0275 (0.260)	-0.1147 (0.082)	-2.9516 (0.090)	15.95
Table 9.3, col. (3)	Y	0.77	0.0715 (0.009)	—	1.6342 (0.157)	1.278
	E	0.65	—	0.1434 (0.023)	3.3265 (0.076)	-6.406
	Y,E	0.89	0.0471 (0.054)	0.0722 (0.112)	2.6896 (0.046)	-3.247
Table 9.3, col. (4)	Y	0.76	0.0716 (0.011)	—	2.1528 (0.098)	1.655
	E	0.67	—	0.1458 (0.022)	3.8919 (0.049)	-6.217
	Y,E	0.88	0.0457 (0.069)	0.0767 (0.115)	3.2740 (0.033)	-3.152
Table 9.4, col. (2)	Y	0.57	-0.0549 (0.040)	—	-2.0615 (0.143)	6.604
	E	0.77	—	-0.1279 (0.010)	-3.7243 (0.019)	13.95
	Y,E	0.82	-0.0241 (0.250)	-0.0915 (0.084)	-3.3988 (0.033)	12.34
Table 9.5, col. (1)	Y	0.48	-0.0506 (0.084)	—	-0.9050 (0.462)	7.080
	E	0.58	—	-0.1046 (0.060)	-2.1154 (0.174)	12.72
	Y,E	0.74	-0.0297 (0.233)	-0.0693 (0.184)	-2.0023 (0.167)	11.60
Table 9.5, col. (3)	Y	0.34	-0.0397 (0.136)	—	-1.5879 (0.232)	5.334
	E	0.78	—	-0.0959 (0.023)	-2.8564 (0.032)	10.93
	Y,E	0.82	-0.0166 (0.319)	-0.0762 (0.093)	-2.7931 (0.054)	10.30
Table 9.6, col. (2)	Y	0.58	-0.0928 (0.037)	—	-3.3733 (0.146)	10.49
	E	0.70	—	-0.2077 (0.019)	-6.0117 (0.034)	22.22
	Y,E	0.76	-0.0463 (0.252)	-0.0138 (0.141)	-5.3855 (0.054)	19.12
Table 9.6, col. (6)	Y	0.57	-0.0579 (0.046)	—	-2.7133 (0.098)	6.972
	E	0.87	—	-0.1420 (0.004)	-4.6136 (0.005)	15.30
	Y,E	0.90	-0.0204 (0.250)	-0.1111 (0.035)	-4.3375 (0.011)	13.94

(cont.)

TABLE 10.6 (cont.)

Observations on dependent variable (X)	Independent variable(s)	r^2	a	b	c	k
Table 10.1, col. (1)						
1955-1970	Y	0.40	-0.0838 (0.071)	—	-1.6004 (0.495)	9.170
	E	0.52	—	-0.1822 (0.059)	-3.8716 (0.186)	19.32
	Y,E	0.58	-0.0457 (0.408)	-0.0113 (0.343)	-3.2544 (0.290)	16.26
1960-1970	Y	0.21	-0.0771 (0.134)	—	-1.7987 (0.519)	9.004
	E	0.36	—	-0.18030 (0.082)	-4.1492 (0.202)	19.38
	Y,E	0.23	-0.0332 (0.606)	-0.0130 (0.365)	-3.7008 (0.316)	17.16
Table 10.1, col. (3)						
1955-1970	Y	0.36	-0.0625 (0.083)	—	-1.4600 (0.435)	7.697
	E	0.52	—	-0.1444 (0.044)	-3.3304 (0.126)	15.97
	Y,E	0.61	-0.0281 (0.482)	-0.1020 (0.264)	-2.9509 (0.213)	14.09
1960-1970	Y	0.22	-0.0594 (0.130)	—	-1.6392 (0.445)	7.755
	E	0.67	—	-0.1606 (0.021)	-3.8945 (0.061)	17.52
	Y,E	0.68	-0.0107 (0.769)	-0.1444 (0.132)	-3.7503 (0.124)	16.81
Table 10.1, col. (4)						
1955-1970	Y	0.51	-0.0635 (0.050)	—	-2.1287 (0.207)	8.007
	E	0.75	—	-0.1502 (0.013)	-4.0991 (0.028)	16.69
	Y,E	0.77	-0.02627 (0.328)	-0.1105 (0.103)	-3.7440 (0.053)	14.93
1960-1970	Y	0.54	-0.0728 (0.050)	—	-3.1080 (0.129)	8.849
	E	0.91	—	-0.1834 (0.002)	-5.5964 (0.003)	19.72
	Y,E	0.95	-0.0224 (0.223)	-0.1495 (0.017)	-5.2934 (0.007)	18.22
Table 10.2 col. (2)						
1955-1970	Y	0.47	-0.0616 (0.056)	—	-1.8117 (0.275)	8.415
	E	0.70	—	-0.1455 (0.017)	-3.7193 (0.044)	16.83
	Y,E	0.78	-0.0256 (0.374)	-0.1069 (0.132)	-3.3736 (0.082)	15.11
1960-1970	Y	0.51	-0.0776 (0.057)	—	-3.3079 (0.142)	9.734
	E	0.92	—	-0.1995 (0.001)	-6.0432 (0.002)	21.65
	Y,E	0.93	-0.0210 (0.622)	-0.1677 (0.014)	-5.7588 (0.006)	20.24

11. Comparative Growth in COMECON and OECD since 1950

A familiar but still notable feature of socialism is the nature of the countries where that form of social organization prevails. With few exceptions, all are economically among the less advanced countries of the world. At least they were at the time they became socialist. In those countries, then, socialism has been the instrument for further economic development. How have they fared in consequence? How accurate is the claim of its proponents that socialism is a superior system for such development?

Both the nature of socialist countries and the socialist claim are paradoxical, to say the least. Among composers of encomiums of capitalism as a vehicle for economic advance, few surpass Karl Marx. We must still be somewhat incredulous that, for example, the *Communist Manifesto* contains such lines as these:

> The bourgeoisie . . . has been the first to show what man's activity can bring about. It has accomplished wonders far surpassing Egyptian pyramids, Roman aqueducts, and Gothic cathedrals . . . The bourgeoisie, during its rule of scarce one hundred

This is a somewhat edited version of an essay that appeared in *World Politics*, July 1971. The essay revised and expanded upon a John and Dora Haynes Foundation lecture that I gave at the University of California, Santa Barbara, in May 1970. In preparing the lecture for publication, I benefited from advice of Professors Simon Kuznets and Zvi Griliches. The work was aided by a grant from the National Science Foundation.

> years, has created more massive and more colossal productive forces than have all preceding generations together.[1]

For Marx, it is true, socialism was economically superior to and on that account was ultimately to supersede capitalism. In any particular country, however, socialism would supplant capitalism only after the latter had run its course; only, that is, after capitalism had ceased to be the great engine for material advance that, in Marx's view, it must prove to be in earlier phases.

These proverbial Marxian theories rarely come up in socialist discussion of economic modernization. As every sophomore knows, Marx stood Hegel on his head. Proponents of socialism who urge that it is relatively meritorious at earlier economic stages now seem to be performing a similar stunt with respect to Marx himself.

The fact remains that socialism has tended to come into existence primarily in less advanced countries. And, whether Marxian or not, the view that socialism is especially meritorious in promoting economic development in such countries has enjoyed wide currency even among nonsocialists. It is a view that could easily become the subject of a lengthy inquiry, but a summary appraisal, which I undertake here, may be of value. The appraisal must be very selective. Most important, I focus exclusively on socialism in the USSR and Eastern Europe. Regrettably I bypass the socialist variants in China and other Asiatic countries, the only areas in which socialism exists at an especially early economic stage. Some would contend that it is particularly at such a stage that socialism is advantageous. Yugoslavia, too, is well-known as a special case. Therefore, interesting as the experience there is, I also leave it for separate inquiry.

In sum, attention is directed to European members of COMECON, that is (in addition to the USSR) Bulgaria, Rumania, Poland, Hungary, East Germany, and Czechoslovakia.[2] It seems fitting to juxtapose the experience under COMECON with that under its Western counterpart, OECD. With minor exceptions, I consider all member countries of that organization.[3]

1. Karl Marx, *Communist Manifesto,* International Publishers edition (New York, 1932), pp. 11-14.

2. COMECON stands for the Council for Mutual Economic Assistance, which was founded in 1949. Yugoslavia has been associated with this agency as an observer, not as a member. I shall also bypass Albania, even though it is a European member.

3. The Organization for Economic Cooperation and Development was established in 1960 as the successor to the Organization for European Economic Cooperation. Among OECD members, I omit Luxembourg and Iceland from this investigation because of their tiny size, Spain because of the lack of needed data, and Finland because of its somewhat special status. I again bypass Yugoslavia, though it participates in some OECD activities.

Inquiry into economic development must start somewhere. Socialism has its beginnings in Eastern Europe at the end of and right after the second World War. For all these countries I shall focus on the period since 1950 because earlier postwar years were remarkably turbulent and hence can be of little interest for our purposes. In the USSR, socialism dates from World War I, but the extraordinary experience there in the interwar years would make a study by itself. Hence I focus on the years since 1950 for the Soviet Union, as well. It seems best to consider the OECD trends for the same years.

APPRAISAL OF PERFORMANCE

How may we gauge comparative performance in economic development? Only a few of many diverse criteria that could be applied are very comprehensive. One of the most outstanding is the growth of labor productivity, represented by national income or output per worker. A summary account may properly use that yardstick.

The social system may promote growth of output per worker, however, in various ways that are not all equally beneficial. It may induce such growth simply by stimulating expansion of the stock of reproducible capital (plant, machinery, and other facilities) that is available to collaborate with labor. But, if it is to be widespread, capital stock expansion requires allocation of some part of the national income or output to investment and so necessarily entails a cost in the form of a sacrifice of other uses of income, mainly consumption.

The social system may also promote labor productivity growth through its favorable impact on labor quality, as manifest in worker attitudes and skills, and on "technological progress," that is, innovations in productive technologies and gains in productive efficiency due to redesign of the working arrangements (institutions, policies, and practices) by which the economy is organized. To be sure, costs are apt to be incurred, on the one hand in the form of "investment of human capital" and on the other hand as outlays for research and development. But relative to the gain in productivity, such costs should often not be comparable to those represented by an increase in investment in physical capital. That should be true especially in the case of technological progress. Costs incurred may also be offset by intrinsic benefits generated quite apart from the effect on productivity. For well-known reasons, such benefits are usually regarded as especially noticeable in the category of labor quality improvement, particularly when it reflects additional education.

Sources of productivity growth should differ in these ways under one system as well as under another but not necessarily to the same degree. The reasons are diverse. Suffice it to recall the familiar contention that one system may be inherently more favorable than another to workers' attitudes. If that is so, the effect should be primarily of a once-and-for-all sort, but a continuing improvement in labor quality may also occur. If it does, the cost of the improvement of labor quality must be less. That is apt to be so, too, in the case of technological progress inasmuch as systems differ in incentive arrangements. Although innovators may profit more in one case than another, the same technological progress may be achieved at less cost to the community generally. In addition, gains in the efficiency of economic working arrangements are presumed here to be a factor in technological progress. Hence the costs of such progress should diminish if, as is possible, one system is inherently more favorable than another to the achievement of such gains. The difference in gains in efficiency would manifest, in effect, a corresponding difference between the two systems in the capacity for economic self-improvement.

Even if productivity should grow at the same rate under one system as under another, then, growth could be more costly in one case than in the other. In a performance appraisal that possibility must be considered. Of particular interest are the comparative roles of capital investment, on the one hand, and labor quality improvement and technological progress, on the other. Other possible causes of a difference in costs are also of concern, although they are not often as easy to delineate.

Investment, labor quality improvement, and technological progress must usually be the most important forces in labor productivity growth on which the social system impinges, but the social system may also affect the growth of the labor force itself and hence labor productivity. The effect almost inevitably is of a perverse nature, for, other things being equal, increasing numbers of workers should yield diminishing returns in output. Even so, in an appraisal of performance, this consequence must be considered. Labor growth, however, may reflect demographic and other forces that are partly independent of the social system, at least in any short period. To that extent, therefore, productivity growth must vary quite apart from the social system rather than in dependence on it. That is also the case so far as the growth depends on physical endowment in the form of natural resources, for that too is beyond the reach of the social system. What can be achieved in respect to labor productivity in any period must additionally depend on labor quality at the outset of the period and on the inherited reproducible capital stock and state of technology. Here too, therefore, growth of labor productivity must vary independently of the social system, at least as that system functions during any period in question. How it functioned previously, however, would still be material. Difficlt as it is to do, a performance evaluation must seek to disentangle the role of the social system from these and other extrasystem factors.

An inquiry such as this one requires much quantitative data. For OECD countries I utilize well-known materials, principally publications of the OECD itself. For COMECON countries I draw heavily on Western research, as I have implied. I have also made selective use of official data released in different countries, but at important points such data are superceded by Western findings.[4] Western scholars have had many reasons to undertake independent calculations regarding socialist economic development, and, curiously, even socialist scholars do not always conceal their skepticism of the official figures. Of course the Western calculations, too, have their limitations.

POSTWAR RECOVERY

By 1950, the countries studied had already left behind them the immediate aftermath of the war. Recovery from wartime destruction and dislocations had proceeded rapidly almost everywhere, but different countries had suffered unequally and, partly for that reason, had by 1950 regained prewar levels of economic activity in varying degrees. That that was so is indicated by per capita national income (Table 11.1). So far as the wartime and immediate postwar experience of different countries varied, the extent and sources of gains in labor productivity after 1950 may have varied as well.

How one would have affected the other must have depended on the specific circumstances of each case, but paradoxically a lag in recovery could easily have been favorable to subsequent growth, for it is a familiar fact that it may often be easier to reattain previous levels of activity than to surpass them. And, even after prewar per capita national output has been reattained, one country may be favored over another if it still has more devastation to make good than does the other. Previous turmoil may also leave different countries with varying opportunities for further growth in other complex areas, for example, in making up arrearage in technology. Although growth usually should be favored especially in terms of output, the increase of productivity should commonly be hastened or made less costly.

4. The USSR apart, this means primarily the work of Thad P. Alton and his associates in the Research Project on National Income in East Central Europe at Columbia University, as collated in Maurice Ernst, "Postwar Economic Growth in Eastern Europe," for the JEC, *New Directions in the Soviet Economy,* pt. 4 (Washington, D.C., 1966); and in Thad P. Alton, "Economic Structure and Growth in Eastern Europe," for the JEC, *Economic Developments in Countries of Eastern Europe* (Washington, D.C., 1970). From one standpoint, the present essay might be considered in good part as an attempt to round out and explore the import of the voluminous data on Eastern Europe compiled in the studies of Ernst and Alton, although I have had to rework some of the data. For more details on sources and methods, see the appendix referred to in the Preface to this volume.

TABLE 11.1. Comparison of prewar and 1950 real national income per capita, COMECON and OECD countries (prewar = 100)[1]

Country	Prewar year	1950
COMECON		
Bulgaria	1939	103
Rumania	1938	96
Poland	1937	141[2]
Hungary	1938	93
USSR	1940	134
East Germany	1936	75
Czechoslovakia	1937	121
OECD		
Turkey	1938	100
Greece	1938	73
Portugal		—
Japan	1939	72
Ireland	1938	119
Italy	1939	99
Austria	1938	102
Netherlands	1937	110
Belgium	"Prewar"	121
France	1937	108
Norway	1939	119
United Kingdom	1937	103
Denmark	1939	116
West Germany	1936	94
Switzerland	1938	114
Canada	1939	152
Sweden	1939	150
United States	1939	147

[1]For COMECON countries reference is to gross national product; for OECD countries it is sometimes to national income as such and sometimes to some other concept of total output, including gross national product, net national product, and so on. For Denmark reference is to "total available supply," and for Ireland, to consumer expenditures. On sources and methods for this table and Tables 11.2-11.6, see the Preface.

[2] See text footnote 6, this chapter.

Although I focus on a period five years removed from the war, then, in assessing comparative performance we must still reckon with differential manifestations of "catch-up" phenomena, which have become a well-known theme in analyses of postwar economic growth.[5] I am concerned particularly with COMECON and OECD countries. As my data on relative prewar and postwar per capita national income (Table 11.1) underline, wartime and immediate postwar experience varied widely even among countries on the same side,[6] but it should be borne in mind that catch-up phenomena may still affect comparative performance.

GROWTH OF PRODUCTIVITY

Data on the growth of national income per worker in COMECON and OECD countries for the period 1950-1967 indicate that during that interval, COMECON countries tended neither to surpass nor to lag behind OECD countries but simply to match them. Output per worker during 1950-1967 grew by 4.1 percent a year on the average in COMECON countries, or at essentially the same tempo as in OECD countries—4.0 percent (Table 11.2).

Together with rates of growth of output per worker for different countries, the table shows a corresponding index of the level of output per worker in 1960 for each country compared to that of the United States. Just as the increase in labor productivity epitomizes a country's progress in economic development, the relative level of such productivity serves at once as an indicator of comparative stages of economic development in different countries. Reference to such an indicator is in order, for, as I have explained, many causes of labor productivity growth are more or less beyond the reach of the social system, at least during the period studied. Clearly some of the causes that were discussed must be related to the stage of development and other, similar ones readily come to mind. Such causes must be rather consequential.

Thus, among OECD countries, the rate of growth of output per worker varies widely but very broadly tends to be higher the lower the level of output per worker and conversely. The inverse relation is apparent from the data, particularly when represented graphically (Figure 11.1). Such a relation could not have been predicted with any confidence, but is not too difficult to understand in terms of the "advantages of backwardness" that a

5. See Simon Kuznets, *Postwar Economic Growth* (Cambridge, Mass., 1964), pp. 69 ff., 99 ff.

6. The incongruously high 1950 figure, compared to the prewar figure, for Poland apparently reflects, in part, the wholesale boundary changes that were a result of the war. Per capita national income in 1950 in the postwar territory is compared with per capita national income in 1937 within the prewar boundaries.

TABLE 11.2. Comparative real national income per employed worker, 1960, and average annual increase, real national income per employed worker, 1950-1967 and 1955-1967, COMECON and OCED countries

Country	Real national income per employed worker[1] (USA = 100)	Rate of growth of real national income per employed worker[2] (%)	
		1950-1967	*1955-1967*
COMECON			
Bulgaria	17	5.7	6.2
Rumania	17	4.9	4.9
Hungary	24	3.8	3.9
Poland	24	2.6	2.9
USSR	30	4.4	4.1
East Germany	36	—	3.7
Czechoslovakia	42	3.1	3.5
All	*27*(26)[3]	*4.1*	*4.2*
OECD			
Turkey	8	4.4	4.1
Greece	15	5.4	5.3
Portugal	20	4.7	5.2
Japan	26	7.7	8.4
Ireland	34	3.4	3.2
Italy	34	5.6	5.7
Austria	40	4.8	4.4
United Kingdom	49	2.2	2.4
Denmark	50	3.0	3.6
West Germany	51	4.6[4]	4.1[4]
France	52	4.5	4.6
Switzerland	54	3.1	3.1
Belgium	56	2.9	3.0
Norway	56	3.6	3.6
Netherlands	56	3.7	3.4
Sweden	65	3.1	3.3
Canada	87	2.0	1.7
United States	100	2.4	2.2[5]
All	*47*	*4.0*	*4.0*
All lower-productivity countries[6]	*25*	*5.1*	*5.2*

[1]For each country, reference is either to the geometric mean of alternative in-

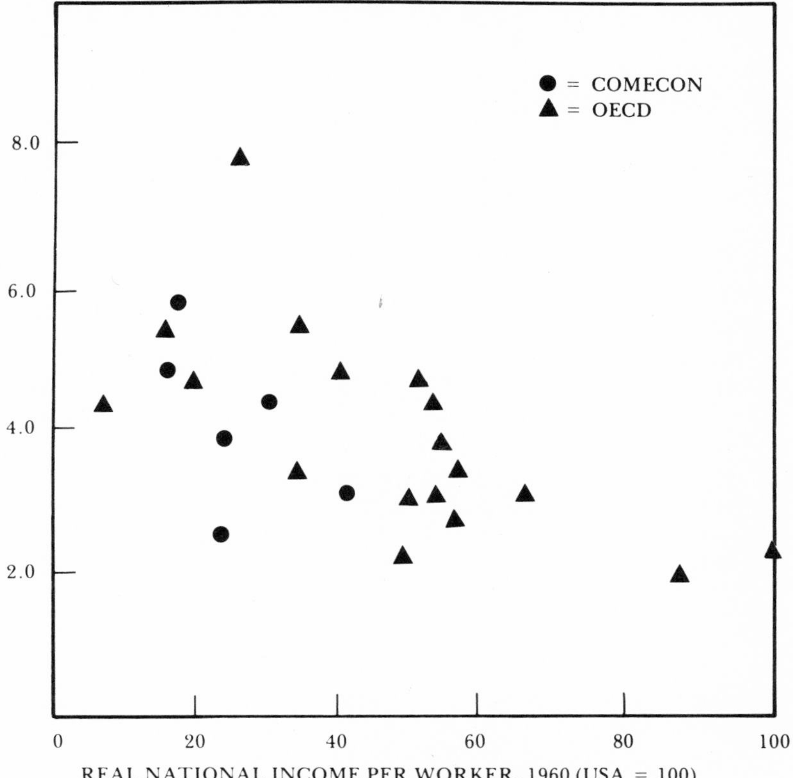

FIGURE 11.1 Rate of growth of GNP per worker, 1950-1967, and real national income per worker, 1960, COMECON and OECD countries

---

dices of GNP per employed worker in national and U.S. prices, or to some alternative measure taken as a surrogate thereof.

[2]Real national income for COMECON countries is given by GNP in constant "adjusted" prices. For OECD countries, reference is to GNP, usually in constant factor cost, though sometimes in market prices. Output as so understood is related to average civilian employment during the year, together with the armed forces. For Turkey, however, reference is instead to the labor force.

[3]In parentheses, average excluding East Germany.

[4]Data adjusted for addition of Saar and West Berlin.

[5]Data *not* adjusted for addition of Hawaii and Alaska.

[6]Turkey, Greece, Portugal, Japan, Ireland, Italy, Austria.

less advanced country can exploit. The advantages can become weighty if the country has gained sufficient momentum to begin with. Perhaps most important, through wholesale borrowing of modern technologies from advanced countries, technological progress can be speeded with only a modest commitment of resources to research and development. It can frequently be hurried even more through transfer to industry of agricultural workers whose productivity is inordinately low.

Among COMECON countries, too, the rate of growth seems generally to vary inversely with the level of output per worker. The relation cannot be considered especially definite, however, in view of the small number of countries in question and the fairly limited variation in productivity level represented.

In sum, the approximate equality of average tempos of productivity growth among COMECON and OECD countries is of interest, but we must consider that COMECON countries tend to be at distinctly lower productivity levels than OECD countries. May not an actual difference in performance between the two systems be obscured on that account? Possibly so, according to this further comparison: whereas the average rate of growth of output per worker in COMECON is 4.1 percent, the corresponding tempo achieved by seven OECD countries at more or less similar productivity levels is 5.1 percent (Table 11.2). The margin between OECD and COMECON seems less than decisive, though, when we consider that the data must be rather inexact for both OECD and COMECON countries of lower productivity. Note also that among OECD countries generally the rate of growth of output per worker varies widely even for countries at fairly similar production levels. As statistical texts caution, under such circumstances limited differences in group summary measures must be of doubtful significance.[7]

7. I have focused on the level of output per worker as of a date (1960) falling within the period 1950-1967 to which the rate of growth of output per worker relates. For present purposes, there is much to recommend using instead the level of output per worker at the beginning of the period, that is, in 1950, but the relationship between level and growth at that time would be especially sensitive to statistical errors. An underestimate in output per worker in 1950, for example, could in itself mean that a low level was associated with rapid growth. I chose 1960 in order to limit the effect of such errors.

Reference is, of course, to the "regression" of the rate of growth on the level of output per worker. Here and wherever else such a relation is considered or where reference is to an issue such as the significance of observed differences in tempo between COMECON and OECD countries, I take into account results of further calculations of a conventional statistical kind set forth in the Technical Note at the end of this chapter.

The relative inexactness of the data for lower productivity OECD and COMECON countries is due partly, if not chiefly, to the limitations in available employment statistics, particularly the incomplete and uneven coverage of "helping family members" in agriculture. I shall consider later, however, comparative data on the rate of growth of national income per

Among causes of productivity growth that are more or less beyond the reach of the system, some must be of a cultural sort not necessarily very dependent even on the stage of development. Some of the complex forces shaping worker attitudes, for example, could be one such cause. Such cultural influences must also vary among countries, but the variation should be relatively limited among three countries that were all once constituents of the Austro-Hungarian Empire. If only for this reason, it is illuminating that productivity growth in Austria, a member of the OECD, appreciably exceeds that in its two former imperial partners, Hungary and Czechoslovakia, both of which are now members of COMECON. Note also that Austria's output per worker in 1960 was about the same as that of Czechoslovakia and higher than that of Hungary.

Among all the countries studied, the one with the highest tempo of productivity growth is a member of OECD rather than of COMECON. That country is, of course, Japan. With output per employed worker increasing at an average rate of 7.7 percent a year, Japan is clearly in a class by itself at this point.

I have been considering growth of output per worker and therefore have taken no account of changes in hours worked. How does the growth of labor productivity in COMECON countries compare to that in OECD countries if allowance is made for such changes? For the USSR and a few OECD countries for which data are available, comparative rates of growth during 1950-1962 do not change much (Table 11.3). How allowance for changes in hours may affect the results generally has to be judged in that light.

Reference, strictly speaking, has also been to output per employed worker. What if we consider instead output per worker in the labor force, including the unemployed? Comparative tempos again seem little affected, at least on the average, for different groups:

	Average annual rate of growth of real national income per worker (1950-1967)	
	For employed workers (Table 11.2)	For the labor force
COMECON, all	4.1%	4.4% (4.6%)
OECD, all	4.0	4.0 (3.9)
OECD, lower-productivity countries	5.1	5.2 (4.8)

person of working age. It is reassuring that these figures seem plausibly related to those in Table 11.2.

TABLE 11.3. Average annual rate of growth, real national income per employed worker, and per employed worker, adjusted for changes in hours, 1950-1962 (percent)[1]

Country	Per employed worker	Per employed worker, adjusted for changes in hours
USSR	4.5	4.7
Italy	5.4	5.3
United Kingdom	1.7	1.9
West Germany	5.2	5.6
France	4.8	4.8
United States	2.2	2.4

[1] For real national income, reference is to net national product in constant prices. Additional working hours are discounted in accord with a scale used by E. F. Denison.

Data on output per worker in the labor force are apt to be less exact than those on output per employed worker. It should be observed, therefore, that the results are still much the same as before if reference is to output per person of working age (fifteen to sixty-four years), though the COMECON performance now appears in a distinctly more favorable light. See the data shown parenthetically above. By implication, COMECON rates of labor participation have tended to rise somewhat relative to those of OECD countries. In view of well-known facts about COMECON labor policies, particularly regarding employment of women, that is not surprising.[8]

I have been discussing rates of growth of output per worker for the entire period 1950-1967. As explained, tempos of labor productivity growth in different countries during this period must have been affected by the tur-

8. In comparing rates of growth set forth in the text, note that the one that relates to output per worker in the labor force for COMECON countries is unchanged if East Germany is excluded, as is done for the corresponding figure from Table 11.2 on output per employed worker. By comparing employment with the labor force in COMECON countries, can we answer, after all, the recurring question concerning the level of unemployment in those countries? Not really, because of the peculiarities of the COMECON concept of and data on the "labor force," at least not in any sense comparable to that in which unemployment is understood in the West. Compilation of meaningful comparative data on the growth of output per worker in the labor force does not seem precluded, although, to repeat, such data are no doubt fairly inexact.

bulent events of the war and of the immediate postwar years. Comparative rates of growth of output per worker in COMECON and OECD countries, however, do not change much if reference is to a period still further removed from the war, 1955-1967 (Table 11.2 and Figure 11.2). That is true whether COMECON countries are compared with OECD countries generally or only with those at lower levels of productivity. As before, Austria outpaces both Hungary and Czechoslovakia, though by a narrower margin. A similar comparison can now be made between East Germany and West Germany. Rates of growth of output per worker in the two countries apparently are practically the same. Japan's tempo, now 8.4 percent yearly, is again the highest by far among all countries considered.

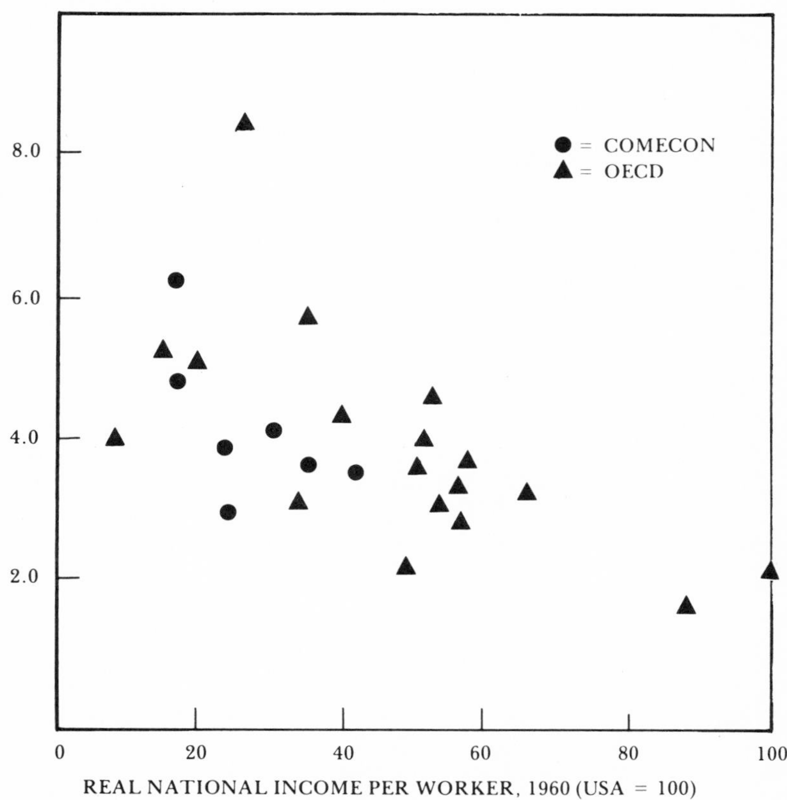

FIGURE 11.2. Rate of growth of GNP per worker, 1955-1967, and real national income per worker, 1960, COMECON and OECD countries

I conclude that in the sphere of labor productivity growth, COMECON countries tend to only hold their own with those in OECD. Perhaps when development stage is taken into account OECD performance is superior.

INVESTMENT RATES

Turning to sources of productivity growth, we may best bring out essentials if we consider that COMECON countries have devoted to capital investment a notably large share of their national income (Table 11.4). COMECON investment rates, even so, are sometimes matched by OECD countries, but often the OECD rates fall well short of those of COMECON. That is the case both during 1950-1966 and during 1955-1966, although data on OECD countries are more complete for the later interval than for the earlier one. For 1955-1966, we can see what could not be seen so easily for 1950-1966: OECD investment rates do not vary much one way or the other with the productivity level. Hence, COMECON rates compare favorably with those not only of OECD countries generally but also of OECD countries at lower productivity levels.

That is so too if, as before, we compare Czechoslovakia and Hungary with Austria. The Hungarian margin over Austria, however, is small. Previously we compared East and West Germany. Regarding the rate of investment, East Germany is at the bottom of the COMECON list and West Germany is nearly at the top of the OECD list. At this point, therefore, it is the OECD rather than the COMECON rate that is higher.

Japan again is in a class by itself among OECD countries. Curiously, however, one COMECON country, Bulgaria, apparently surpasses Japan's rate of capital investment. Even among OECD countries Japan now has a close rival in Norway, but the high investment rate recorded for that country probably is partly statistical rather than real.[9]

I have been referring to investment in fixed capital (plant and equipment, transportation facilities, and so on). That is by far the most impor-

9. Although, according to the usual OECD practice, repairs generally are treated as an expense, in Norway I understand that appreciable outlays of that sort are capitalized and so are included in both investment and national income. It should also be noted, however, that in compiling data on fixed investment shares for COMECON countries, I rather arbitrarily take one-third of so-called "capital repairs" to represent investment and national income. Capital repairs are major renovations that are intended to restore an asset to full working power: replacement of a defective heating system, for example. Such a category of outlay has no counterpart in OECD national income accounts. In practice, the bulk of such repairs must be classified, along with repairs generally, as expense, but most likely appreciable amounts find their way into investment and national income instead. Among COMECON countries, the one-third of capital repairs that are here treated in that way come to an estimated 6.8 percent of gross fixed investment exclusive of such repairs.

TABLE 11.4. Shares of gross investment in gross national product, 1950-1966 and 1955-1966, COMECON and OECD countries (percent)[1]

Country	Gross fixed investment/GNP		Gross domestic investment/GNP	
	1950-1966	1955-1966	1950-1966	1955-1966
COMECON				
Bulgaria	31.3[2]	34.0[2]	—	—
Rumania	—	—	—	—
Hungary	23.8	23.9	—	—
Poland	24.2	25.5	—	—
USSR	25.2	26.6	28.8	30.3
East Germany	19.1	20.7	—	—
Czechoslovakia	24.4	25.2	—	—
All	*24.7*	*26.0*	—	—
OECD				
Turkey	—	15.2[3]	—	—
Greece	21.4	22.8	23.4	24.8
Portugal	—	17.8	—	18.2
Japan	—	32.3	—	36.0
Ireland	16.6	16.9	17.5	17.9
Italy	20.2	20.8	21.2	21.9
Austria	21.3	22.0	—	—
United Kingdom	16.2	17.1	17.2	18.2
Denmark	19.7	20.7	21.2	22.3
West Germany	23.7	24.6	25.6	26.4
France	19.7	20.5	20.9	21.6
Switzerland	—	24.6[3]	—	26.1[3]
Belgium	—	18.1	—	18.6
Norway	29.4	30.0	30.4	30.8
Netherlands	23.2	24.0	25.3	26.1
Sweden	22.0	22.7	23.2	24.1
Canada	23.0	23.2	24.2	24.3
United States	17.3	17.3	18.5	18.3
All	*21.1*	*21.7*	*22.4*	*23.5*
All lower-productivity countries[4]	—	*21.1*	—	—

[1]As implied, reference is to domestic investment in fixed capital. For COMECON countries, investment and output are valued in constant adjusted prices, generally 1955 or 1956, though for East Germany reference is to 1936. For OECD countries, valuation is in market prices of 1955, except for Turkey, for which valuation is at market prices of 1958.

[2]The terminal year is 1965 rather than 1966.

[3]The initial year is 1958.

[4]Turkey, Greece, Portugal, Japan, Ireland, Italy, and Austria.

tant component of investment in any but the most backward countries, but it is, of course, not the only element. It should be noted, therefore, that investment rates for COMECON countries probably compare even more favorably with those of OECD countries when reference is to all investment.

That such is the case for the USSR may be seen from comparative data available on domestic investment (Table 11.4). Comprising investment in both fixed capital and inventories, domestic investment still falls short of all investment, which includes net foreign lending. But relative to output, domestic investment has tended to approximate closely all investment among OECD countries. That must be so for the USSR as well, though highly publicized loan transactions may suggest the contrary. Investment in inventories, it is often supposed, varies with the rate of growth of output. Among OECD countries, if it does, it does not seem to vary at all closely with the rate of growth of output per worker. Note, however, that when inventory additions are included, the Soviet investment rate rises relative even to that of Italy. While on a par with the USSR regarding the level of productivity, Italy surpasses that country in the corresponding tempo of growth.[10]

10. To return to the relation between domestic and all investment among OECD countries studied, as implied, net foreign lending, the source of the difference between the two categories, has lately tended to be limited. That is not necessarily always so, but if my comparison of Soviet and OECD investment errs on that account, the error must generally be in the direction of overstating OECD investment. Where OECD net foreign lending is consequential, it almost always takes the form of net foreign borrowing. That holds true particularly for Greece, Portugal, and Norway, where net borrowing during 1952-1966 amounted to 3.7, 2.9, and 2.3 percent, respectively, and during 1955-1966 to 3.9, 2.8, and 2.1 percent, respectively, of the gross national product. Data on net foreign borrowing are lacking for Turkey and are incomplete for other countries. Canada, too, is probably a net borrower on some scale. Since the USSR was undoubtedly a net lender during the intervals in question, all investment for it must exceed domestic investment, while all investment in Greece, Portugal, Norway, and Canada must fall appreciably short of the domestic kind.

Inclusion of foreign lending in all investment is, of course, the conventional procedure. It is logical, too, for net earnings on foreign assets are included in gross national product. Nevertheless the practice is apt to be misleading, because, as we need not ponder long to realize, a country should usually gain more from borrowing than it remits abroad in the form of earnings on the borrowed assets. Hence all investment, which excludes such borrowing altogether, should understate the increment of capital contribution to growth. By similar reasoning, for a net lender all investment should overstate the additions to capital contributing to growth. In short, even for Greece, Portugal, Norway, and Canada, my comparison of Soviet and OECD investment in terms of rates of domestic investment should not really be far off the mark.

Cited ratios of net foreign lending and borrowing to output are compiled from data on such lending and borrowing and the GNP in current prices. See United Nations, *Yearbook of National Account Statistics, 1959* (New York, 1960), and corresponding volumes for 1961 and 1957; and *National Income, 1966,* pp. 74-75.

I refer elsewhere in the text to investment in a more or less inclusive sense in COMECON countries other than the USSR. Data on net foreign lending by those countries are incomplete

Data on investment for COMECON countries other than the USSR are very incomplete. They point almost unmistakably, however, to the fact that investment generally, compared to fixed investment, must usually be at least as large in those countries as in the USSR. It may be even larger.[11]

My data on investment shares for any country reflect values of investment goods and output generally in the country in question. What of the well-known limitations of the government-controlled prices of COMECON countries? Could not aberrations in such prices distort COMECON compared with OECD shares of investment in national income? To the statistical purist, prices everywhere have their limitations for purposes of national income accounting, but they are no doubt especially dubious in COMECON countries. Revaluation of investment goods and output generally in those countries, in terms of a factor cost standard, however, should have corrected for the more serious of these distortions, and my data may be read accordingly.[12]

Even in a summary inquiry we must consider that what counts for growth of output per worker is not so much gross but net investment, or gross investment less depreciation. Furthermore, depreciation varies with the size of the accumulated capital stock rather than with the volume of current gross investment. As a share of output, therefore, net investment always falls below gross investment by an amount that depends not on gross investment but on the "capital-output ratio," that is, the ratio of the capital stock to output. Depending on that ratio, too, the same rate of net investment may represent a relatively large or small addition to—and so a high or low rate of growth of—capital stock itself. Investment contributes, finally, to growth by determining that tempo. Given the rate of gross investment, then, the lower the capital-output ratio, the higher the rates of net investment and of capital stock growth and vice versa.

---

and obscure. All probably are, like the USSR, net lenders on a very limited scale. Comparative investment there and in OECD countries should be viewed accordingly.

11. See particularly the data on investment rates in the USSR, Hungary, Poland, and Czechoslovakia in *Real SNIP,* pp. 235 ff.; Abraham Becker, *Soviet National Income, 1958-64* (Berkeley, Calif., 1969), pp. 94 ff., 526-529; and Alton, "Economic Structure and Growth in Eastern Europe," p. 59.

12. This presupposes that each country's output ideally should be measured in terms of its own scarcity values. That is indeed the case for an inquiry such as this one, but it is illuminating that a further revaluation of output in terms of United States dollar prices most likely would raise the Soviet investment rate relative to that of Italy, though not relative to that of the United States. We may make this judgment because, relative to a dollar, a ruble of factor cost in 1955 would purchase 94 percent as much investment goods as output generally. The corresponding ratio for the Italian lira was 72 percent; see Chapter 5, this volume. On the valuation problem posed by pricing distortions in COMECON countries, see *Real SNIP.*

The comparative data on gross investment must be seen in that perspective. Figures on capital output ratios are difficult to come by, but those for COMECON countries cannot usually be especially high by OECD standards. That may perhaps be surmised from the rather low COMECON productivity levels, although information on how, in general, capital-output ratios vary with the productivity level is also surprisingly incomplete.[13] COMECON capital stocks, however, do in fact grow notably rapidly, and that is as should be expected if their capital-output ratios are not very high. Stocks of reproducible capital, exclusive of housing in the USSR and the West, for example, grew at these average rates during 1950-1962:[14]

	Percent
USSR	9.3
Italy	3.5
United Kingdom	3.4
West Germany	6.4
France	4.2
Northwestern Europe	4.5
United States	3.6

In Czechoslovakia, gross fixed capital, exclusive of housing, reportedly grew during 1950-1962 at an annual rate of 5.3 percent. Gross fixed productive assets grew in Bulgaria during 1952-1958 by 8.8 percent annually and net fixed productive assets in Hungary grew during 1950-1959 by 8.3 percent.[15]

None of these facts, however, are very surprising. Indeed what may be

13. There can be no question about capital stock per worker. That coefficient is, almost as much as output per worker, the hallmark of a country's economic development. Capital per worker should also vary with output per worker as between countries. Evidence regarding capital stock per unit of output, however, is meager and somewhat conflicting, at least for reproducible capital, which is of concern here.

14. Reproducible capital here also omits net foreign assets, and for OECD countries, stocks in "general government" are also excluded. For fixed capital, reference à la Denison is to an average of two index numbers, one representing gross and the other net assets. While housing was proverbially neglected in the USSR under Stalin, the stock increased at an impressive rate during 1950-1962. Including housing, Soviet reproducible capital grew during that period at a rate of 8.9 percent yearly. See Abram Bergson, *Planning and Productivity Under Soviet Socialism* (New York, 1968), pp. 81-82, 92-95, and the sources cited there.

15. Inclusive of housing, the Czech stock of gross fixed capital grew during 1950-1962 by 4.8 percent yearly. See Gregor Lazarcik, *Czechoslovak Gross National Product by Sector of Origin and by Final Use, 1937 and 1948-65,* Research Project on National Income in East Central Europe, OP-26 (New York, 1969), pp. 71-73; and United Nations, *Economic Survey of Europe in 1961,* pt. 2 (Geneva, 1964), p. 26.

surprising is that in capital accumulation, COMECON has not outpaced the West by an even larger margin than that shown. The moral must be, in part, that capabilities of Western countries for generating investment are greater than is often supposed. But two of the OECD countries whose investment rates were especially high are Germany and Japan. In accumulating capital, both countries, of course, have been fortunate in having to devote very limited output to defense. Among COMECON countries, moreover, it has been possible not only to achieve notably high investment rates but also to attain them even at an early stage and with striking speed. That was the case in the USSR in the thirties, and it must have been so in the two other COMECON countries studied where socialism arrived before development had proceeded very far, namely, Bulgaria and Rumania. The West probably has not been able to match that feat very often.[16]

TECHNOLOGICAL PROGRESS

We want to explain not so much comparative investment rates, as comparative tempos of growth of output per worker. From that standpoint the chief finding is already fairly evident but becomes more so if we relate rates of investment to corresponding rates of increase of output per worker. In that way we may determine for each period and country how costly it was, in terms of investment, to achieve a 1 percent increase in output per worker. Productivity cost increases, as so reckoned, apparently tend to be higher among COMECON than among OECD countries generally (Table 11.5 and Figure 11.3). But of special interest here is the comparative performance of COMECON and OECD countries with lower productivity. The COMECON cost disadvantage is marked at this point. Productivity increases have almost always been distinctly more costly for COMECON than for OECD countries.

The same is true for Hungary and Czechoslovakia by comparison with Austria. East Germany, however, apparently enjoys a slight cost advantage over West Germany. Interestingly Japan ceases to be a special case in this assessment. High as its investment rate is, it is not inordinate relative to its dramatic rate of increase in output per worker.

The COMECON cost disadvantage in the area of gross fixed capital investment probably persists in calculations of all net investment and capital stock growth.[17]

16. Compare Simon Kuznets, "A Comparative Appraisal," in Abram Bergson and Simon Kuznets, eds., *Economic Trends in the Soviet Union* (Cambridge, Mass., 1963), p. 357.

17. As the more specialized reader will be aware, the coefficient that has been computed is similar to the incremental capital-output ratio (ICOR) familiar in economic growth analysis. In the ICOR, one compares the increment of capital with the increment in output that is asso-

TABLE 11.5. Ratio of gross investment share in gross national product to rate of growth of gross national product per employed worker, 1950-1967 and 1955-1967, COMECON and OECD countries (percent)[1]

	Ratio, gross fixed investment share to rate of growth of GNP per employed worker		Ratio, gross domestic investment share to rate of growth of GNP per employed worker	
Country	1950-1967	1955-1967	1950-1967	1955-1967
COMECON				
Bulgaria	5.5[2]	5.5[2]	—	—
Rumania	—	—	—	—
Hungary	6.3	6.1	—	—
Poland	9.3	8.8	—	—
USSR	5.7	6.5	6.6	7.4
East Germany	—	5.6	—	—
Czechoslovaki	7.9	7.2	—	—
All	*6.9*	*6.6*	—	—
OECD				
Turkey	—	3.7[3]	—	—
Greece	4.0	4.3	4.3	4.7
Portugal	—	3.4	—	3.5
Japan	—	3.8	—	4.3
Ireland	4.9	5.3	5.1	5.6
Italy	3.6	3.6	3.8	3.8
Austria	4.4	5.0	—	—
United Kingdom	7.4	7.1	7.8	7.6
Denmark	6.6	5.8	7.1	6.2
West Germany	5.2	6.0	5.6	6.4
France	4.4	4.5	4.6	4.7
Switzerland	—	7.9[3]	—	8.4[3]
Belgium	—	6.2	—	6.2
Norway	8.2	8.3	8.4	8.6
Netherlands	6.3	7.1	6.8	7.7
Sweden	7.1	6.9	7.5	7.3
Canada	11.5	13.6	12.1	14.3
United States	7.2	7.9	7.7	8.3
All	*6.2*	*6.1*	*6.7*	*6.7*
All lower-productivity countries[4]	—	*4.2*	—	—

[1]Except as noted, investment shares relate to 1950-1966 and 1955-1966.

[2]Investment shares for 1950-1965 and 1955-1965.

[3]Investment shares for 1958-1966.

[4]Turkey, Greece, Portugal, Japan, Ireland, Italy, Austria.

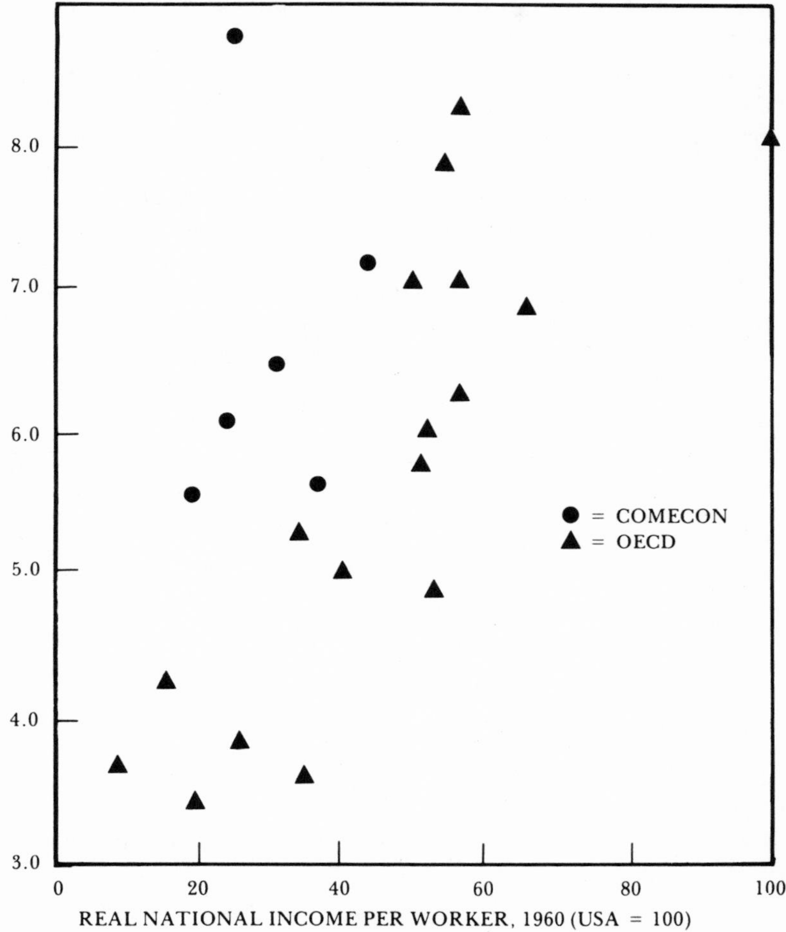

FIGURE 11.3. Ratio of gross fixed investments share in GNP to rate of growth of GNP per worker, 1955-1967, and real national income per worker, 1960, COMECON and OECD. Not shown, Canada (87, 13.6).

If productivity increases have been relatively costly in capital for COMECON, may we conclude that other sources of such increases have been less potent there? What, particularly, of technological progress? Has it been less rapid in COMECON than in OECD countries? In trying to answer, we must consider that one country may require more capital than another to assure the same increase in productivity even though technological progress is fully as rapid in the one case as in the other. That may be so especially if the labor force is increasing more rapidly in one country than in the other, for more capital is then required simply to provide additional workers with as much plant and equipment as was available to those previously employed. Without the inordinate increase in labor, the same increase in capital stock should have permitted productivity to rise more rapidly. In fact, employment increased at diverse tempos among both COMECON and OECD countries, but, as I have implied, tended to grow more rapidly among the former. The gap between the two groups at this point is small, however, and could hardly be very consequential, as these data indicate:

	Ratio of gross fixed investment to rate of increase of GNP per worker (Table 11.5)		Ratio of gross fixed investment to rate of increase in GNP per worker, adjusted	
	1950-1967	1955-1967	1950-1967	1955-1967
COMECON, all	6.9	6.6	6.7	6.6
OECD, all	6.2	6.1	6.3	6.1
OECD, lower-productivity countries	—	4.2	—	4.4

Average ratios in the two columns on the right are obtained after adjusting hypothetically, for inordinate employment changes, the rates of increase in

ciated with it. For the coefficient computed here—perhaps it should be called the "incremental capital-productivity ratio" (ICPR)—one compares the increment of capital with that of output, after the latter has been reduced by an amount proportional to the increase in employment. Neither the ICOR nor the ICPR represents the marginal cost of production in terms of capital input, as it is understood in economic theory, for the increment of output considered in both cases results not only from the increase in capital but also from technological progress. For the ICOR, it results from the increase in employment as well. For the ICPR, the output increment is in effect discounted for the increase in employment crudely, in a proportional way.

The ICPR has been computed previously in Simon Kuznets, "Long-Term Trends in Capital Formation Proportions," *Economic Development and Cultural Change,* July 1961, pt. 2, pp. 27 ff.

output per worker for different countries. The adjustment is rather arbitrary, but the results should not be far off the mark.[18]

Reference has been to *physical* capital, but one country may also have to invest more of such capital than another to assure the same productivity increase because it chooses to invest less in *human* capital and so is able to improve the quality of labor less rapidly. More physical capital may be required on that account without technological progress being less rapid. The higher COMECON requirements for physical capital, however, cannot easily be explained in that way. If we may judge from somewhat dated information (Table 11.6), COMECON educational outlays tend to be fully comparable to those of OECD. COMECON requirements for physical capital should have been no greater than those of OECD at this point.

Requirements for capital of any sort to achieve given productivity increases depend also on a country's natural endowment. The less favorable that endowment is, the greater the capital requirements. Again, techno-

TABLE 11.6. Education outlays as a share of the gross national product, COMECON and OECD countries, 1950 and 1955 (percent)

Country	1950	1955
COMECON		
Hungary	—	2.0
Poland	—	2.2
USSR	—	5.0
Czechoslovakia	—	2.9
OECD		
Italy	3.2	—
United Kingdom	2.5	—
Denmark	2.0	—
West Germany	2.1	—
France	2.2	—
Belgium	2.6	—
Norway	2.4	—
Netherlands	2.1	—
United States	2.4	2.8

18. See the Technical Note at the end of the chapter.

logical progress need not be less rapid as a result. Among both COMECON and OECD countries, natural endowments must have varied widely. That countries in one group have been favored systematically in my calculations over those in another on that account seems doubtful.[19]

Very possibly, then, technological progress tended to be less rapid among COMECON than among OECD countries. At least there is no evidence of COMECON superiority.

CONCLUSION

COMECON countries, as commonly supposed, appear generally to have surpassed those of OECD in postwar years with respect to the share of national income going to investment. Relatively high rates of investment probably have often been achieved speedily even at early stages of development. Capital investment, however, is necessarily costly to consumers, and the returns on the extra costs incurred in COMECON are by no means clear. In the cardinal sphere of productivity growth, COMECON countries, on the average, have no more than matched those of OECD. Among OECD countries, the rate of growth of output per worker has tended to vary inversely with the level of productivity. Growth of output per worker in OECD countries may have been superior if allowance is made for differences in the productivity levels of OECD and COMECON countries.

These briefly are the principal findings of our attempt to gauge summarily the comparative performance of the two groups of countries with respect to growth. By implication, the familiar claim as to the superiority of socialism over capitalism in that sphere appears to have little basis. On the contrary, the latter system may be advantageous. So far as attention has been directed to COMECON, however, reference has been to one

19. Could COMECON capital requirements also be inordinately large because the COMECON countries have concentrated especially on investment projects in "capital-intensive" industries—that is, in industries where capital-output ratios tend, for technological reasons, to be high? Is that not likely to be so particularly for the investment goods whose production the COMECON countries have so striven to expand? In other words, could not COMECON investment rates be high, at least in part simply because they are high, and without technological progress being any slower?

Such queries are familiar, but as already explained, for the economy as a whole, capital-output ratios do not appear to have been notably high in COMECON countries. Even so, the volume of new investment evidently does turn out to be inordinately large there, relative to the increment of output per worker, if not of output, with which it is associated. But COMECON preferences and technology still seem improperly interpreted as the questions suggest: as an additional, consequential cause of that relation.

What is in question essentially, I believe, is whether the nature of their preferences and the technological constraints on factor proportions have led COMECON countries to undertake investment projects that were not only capital-intensive but also relatively unprofitable. While the technologies available to a country at any time are not very susceptible to generali-

brand of socialism, as the development model that originated in the USSR has been emulated fundamentally by all the other COMECON countries in question. Like the USSR, they have applied, among other things, a system of planning, which stresses bureaucratic rather than market controls, and a development strategy, which emphasizes growth.[20] My findings must be interpreted accordingly.

Of the OECD countries in Western Europe and elsewhere that I have discussed, a number are at stages of development similar to those of the USSR and Eastern European socialist countries. That parallel greatly facilitates comparative appraisal of performance. The fact that many of the OECD countries are culturally not very different from those of COMECON also helped to ease the task. Cultural factors most frequently affect economic development quite apart from the nature of the social system. There are, of course, capitalist countries other than those of the OECD. Comparison of the European COMECON experience with that of such countries could further illuminate the relative performances of the two systems.

But the reader may have wanted to demur long ago about the direction of this inquiry. Have I not expressed, throughout, Western values inappropriate to an examination of the comparative performances of socialism and capitalism? Most important, is not productivity growth an illegitimate yardstick to apply in that context? After all, under the development strategy pursued has not the overriding concern in the USSR and Eastern Europe simply been expansion of production, and have not costs of any sort really been immaterial? In the USSR and Eastern Europe, growth of output no doubt has been a cardinal imperative. That goal has always dictated a concern for productivity as well and, if only on that account, for

---

zation, presumably there is, in the expansion of one or another industry, usually a decided latitude to determine factor proportions in light of relative factor scarcities in the economy in general. It should be possible, therefore, to extract from any project a rate of return comparable to that earned on capital in the economy generally. Foreign trade may assure the same result in determining the comparative stress on different industries.

COMECON countries admittedly have hesitated to conduct foreign trade on such principles, and there is much evidence that, even apart from that, they have tended to overcapitalize some economic branches at the expense of others. The resultant sacrifice of efficiency, however, is properly seen here as a factor in rather than apart from COMECON technological progress.

On the subject of capital intensities in different industries, data at hand for the United States are also illuminating. According to a study in progress by Peter Petri, American capital-output ratios tend to be somewhat higher for consumption than for investment goods. At least that is so for fixed capital in 1958, the year investigated.

20. Planning organization and development strategy in both the USSR and Eastern Europe, however, have been evolving, and in Hungary centralist planning of the Soviet sort appears to have been abandoned for a form of market socialism in 1968, following the period on which I have focused. See Chapters 1 and 2, this volume.

residual supplies available to consumers. For some time these concerns have been gaining force. The change in priorities has long been manifest and is sufficiently familiar that I need not go into it. Growth of output continues to be pursued, but it is sought at less cost than in the past in terms of both labor and capital. Perhaps, then, the COMECON values relating to development have not differed from those in the West quite so much as many suppose. They differ even less now than formerly.

If COMECON countries have not performed outstandingly well with respect to economic development, could part of the reason be their greater concern for equity of income distribution? Is not equity itself a redeeming feature? Does not COMECON compare more favorably with OECD according to other yardsticks? In particular, what of the pervasive environmental pollution in the West? Must we not set that against more material Western achievements? If equity of income distribution turns on the degree of equality, greater equity probably has often been achieved in COMECON than in OECD, and at the expense of incentives and hence of economic performance generally. That judgment is somewhat difficult to make, though, if only because COMECON governments have tended to be rather secretive about income inequality. And no one needs to be told that pollution is an offsetting consequence of Western material achievements. But, as is rarely considered, pollution is a problem not only in the West. As the daily newspaper often reminds us, it is pervasive in the East as well.

If we extend the appraisal of the two systems to such considerations, must we not extend it still further, especially to the authoritarianism that has permitted COMECON countries, via control of capital formation, to achieve much of their success in economic development? The question still seems in order after due allowance for familiar political vicissitudes in the West, but that and other questions raised only highlight what is already evident: the comparative merit of the two systems is an issue with many sides, of which comparative performance in economic development is but one. Evaluating such merit should be facilitated, however, by the understanding that, in the context of economic development, it may well be that capitalism as it exists in OECD, rather than socialism such as prevails in COMECON, is the more advantageous system.

TECHNICAL NOTE[21]

Regression relations. Table 11.7 sets forth selected data concerning various regression relations alluded to in the text. Rows I A-C all pertain to such relations of the form:

$$Y = aX + k \tag{11.1}$$

21. I am indebted to Robert Allen for assistance in carrying out the calculations of regression relations presented here and to Earl R. Brubaker for helpful advice on the derivation of formula (11.3).

TABLE 11.7. Selected data on various regressions relating to COMECON and OECD growth

Item		Text table	No. of observations	r^2	a		b		k	
I	A	11.2	18	0.46	−0.041	(3.690)	—		5.914	(10.03)
	B	11.2	16	0.34	−0.047	(2.713)	—		6.115	(7.931)
	C	11.2	15	0.36	−0.035	(2.693)	—		5.436	(9.089)
II	A	11.2	24	0.43	−0.043	(4.011)	−0.800	(1.462)	5.986	(10.60)
	B	11.2	22	0.34	−0.049	(3.130)	−0.872	(1.511)	6.222	(8.766)
	C	11.2	21	0.33	−0.039	(2.990)	−0.514	(1.076)	5.600	(9.308)
III	A	11.2	18	0.45	−0.045	(3.623)	—		6.077	(9.394)
	B	11.2	16	0.31	−0.047	(2.502)	—		6.187	(7.294)
	C	11.2	15	0.35	−0.033	(2.664)	—		5.352	(9.381)
IV	A	11.2	25	0.44	−0.046	(4.096)	−0.722	(1.329)	6.144	(10.35)
	B	11.2	23	0.31	−0.050	(3.031)	−0.764	(1.337)	6.292	(8.462)
	C	11.2	22	0.34	−0.038	(3.048)	−0.345	(0.808)	5.536	(9.742)
V	A	11.5	18	0.63	0.084	(5.175)	—		2.170	(2.558)
	B	11.5	16	0.64	0.076	(5.008)	—		2.411	(3.572)
	C	11.5	15	0.62	0.073	(4.594)	—		2.551	(3.502)
VI	A	11.5	24	0.57	0.081	(5.226)	1.979	(2.579)	2.314	(2.846)
	B	11.5	22	0.55	0.070	(4.398)	1.957	(3.478)	2.638	(3.675)
	C	11.5	21	0.52	0.067	(4.058)	1.897	(3.211)	2.788	(3.635)
VII	A	—	18	0.60	0.064	(4.908)	—		3.085	(4.477)
	B	—	16	0.62	0.077	(4.736)	—		2.597	(3.573)
	C	—	15	0.59	0.074	(4.334)	—		2.791	(3.591)
VIII	A	—	24	0.57	0.063	(5.194)	1.626	(2.704)	3.164	(4.968)
	B	—	22	0.57	0.072	(4.803)	1.727	(3.243)	2.784	(4.098)
	C	—	21	0.54	0.069	(4.434)	1.624	(2.964)	2.980	(4.148)

where, for any country, X is the index of GNP per worker in 1960 as a percentage of that of the USA and Y is the corresponding rate of growth of GNP per worker during 1950-1967. Reference is only to OECD countries. I consider in I A all such countries, in I B all such countries exclusive of Canada and the United States, and in I C all such countries exclusive of Canada, the United States, and Japan.

Rows II A-C pertain to regression relations of the form:

$$Y = aX + bS + k \tag{11.2}$$

where X and Y are as before and S is a dummy variable representing the presence or absence of socialism. Reference here, therefore, is to both COMECON and OECD countries. I consider in II A all OECD countries, in II B all such countries other than Canada and the United States, and in II C all such countries other than Canada, the United States, and Japan.

Rows III A-C and IV A-C show the results obtained by repeating calculations for I A-C and II A-C for the period 1955-1967.

Rows V A-C pertain to regression relations of the form (11.1), except that Y stands for a country's "incremental capital-productivity ratio" (ICPR), that is, the ratio of the share of GNP invested in fixed capital to the rate of growth of GNP per worker. Reference is to the ICPR for 1955-1967. Among OECD countries the three variants relate, as before, to all of these countries, all OECD countries other than Canada and the United States, and all such countries other than Canada, the United States, and Japan. Rows VI A-C pertain to regression relations of the form (11.2), on the understanding that Y is as in V A-C. Whereas the calculations relate to the ICPR during 1955-1967 in COMECON and OECD countries, reference for the latter is again to the three variants just identified.

In rows VII A-C and VIII A-C, I show the results obtained by repeating the calculations considered in V A-C and VI A-C, except that for each country reference is to an adjusted ICPR.

In Table 11.7, r stands for the coefficient of correlation. Parenthetic figures are t values. Each has the sign of the constant to which it refers. The dash stands for "not applicable."

Adjustment of ICPR. For any country an adjusted ICPR is the ratio of the share of GNP invested in fixed capital to an adjusted rate of growth of GNP per employed worker. The latter is a hypothetical rate of growth that is intended to represent what the rate of growth of GNP per worker would have been if technological progress and the growth of capital stock had proceeded as they do in fact and employment had grown not at the actual rate but at a rate of 1.0 percent annually, or about the average rate of growth of employment in all the countries studied during the period 1955-1967.

I assume that for any country output is given by the well-known formula,

$$Y(t) = A(t)F[K(t), L(t)]$$

where $A(t)$ represents the level of factor productivity at time t, as determined by technological progress; $Y(t)$, $K(t)$, and $L(t)$ represent output, capital stock, and employment at time t; and F is a linear homogeneous function. According to familiar reasoning,

$$\dot{Y} = \dot{A} + a\dot{K}(1 - a)\dot{L}$$

where Y, K, and L represent relative rates of growth of the corresponding variables, a represents capital's share in output, and $(1 - a)$ is labor's share in output. But:

$$(\dot{Y/L}) = \dot{Y} - \dot{L},$$

where $(\dot{Y/L})$ represents the relative rate of growth of output per worker. Hence

$$(\dot{Y/L}) = \dot{A} + a\dot{K} - a\dot{L},$$

and

(11.3) $$(\dot{Y/L})_C = (\dot{Y/L}) + a(\dot{L} - 0.01),$$

where it is now understood that $(\dot{Y/L})$ is the actual and $(\dot{Y/L})_C$ the adjusted rate of increase in output per worker.

In applying (11.3), I assume rather arbitrarily that a is 0.3 for Belgium, Denmark, France, West Germany, the Netherlands, Norway, United Kingdom, United States, Canada, Sweden, and Switzerland, and that it is 0.4 for all other OECD countries as well as all COMECON countries. Note that reference is to the share of capital gross of depreciation.

Strictly speaking, formula (11.3) should be applied only to variations over a very short interval of time. Where reference is to variations over a protracted period, as it is here, the adjusted rate of growth of output per worker for the entire period should ideally be calculated by applying (11.3) to successive short intervals, the adjusted rate of growth of output per worker for the entire period then being obtained as an average of corresponding adjusted rates for the successive short intervals. At least it should be done insofar as the elasticity of substitution differs from unity and factor shares vary. The data available, however, do not permit such a refinement.

APPENDIX

INDEX

Appendix

Each of the tables that follow should be read in conjunction with the chapter in question. Appendix Tables 1-3 pertain to Chapter 5, Appendix Tables 4-11 to Chapter 6, Appendix Tables 12-18 to Chapter 7, and Appendix Tables 19-25 to Chapters 9 and 10. Sources and methods for the tables are supplied in the appendix from which they are taken; on the appendixes see the Preface. In the tables the symbol "—" stands for "not available" or "not applicable."

APPENDIX TABLE 1. Gross national product of the USSR by final use, 1955, in prevailing and adjusted rubles and in United States dollar prices of 1955

Final use	Prevailing rubles (bil.)	Adjusted rubles (bil.)	U.S. dollars (bil.)
Retail sales to households			
In state and cooperative shops	442.2	253.1	33.4
In collective farm markets	51.1	50.1	2.7
All outlets			
Food	(300.7)	—	25.0
Nonfood	(192.6)	—	11.1
All	*493.3*	*303.2*	*36.1*
Housing: services			
Housing	8.4	58.1	6.4
Utilities, misc. services	50.3		12.0
Trade union and other dues	5.2	5.2	2.5
All	*63.9*	*63.3*	*20.9*
Consumption of farm income in kind	80.4	90.3	5.8
Military, including internal security, subsistence	21.6	16.7	1.6
Household consumption, all	659.2	473.5	64.4
Communal services			
Wages	61.6	61.6	31.0
Nonwages	40.9	31.6	3.7
All	*102.5*	*93.2*	*34.7*
Government administration, internal security, Party			
Wages	22.1	21.6	8.1
Nonwages	7.4	5.8	0.7
All	*29.5*	*27.4*	*8.8*
Defense (as recorded in budget)			
Military pay	23.4	23.4	—
Military subsistence	19.8	15.4	—
Military services, all	43.2	38.8	17.7
Munitions	39.8	60.7	9.7
Other	22.4		2.5
All	*105.4*	*99.5*	*29.9*

(*cont.*)

APPENDIX TABLE 1 (cont.)

Final use	Prevailing rubles (bil.)	Adjusted rubles (bil.)	U.S. dollars (bil.)
Gross investment			
Household livestock investment in kind; socialist money investment in livestock	4.5	4.7	0.2
Fixed capital			
New machinery	63.3	—	15.4
Capital repairs to machinery	7.8	—	1.9
Construction	131.8	—	18.8
All	*202.9*	*201.4*	*36.1*
Public sector inventory investment, misc.	39.2	32.0	6.7
All	*246.6*	*238.1*	*43.0*
Gross national product	1143.2	931.7	180.8

APPENDIX TABLE 2. Calculation of net adjustment, gross national product by final use, USSR, 1955

Final use	(1) Outlays in prevailing rubles (bil.)	(2) Assumed effective turnover tax rate (%)	(3) Indicated taxes (bil. rubles)	(4) Assumed subsidies (bil. rubles)	(5) Net adjustment (bil. rubles) [(3)-(4)]
Retail sales to households					
In state and cooperative shops	442.2	—[1]	206.3	17.2	189.1
In collective farm markets	51.1	2	1.0	0	1.0
All	*493.3*				*190.1*
Housing; services					
Other than dues	58.7	1	0.6	0	0.6
Trade union and other dues	5.2	0	0	0	0
All	*63.9*				*0.6*
Consumption of farm income in kind	80.4			(9.9)	−9.9
Military, including internal security, subsistence	21.6	26	5.6	0.7	4.9
Household consumption, all	659.2				185.7
Communal services					
Labor	61.6	0	0	0	0
Nonlabor	40.9	26	10.6	1.3	9.3
All	*102.5*				*9.3*
Government administration, internal security, Party					
Labor: money pay	20.3	0	0	0	0
Labor: subsistence	1.8	(26)[2]	(.5)	0	0.5
Nonlabor	7.4		1.9	0.3	1.6
All	*29.5*				*2.1*

(*cont.*)

APPENDIX TABLE 2 (cont.)

Final use	(1) Outlays in prevailing rubles (bil.)	(2) Assumed effective turnover tax rate (%)	(3) Indicated taxes (bil. rubles)	(4) Assumed subsidies (bil. rubles)	(5) Net adjustment (bil. rubles) [(3)-(4)]
Defense					
Military pay	23.4	0	0	0	0
Military subsistence	19.8	(26)	(5.1)	(1.7)	4.4
Munitions and other	62.2	4	2.5	1.0	1.5
All	*105.4*				*5.9*
Gross investment					
Household livestock investment in kind; socialist money investment in livestock	4.5	0	0	(0.2)	−0.2
Fixed capital	202.9	2.5	5.1	3.6	1.5
Public sector inventory investment					
Trade	14.0	—[1]	6.4		
Industry	−3.3	26	−0.9	1.1	7.2
All	*10.7*				
Miscellaneous	28.5	10	2.8		
All	*246.6*				*8.5*
Gross national product	1143.2		247.5	36.0	211.5

[1] Tax calculated as residual.
[2] Figures in parentheses represent duplications of amounts recorded elsewhere or imputations.

APPENDIX TABLE 3. Gross national product of the United States by final use, 1955, in United States dollar prices of 1955 and in established and adjusted ruble prices of 1955

Final use	U.S. dollars (bil.)	Established rubles (bil.)	Adjusted rubles (bil.)
Household food consumption			
Purchased	64.34	1126.0	1973.1[1]
Farm income in kind	1.56	22.8	
All	*65.90*	*1148.8*	
Household nonfood consumption	91.72	1687.6	
Housing	33.74	44.5	403.7
Utilities, miscellaneous services	46.58	363.3	
Military consumption	1.34	23.2	—
Household consumption, all	239.28	3267.4	2376.8
Communal services			
Wages	19.27	36.4	36.4
Nonwages	10.59	161.7	124.5
All	*29.86*	*198.1*	*160.9*
Defense			
Military pay and subsistence	9.78	23.8	21.4
Munitions	13.29	85.1	184.5
Military construction	1.83	13.4	
Civilian wages	5.08	11.8	
Other goods and services	6.31	68.1	
Other, including atomic energy development	1.77	9.9	
All	*38.06*	*212.1*	*205.9*
Gross investment			
Producers' durables	27.40	175.4	511.4
Construction	48.05	341.2	
Change in business inventories	5.95	85.4	94.2
Net exports	2.01	26.7	
Stockpiling	0.66		
All	*84.07*	*628.7*	*605.6*
Government purchases not classified elsewhere			
Wages	6.49	15.1	15.1
Nonwages	1.80	27.7	21.3
All	*8.29*	*42.8*	*36.4*
Gross national product	399.56	4349.1	3385.6

[1] Including military consumption.

APPENDIX TABLE 4. Output and factor inputs, USSR and United States, 1960

Item	Nature of measurement	USSR				U.S.			
		All sectors	Farm	Nonfarm	Selected final services	All sectors	Farm	Nonfarm	Selected final services
Gross product	In 1955 ruble factor cost (bil.)	1278.6	260.1	884.4	134.1	3768.2	331.9	3300.1	136.2
	In 1955 dollars (bil.)	247.2	17.5	163.0	66.7	44.8	19.4	343.7	81.7
Net product	In 1955 ruble factor cost (bil.)	1182.2	247.9	824.9	109.4[1]	3406.1	310.8	3079.4	15.9[1]
	In 1955 dollars (bil.)	231.0	15.3	152.3	63.4[1]	391.4	16.3	311.1	64.0[1]
Employment	Workers engaged (mil.)	102.1	39.3	47.3	15.5	65.8	4.4	48.2	13.2
Employment (adjusted)	Workers engaged (adjusted hypothetically to equivalent male eighth-grade graduate; mil.)	81.9[2]	25.8	40.6	15.5[2]	67.5[2]	4.4	49.9	13.2[2]
Reproducible capital, including gross fixed assets	In 1955 rubles (bil.)	3789.7	495.7	2055.6	1238.4[3]	12,580.9	715.4	6031.8	5833.7[3]
	In 1955 dollars (bil.)	606.4	68.0	352.7	185.7[3]	1785.8	81.6	820.3	883.9[3]
Reproducible capital, including net fixed assets	In 1955 rubles (bil.)	3030.1	397.2	1658.9	974.0[3]	7923.1	495.7	3927.4	3500.0[3]
	In 1955 dollars (bil.)	474.7	51.0	278.4	145.3[3]	1100.0	50.4	51.3	530.3[3]
Cultivated arable land	Million acres	549	549			359	359		
Cultivated arable land (adjusted to U.S. equivalent)	Million acres	275	275			359	359		

[1] Relatively limited magnitudes reflect depreciation accounting.
[2] Selected final services unadjusted.
[3] Fixed assets only.

APPENDIX TABLE 5. Elements in calculation of gross and net national product of USSR by sector, 1960, in 1955 Ruble factor cost and 1955 United States dollars (billions)

Sector	Gross product, 1955		Gross product, 1960		Depreciation, 1960		Net product, 1960	
	In 1955 ruble factor cost	In 1955 dollars	In 1955 ruble factor cost	In 1955 dollars	In 1955 ruble factor cost	In 1955 dollars	In 1955 ruble factor cost	In 1955 dollars
Farm	218.6	14.7	260.1	17.5	12.2	2.2	247.9	15.3
Nonfarm	586.4	102.9	884.4	163.0	59.5	10.7	824.9	152.3
Selected final services								
Health care, education	61.6	31.0	79.1	39.8				
Government administration, including internal security,					5.3	0.4	117.5	57.6
Party	21.6	8.1	20.4	7.6				
Armed forces	38.8	17.7	23.3	10.6				
Housing	8.3	6.4	11.3	8.7	19.4	2.9	(−)8.1	5.8
All	*130.3*	*63.2*	*134.1*	*66.7*	*24.7*	*3.3*	*109.4*	*63.4*
All	*935.3*	*180.8*	*1278.6*	*247.2*	*96.4*	*16.2*	*1182.2*	*231.0*

APPENDIX TABLE 6. Elements in calculation of gross and net national product of United States by sector, 1960, in United States dollars and ruble factor cost of 1955 (billions)

Sector	Gross product, 1955		Gross product, 1960		Depreciation, 1960		Net Product, 1960	
	In 1955 dollars	In 1955 ruble factor cost	In 1955 dollars	In 1955 ruble factor cost	In 1955 dollars	In 1955 ruble factor cost	In 1955 dollars	In 1955 ruble factor cost
Farm	18.58	318.2	19.4	331.9	3.1	21.1	16.3	310.8
Nonfarm	311.70	2950.4	343.7	3300.1	32.6	220.7	312.8	3079.4
Selected final services								
Health care, education, government purchases, n.e.c., armed forces	35.54	72.9	39.3	80.7	4.2	31.4	35.1	49.3
Housing	33.74	44.1	42.4	55.5	13.5	88.9	28.9	(−)33.4
All	*69.28*	*117.0*	*81.7*	*136.2*	*17.7*	*120.3*	*64.0*	*15.9*
All	*399.56*	*3385.6*	*444.8*	*3768.2*	*53.4*	*362.1*	*391.4*	*3406.1*

APPENDIX TABLE 7. Employment by sector and sex, USSR, 1960 (millions)

Sector	All	Male	Female
Farm			
Collective farmers, in 280-day man-years	19.0	9.7	9.3
Collective farmers and others on household plots, in 280-day man-years	16.1	3.2	12.9
Employees, state farms	6.3	3.6	2.7
Other	0.5	0.3	0.2
All	*41.9*	*16.8*	*25.1*
Less:			
Collective farmers, nonfarm activities	2.1	1.1	1.0
Employees, state farm, nonfarm activities	0.5	0.3	0.2
All, farm activities only	*39.3*	*15.4*	*23.9*
Nonfarm			
Collective farmers, nonfarm activities	2.1	1.1	1.0
Employees, state farm, nonfarm activities	0.5	0.3	0.2
Employees, repair-technical stations	0.3	0.3	—[1]
Employees, including artisans, nonfarm enterprises	42.9	24.3	18.6
Other	1.5	1.0	0.5
All	*47.3*	*27.0*	*20.3*
Selected final services			
Health care	3.5	0.5	3.0
Education	5.7	2.2	3.5
Government administration, etc.	2.0	1.2	0.8
Armed forces	3.3	3.3	—[1]
Housing	1.0	0.5	0.5
All	*15.5*	*7.7*	*7.8*
All	*102.1*	*50.1*	*52.0*

[1] Negligible.

APPENDIX TABLE 8. Employment by sector, United States, 1960 (millions)

Sector	All
Farm	4.4
Nonfarm	48.2
Selected final services	
Health care, private	2.0
Education, private	0.8
Federal, general government, civilian	1.7
State and local, general government	5.2
Military	2.5
Housing	1.0
All	*13.2*
All	*65.8*

APPENDIX TABLE 9. Adjustment of employment to male eighth-grade equivalent, USSR and United States, 1960 (millions)

	All sectors, excluding selected final services		Nonfarm	
Item	USSR	U.S.	USSR	U.S.
Workers engaged	86.6	52.6	47.3	48.2
Workers engaged (adjusted to male equivalent)	68.5	46.4	39.0	42.3
Average male worker in male eighth-grade graduate equivalent	0.97	1.17	1.04	1.18
Workers engaged (adjusted to male eighth-grade graduate equivalent)	66.4	54.3	40.6	49.9

APPENDIX TABLE 10. Reproducible capital, USSR and United States, July 1, 1960, in 1955 rubles and United States dollars (billions)

Type of capital	All sectors		Farm		Nonfarm		Selected final services	
	In 1955 rubles	In 1955 dollars	In 1955 rubles	In 1955 dollars	In 1955 rubles	In 1955 dollars	In 1955 rubles	In 1955 dollars
USSR								
Fixed capital, gross	3,045.0	510.4	308.4	53.4	1498.2	271.3	1238.4	185.7
Fixed capital, net	2,285.4	378.7	209.9	36.4	1101.5	197.0	974.0	145.3
Inventories	604.6	88.3	47.2	6.9	557.4	81.4	—[2]	—[2]
Livestock	140.1	7.7	140.1	7.7	—[1]	—[1]	—[1]	—[1]
All, including gross fixed capital	3,789.7	606.4	495.7	68.0	2055.6	352.7	1238.4	185.7
All, including net fixed capital	3,030.1	474.7	397.2	51.0	1658.9	278.4	974.0	145.3
U.S.								
Fixed capital, gross	11,273.3	1662.5	443.2	62.9	4996.4	715.7	5883.7	883.9
Fixed capital, net	6,615.5	976.7	223.5	31.7	2892.0	414.7	3500.0	530.3
Inventories	1,115.7	112.7	80.3	8.1	1035.4	104.6	—[2]	—[2]
Livestock	191.9	10.6	191.9	10.6	—[1]	—[1]	—[1]	—[1]
All, including gross fixed capital	12,580.9	1785.8	715.4	81.6	6031.8	820.3	5833.7	883.9
All, including net fixed capital	7,923.1	1100.0	495.7	50.4	3927.4	519.3	3500	530.3

[1] Negligible.
[2] Included in nonfarm sector.

APPENDIX TABLE 11. Weights used in aggregating factor input[1]

Factor input	USSR				U.S.			
		Percent				Percent		
	Billion rubles	(1)	(2)	(3)	Billion dollars	(1)	(2)	(3)
All sectors								
Employment	743.6	61.8	67.2	56.3	258.4	67.2	78.1	66.7
Reproducible capital								
Gross services	460.1	38.2	—	34.8	126.0	32.8	—	32.5
Net services	363.6	—	32.8	—	72.6	—	21.9	—
Cultivated arable land	117.9	—	—	8.9	2.9	—	—	0.7
All	(1) 1203.7	100.0	—	—	384.4	100.0	—	—
	(2) 1107.2	—	100.0	—	331.0	—	100.0	—
	(3) 1321.6	—	—	100.0	387.3	—	—	100.0
All sectors, excluding selected final services								
Employment	612.2	65.8	71.3	58.4	216.3	71.2	80.0	70.5
Reproducible capital								
Gross services	318.4	34.2	—	30.4	87.7	28.8	—	28.6
Net services	246.7	—	28.7	—	54.1	—	20.0	—
Cultivated arable land	117.9	—	—	11.2	2.9	—	—	0.9
All	(1) 930.6	100.0	—	—	304.0	100.0	—	—
	(2) 858.9	—	100.0	—	270.4	—	100.0	—
	(3) 1048.5	—	—	100.0	306.9	—	—	100.0

Nonfarm									
Employment		429.2	62.4	68.3	—	210.3	72.5	81.0	—
Reproducible capital									
Gross services		258.6	37.6	—	—	79.6	27.5	—	—
Net services		199.1	—	31.7	—	49.3	—	19.0	—
All	(1)	687.8	100.0	—	—	289.9	100.0	—	—
	(2)	628.3	—	100.0	—	259.6	—	100.0	—

[1] Percentage data and totals designated (1) refer to weights in which capital services are gross and land is omitted. Those designated (2) refer to weights in which capital services are net and land is omitted. Those designated (3) refer to weights in which capital services are gross and land is included. Differences between sums of figures and indicated total are due to rounding.

APPENDIX TABLE 12. Index numbers of factor inputs and output, total economy (exclusive of selected services), selected countries, 1960

Country	Employment, adjusted for hours	Employment, adjusted for hours, education, sex, and age	Reproducible fixed capital	Inventories	Gross material product
United States	100.0	100.0	100.0	100.0	100.0
France	30.1	25.9	13.4	18.1	15.4
Germany	43.2	35.7	15.4	23.1	21.9
United Kingdom	40.2	36.5	14.1	24.6	19.8
Italy	33.8	26.2	8.6	13.7	11.4
USSR	162.5	120.1	54.6	77.9	50.5

APPENDIX TABLE 13. Index numbers of industrial factor inputs and output, selected countries, 1960

Country	Employment, adjusted for hours	Employment, adjusted for hours, education, sex, and age	Reproducible fixed capital	Inventories	Gross product originating
United States	100.0	100.0	100.0	100.0	100.0
France	24.7	21.9	12.1	16.5	14.8
Germany	40.6	33.8	15.1	24.0	22.1
United Kingdom	42.7	38.5	14.3	27.1	20.3
Italy	24.3	19.8	7.7	13.0	11.1
USSR	98.0	79.6	49.8	77.8	48.7

APPENDIX TABLE 14. Employment by sector, selected countries 1960 (millions)

Country	Agriculture	Industry	Selected final services					All
			Health care	Education	Public admin-istration	Defense	All	
United States	5.46 (5.17)[1]	51.75 (52.04)[1]	2.59	3.32	2.66	2.51	11.08	68.29
France	4.19	12.04		2.48		0.84	3.32	19.55
Germany[2]	3.62	19.80	0.59	0.49	1.45	0.29	2.82	26.24
United Kingdom	1.03	20.78	1.24		1.21	0.52	2.97	24.78
Italy	6.52	11.87	0.10	0.65	0.86	0.37	1.98	20.37
USSR	(39.3)[1]	(49.0)[1]	3.5	5.0	2.0	3.3	13.8	102.1

[1] Figures shown parenthetically relate to agriculture exclusive, and industry, inclusive of forestry and fisheries.
[2] Including West Berlin.

APPENDIX TABLE 15. Adjustment of employment for education, sex, and age, all sectors (exclusive of selected final services) and industry, selected countries, 1960

Country	(1) Employment, adjusted for hours	(2) Educational quality	(3) Quality as affected by sex and age	(4) Quality as affected by education, sex, and age (adjusted)	(5) Employment, adjusted for hours, education, sex, and age [(1) X (4)]
			ALL SECTORS		
United States	100.0	100.0	100.0	100.0	100.0
France	30.1	86.8	97.8	86.1	25.9
Germany	43.2	85.8	94.8	82.6	35.7
United Kingdom	40.2	91.7	98.2	90.9	36.5
Italy	33.8	74.9	97.6	77.4	26.2
USSR	162.5	81.0	91.2	73.9	120.1
			INDUSTRY		
United States	100.0	100.0	100.0	100.0	100.0
France	24.7	89.3	97.8	88.7	21.9
Germany	40.6	86.3	94.8	83.3	33.8
United Kingdom	42.7	90.8	98.2	90.2	38.5
Italy	24.3	77.1	97.6	81.5	19.8
USSR	98.0	86.7	93.6	81.2	79.6

APPENDIX TABLE 16. Gross domestic product by sector, selected Western countries in United States factor cost of 1960 (billions of dollars)

Sector	United States	France	Germany	United Kingdom	Italy
Agriculture	21.0	5.7	3.9	2.3	3.7
Industry	355.7	52.5	78.6	72.3	39.4
Selected final services					
Health care	13.6	11.9 (health care, education, and public administration combined)	3.4	5.1 (health care and education combined)	0.5
Education	14.9		2.2		2.9
Public administration	14.6		8.0	6.6	4.7
Defense	10.6	3.5	1.2	2.2	1.6
Housing	33.4	3.9	6.1	6.6	1.9
All	*87.1*	*19.3*	*20.9*	*20.5*	*11.6*
All sectors	463.8	77.5	103.4	95.1	54.7

APPENDIX TABLE 17. Gross national product by sector, United States and USSR, in 1960, in United States market prices of 1960 (billions of dollars)

Sector	United States	USSR
Agriculture	20.5	17.4
Industry	391.5	190.8
Selected final services		
Health care	13.6	18.4
Education	14.9	22.4
Public administration	14.6	11.0
Defense	10.6	13.9
Housing	36.5	7.5
All	*90.2*	*73.2*
All sectors	502.2	281.4

APPENDIX TABLE 18. Factor income shares, United States, 1960

	All sectors, excluding selected final services		Industry	
Item	Dollars (bil.)	Percent	Dollars (bil.)	Percent
Labor	270.8	74.15	260.1	75.37
Reproducible fixed capital				
Net	45.7	—	41.6	—
Depreciation	37.5	—	33.9	—
Gross	83.2	22.78	75.5	21.88
Inventories	11.2	3.07	9.5	2.75
All	*365.2*	*100.00*	*345.1*	*100.00*

APPENDIX TABLE 19. Gross domestic product originating and employment by sector, selected countries, 1955, 1960, 1970

Country and sector	Gross product originating (bil. units of national currency)[1]			Employment (mil.)		
	1955	1960	1970	1955	1960	1970
United States[2]						
All sectors	475.4	528.3	788.3	65.08	68.29	81.82
				(65.83)[3]	(68.29)	(80.19)
Agriculture[4]	20.3	20.7	25.6	6.72	5.46	3.46
Industry	335.2	364.6	546.5	41.72	44.36	52.61
				(42.47)	(44.36)	(50.98)
Selected services	119.9	143.0	216.2	16.64	18.47	25.75
France						
All sectors	274.4	346.1	606.9	19.46	19.55	20.97
				(20.18)	(20.26)	(21.54)
Agriculture[4]	29.3	34.1	40.0	5.00	4.19	2.86
Industry	169.0	220.5	411.0	10.19	10.87	12.96
				(10.91)	(11.58)	(13.53)
Selected services	76.1	91.5	155.9	4.27	4.49	5.15
Germany[5]						
All sectors	231.5	332.5	532.2	22.83	26.24	27.20
				(24.20)	(27.39)	(27.74)
Agriculture[4]	15.9	18.4	20.6	4.25	3.62	2.41
Industry	168.6	250.4	409.2	14.28	17.46	18.68
				(15.65)	(18.61)	(19.22)
Selected services	47.0	63.7	102.4	4.30	5.16	6.11
United Kingdom						
All sectors	22.23	25.10	32.50	24.28	24.78	25.08
				(25.62)	(25.97)	(25.58)
Agriculture[4]	0.78	0.92	1.13	1.09	1.00	0.71
Industry	15.50	17.46	23.00	16.95	17.47	17.11
				(18.29)	(18.66)	(17.61)
Selected services	5.95	6.72	8.37	6.24	6.31	7.26

(*cont.*)

APPENDIX TABLE 19 (cont.)

Country and sector	Gross product originating (bil. units of national currency)[1]			Employment (mil.)		
	1955	1960	1970	1955	1960	1970
Italy						
All sectors	17.37	23.04	39.49	19.25 (19.92)	20.37 (21.24)	19.17 (19.05)
Agriculture[4]	3.24	3.50	4.58	7.79	6.57	3.69
Industry	9.06	13.50	26.05	8.66 (9.33)	10.87 (11.74)	12.29 (12.17)
Selected services	5.07	6.04	8.86	2.80	2.93	3.19
Japan						
All sectors	10.87	16.64	47.68	40.96 (42.27)	44.36 (46.43)	50.94 (52.36)
Agriculture[4]	—	—	—	15.35	13.40	8.86
Industry	—	—	—	19.62 (20.93)	23.80 (25.87)	32.96 (34.38)
Selected services	—	—	—	5.99	7.16	9.12
USSR						
All sectors	98.1	132.6	226.7	93.74 (97.17)	99.00 (100.83)	122.17 (121.84)
Agriculture	26.1	30.9	43.1	41.44	38.39	36.31
Industry	51.3	78.7	150.5	36.87 (40.30)	45.64 (47.47)	64.26 (63.93)
Selected services	20.7	23.0	33.1	15.43	14.97	21.60

[1] For Italy and Japan, 1000 billion. All data in constant prices.
[2] For 1955, exclusive of Hawaii and Alaska.
[3] For parenthetical data, industrial employment has been adjusted for hours.
[4] Including forestry and fishing.
[5] For 1955, exclusive of Saar and West Berlin.

APPENDIX TABLE 20. Gross domestic product, gross fixed investment, and gross domestic investment, selected countries, 1955-1969 and 1960-1969 (bil. units of national currency)[1]

	Gross domestic product		Gross fixed investment		Gross domestic investment	
Country	1955-1969	1960-1969	1955-1969	1960-1969	1955-1969	1960-1969
United States[2]	8940	6534	1596	1144	1674	1206
France	5973	4506	1362	1076	1486	1176
Germany[3]	5473	4181	1366	1067	1459	1130
United Kingdom	443.2	317.6	75.3	57.0	79.6	60.1
Italy	431.5	333.9	89.0	69.6	93.4	73.2
Japan	368.2	299.9	116.5	101.2	131.3	113.8
USSR	2769	2020	668	521	764	587

[1] For Italy and Japan, 1000 billion. All data in constant prices.
[2] For 1955-1959, exclusive of Hawaii and Alaska.
[3] For 1955-1959, exclusive of Saar and West Berlin.

APPENDIX TABLE 21. Index numbers of enterprise fixed capital for total economy and industry, selected countries, 1955-1970 (percent)

	Index numbers of net fixed capital		Index numbers of gross fixed capital		Average of index numbers of net and gross fixed capital	
Country	1970/1955	1970/1960	1970/1955	1970/1960	1970/1955	1970/1960
			TOTAL ECONOMY			
United States	182.4	155.3	171.9	147.5	177.2	151.4
France	227.3	181.5	209.8	181.5	218.6	181.5
Germany	288.2	189.2	243.0	170.3	265.6	179.8
United Kingdom	197.4	157.8	172.4	149.3	184.9	153.6
Italy	235.5	174.8	217.3	174.8	226.4	174.8
Japan	545.2	359.5	409.0	292.0	477.1	325.8
USSR	388.4	231.1	383.1	232.3	385.8	231.7
			INDUSTRY			
United States	189.4	158.9	176.8	150.7	183.1	154.8
France	224.9	180.7	207.6	180.7	216.3	180.7
Germany	—	—	—	—	—	—
United Kingdom	200.5	159.9	175.1	151.3	187.8	155.6
Italy	245.5	181.4	226.6	181.4	236.0	181.4
Japan	—	—	—	—	—	—
USSR	392.0	232.6	383.2	232.3	387.6	232.4

APPENDIX TABLE 22. Gross income shares imputed to enterprise capital stock for total economy and industry, selected countries (percent)

Country	Total economy	Industry
United States	20	22
France	22	26
Germany	25	27
United Kingdom	20	23
Italy	25	30
Japan	31	—
USSR	23	33

APPENDIX TABLE 23. Hypothetical gross domestic product by sector and type of factor charge, USSR, 1959 (billions of rubles)

Sector	Labor earnings	Interest on		Depreciation	All charges
		Fixed capital	Inventories		
Agriculture	25.0	3.8	0.6	1.3	30.7
Industry	45.9	11.8	5.6	4.8	68.1
Selected services	17.4	4.2	0.2	2.4	24.2
All sectors	88.3	19.8	6.4	8.5	123.0

APPENDIX TABLE 24. Population, July 1, 1955, 1960, and 1970, selected countries (millions)

Country	1955	1960	1970
United States	165.3[1]	180.7	204.8
France	43.4	45.7	50.8
Germany	49.2[2]	55.4	60.6
United Kingdom	51.2	52.6	55.8
Italy	47.4	49.0	53.5
Japan	89.1	93.3	103.6
USSR	196.2	214.3	242.8

[1] Excluding Hawaii and Alaska.
[2] Excluding Saar and West Berlin.

APPENDIX TABLE 25. Consumption by category, 1955, 1960, and 1970, selected countries (bil. units of national currency)[1]

Country and category	1955	1960	1970
United States			
Consumption (all private), including	290.0	336.6	507.7
Food	64.9	72.1	90.7
Clothing	26.0	30.0	43.7
Durables	36.0	36.3	65.1
Rent	38.0	48.0	76.5
Consumption (all)	308.1	359.5	550.3
France			
Consumption (all private), including	171.7	208.8	364.2
Food	60.3	69.2	98.4
Clothing	19.4	23.4	40.2
Durables	12.0	17.1	40.2
Rent	12.7	15.7	28.2
Consumption (all)	—	—	—
Germany			
Consumption (all private), including	128.3 (155.8)[2]	188.1	306.7
Food	(59.1)[2]	69.2	96.3
Clothing	(18.9)[2]	22.6	36.0
Durables	—	—	—
Rent	(11.8)[2]	14.9	26.7
Consumption (all)	—	—	—
United Kingdom			
Consumption (all private), including	16.1	18.4	23.2
Food	4.72	5.13	5.72
Clothing	1.67	2.02	2.50
Durables	1.09	1.52	2.19
Rent	1.76	1.97	2.60
Consumption (all)	17.5	20.1	25.6

(*cont.*)

APPENDIX TABLE 25 (cont.)

Country and category	1955	1960	1970
Italy			
Consumption (all private), including	12.970	16.189	29.241
Food	5.372	6.555	10.632
Clothing	1.238	1.514	2.746
Durables	0.900	1.155	2.856
Rent	1.552	1.771	2.432
Consumption (all)	—	—	—
Japan			
Consumption (all private), including	7.216	10.538	25.076
Food	3.478	4.615	8.268
Clothing	0.846	1.382	2.753
Durables	—	—	—
Rent	0.765	1.074	2.333
Consumption (all)	—	—	—
USSR			
Consumption (all private), including	89.5	118.2	193.6
Food	54.8	68.9	98.1
Clothing	15.9	22.7	38.1
Durables	2.06	4.19	10.58
Rent	1.54	1.93	2.72
Consumption (all)	98.7	131.0	216.8

[1] For Italy and Japan, 1000 billion. All data in constant prices.

[2] Parenthetical figures are for 1958.

Index